OF MISTLETOE AND SNOW

AN ANTHOLOGY

Edited by
TIFFANY CURRY, TARA JAZDZEWSKI, SEAMUS
KING, AND ALEXA ROSE

Printed in the United States of America

First Printing, 2020

ISBN 978-1-7357905-3-4

Jazz House Publications
300 Lenora Street # 1119
Seattle, WA 98121
www.JazzHousePublications.com

Supervising Editor: Tiffany Curry
Cover art: Fay Lane
Formatting: Nicole Scarano

CONTENTS

THE HEARTH IN THE HILLS

SEAMUS KING

*D*ark grey clouds hung over the peak of High Fadr. The temperature plummeted from crisp to bone chilling. Brandr swore. Winter in the Northern Crown was cold at the best of times. Winter storms would make it worse.

Brandr sighed. The sky had been clear when he left home two days past, painted a washed-out robin's egg blue. Langenacht was mere days away, and so far the winter storms had not yet raked across the mountains. But heavy snow was inevitable this far north; the rime-kissed cost of life in the mountains.

"Of all times to be on the road," he muttered, tugging his sky-blue woolen hood up over his ears. "Well. Best to hurry and find some shelter. Move your feet, Ulf-hadin."

The hike down the mountains was not fast-going. It became easier with the passing of time; it was a year since he'd come here, and already his feet knew how best to move on narrow paths and traverse steep climbs; but he was a man and not a mountain goat. Brandr had lived near mountains when he was a boy on Long Winter, but they had been great crags with few paths to navigate. Most of his days had been spent in the great hall of the Wynterwyrm, on the sea, or on the far-shores his longship had led him to. These endless mountains had been challenging, but after a year hunting and tracking and trapping, he had learned a great deal about these hills and their hidden ways.

Brandr followed the winding road, switching back and forth on paths beneath bare trees that had just a month or ago had still been crowned with autumn's splendor, now grasping, skeletal fingers reaching towards the sky.

The wind kicked up. The storm drew closer, wind tearing through the bare, spindly branches. Brandr was down from the tops, but still only barely on the Low Road, and the snow was already falling in sheets. He would never make it to Gurrentown.

He huddled next to a massive oak and took shelter in its roots.

THE SNOW BECAME an endless rain of white swirling on the wind; Brandr could see no further than the dark ice-slick bark of the tree. The big Skardr tried to light a fire in a small crook, but his tinder was too wet. It was useless against the relentless wind. The temperature continued to plummet, and the storm's fury showed no sign of abating. Brandr grew colder. He rummaged in his pack, taking out some of the hides and furs he'd planned to sell in Gurretown, and wrapped up. The sound of the wind over the trees took him back. He felt again the wind whipping over white-capped waves, the cold spray of the sea not so different then the snow-flecked gusts now. He saw the stony spires of Long Winter in the tall trees that towered over the now-hidden road.

"You've got me, old man," Brandr said, glancing toward where High Fadr loomed far beyond his sight, his breath curling in fog before it turned to ice and fell to the snow. "Well played." The cold seeped into his bones; the dark drew over him. He saw once more a flash of crimson hair and heard distant laughter like ringing bells. "Sivrid," he murmured. "Your laugh is music."

Brandr thought he heard laughter again, much closer now. He had the feeling of rough hands helping him to his feet, and of being half-carried against a strong shoulder, and then laid down among some furs. Something started moving beneath him, and he thought he heard the braying of sheep.

BRANDR WOKE UP. His head slowly cleared, and he felt the warmth and could hear the soothing cackling of a fire earby. His fingers and toes hurt wildly. That was a good sign, too. It meant he still had them. He opened his eyes. He lay on a linden-wood bench in an old hall, hung with holly and ivy all 'round, and the fire flickered in a long stone hearth. The walls were decorated with intricately woven wool tapestries. One showed Earin, the huntress, leading the chase through the forest amid a pack of hounds. Another had two young men pulling a sled over a mountain top, bringing the sun (woven with threads of real gold), back to the world, and with it came spring.

An old man sat across from him, watching. His face was a cobweb of wrinkles, though his luxuriously long white beard was still shot through with streaks and slivers of crimson. His bald head gleamed in the firelight, and his small but merry eyes were clear and bright as blue stars.

"You're awake," he said. "That's a good lad."

"There, you see," a woman's voice said, creaky and welcoming like old stairs. Brandr turned. She tended a great black iron pot over the hearth, from which the rich strong smell of stewing apples rolled out on delicious currents of steam. Her long hair fell to the middle of her back in snow-white curls, and her long tunic-dress, which may have once been crimson, brushed the planks of the hall as she dipped a ladle into the black cauldron. "He'll be fine, Gavfar."

"Of course you're right, mother," the man replied in a voice like warm leather. "I never doubted your skills. There is no winter chill that you can not master."

"He says that now," the elderly woman told Brandr. "But you should have seen him worried after you. Clucking like an old hen." She walked over, her dark eyes twinkling, and she lifted the ladle towards him. "Drink, duckling. It will warm your bones."

He drank the hot cider, and she was right. The warmth of the liquid spread over him, and the chill faded away like the winter snow melted from the sun. "That's amazing," he said.

Her smile could have lit up midnight. "Good lad," she said. "I'm glad you like it. I…"

Loud voices echoed outside the hall, and a man pushed in through the heavy doors and strode into the hall. He was nearly as tall as Brandr and broad across the shoulder; he wore a tunic of forest green and carried a fine doe over his shoulder. "It's cold as the ice flats out there," he said, laying the doe down across one of the benches. "But the reindeer should be safe. They're all gathered on the western bluff. And I've brought dinner."

"But Vriya shot it," said a younger man, following him in, the beginnings of a crimson beard thin and fuzzy on his face and cheeks. "You should have seen the shot, father. Vrey couldn't have done it. I don't think he could have even seen it."

"I could have seen it," the other man, Vrey, replied. "If I weren't trying to make sure our herd all made it to their pasture."

"Excellent either way," their father said, and his merry eyes twinkled. "We have need of a feast tonight. We have a guest. And where is Vriya? Where is my firstborn daughter?"

"Coming soon enough," Vrey said. "She's seeing to our mounts."

Two children ran in, a little girl with ribbons in her hair and a boy that was nearly her mirror image, laughing as they chased each other.

"Mind the fire," the old woman chided, but her eyes twinkled just like her husband's. "Berigal, if you don't stop dancing along the edge of the hearth like a damned fool it'll be no seed cakes for a month, do you understand?"

"Yes mother," the little boy said with a sulk, but leapt from the edge anyway with that bounding energy that only small children have.

"Who's this then? Is this our guest?" The younger man said, noticing Brandr. "Shoulders like an ox, hair only a few shades paler than good gold bound in the warrior's braid... he has the look of a Skardr. But so far from the sea? Or have I lost track?"

"He's dressed like a trapper instead of a sailor," Vrey said. "And more dour than most."

"A stray your father found on the road," the old woman said. "Frozen near to death. I've warmed him up, sweet chicken, and he's got nowhere to be this coming Langenacht."

"He looks strong," the younger man said. "I bet he'd be a good match. Do you like to wrestle?"

Brandr blinked. He felt overwhelmed by the sudden mass of people in the hall, though it held plenty of space for them all. They were all talking together, their voices as sweet and calming as a babbling brook, but it was more people in one space than Brandr had encountered in some time, had encountered since his father's hall far far away when his cousin had driven him out. There had been a fight then, and blood had spilled on the stone stairs to Long Winter and... Brandr shook his head, trying to clear it out, and he saw the old man looking at him with a sad sympathetic look.

"Memories can be hard this time of year," he said gently. His quiet voice could be clearly heard over all the noise in the hall. "But this is a safe place, friend. I am Gavfar, and you are welcome in this place. You have met my two eldest sons, Vrey and Veny. My eldest daughter will be here soon."

Brandr shifted uncomfortably. "I should warn you, my host. I am an outlaw in my home land, and my cousin has put a price on my head. I would not bring harm to a man who has treated me so well." His voice lowered. "Or his lovely family."

"We are not there, Skardr," the man replied, his voice still calm. "And I think far from the grasp of your cousin. No man yet has done harm to any guest in my hall, and no guest that has not brought ill-will under this roof has been denied hospitality. I brought you to my home willingly. You may have no fear. Will you tell me your name?"

"Brandr. And I am grateful to you."

"Just Brandr? Surely you have a family name, or at least a home."

Brandr looked away. "Just... Brandr. I have no family that would claim me."

A young woman, slight and sharp as a dagger blade came through the back door, a pack of young dogs at her heels, all jumping and hopping, eager for her attention. "The girls are fed," she said, "Though they wish there were more oats. And these damn dogs need something to eat."

Brandr met her gaze, and for a moment the world froze.

"Hello, Stranger," she said. Her eyes were the exact same shade as the northern loch under a night sky, "I see father's brought home another stray."

He nodded, dumb for just a moment.

She smiled, just the corner of her mouth turning up, and warmth and sound and life returned to the world. He shook out of daze. "I'm Brandr," he said at last.

"Vriya," she replied. "Gavfarsdottir. Welcome to our hearth."

"I am grateful for your hospitality," he replied.

Her eyes sparked with good humor. "Thank my father," she said, pulling her hair out of its braid, letting it tumble in flame-kissed summer waves down nearly to the slight curve of her hips. "You're just his type."

Her mother tsked at her, and handed her a cup. "Be Kind, Vriya," she said. "He is of our kind; it is good to see a man like him so far from the sea."

Vriya nodded. "I only tease," she said, and took a sip, then offered it to Brandr. "Take a sip, Brandr of Il-Skardr."

He took the cup from her hands. He searched her face. Her features were as hard and sharp as the rest of her, and her eyes seemed to pierce right through him with harrowing ease. He steeled himself, forcing his nerves to a steady calm. He lifted the cup to his lips, met her gaze, and took a sip. It was like the cider he'd been given earlier, but earthier, hotter, and with an extra punch that spread through his body like a warm flush. He lowered his cup. "il-Skardr will not have me," he murmured.

"Then you are twice as welcome here," she replied, smiling again.

They soon ate together. Gavfar and his wife sat at the end of the hall, and the others at the benches. The doe roasted over the stone hearth, skewered upon a long iron spit that the small children took turns turning. The Mother passed out bread of rye and winter wheat while the doe cooked. The rich dark loaves were still warm from the cooking and brushed with salted butter.

"So you come from Long Winter," she said. "That's one of the northern islands?"

"The largest island in the north of il-Skardr," he replied. "The home of the Wynter Wyrm tribe."

"The Winter Wyrm? You mean old Isfar?"

"You know of him?"

"There were stories," she said.

"You are long since out of touch. He was killed in my grandfather's grandfather's time."

"Long out of touch," she agreed. "But you are far from home. Men like you don't travel far from the sea."

He saw his home again, the jagged teeth rising toward the sky, the hall not so unlike this one lit by many fires. Blood on the steps, his crew swirling around him as they fought their way back to the piers. He saw Ivar's head half-split by a two-handed axe, saw Astrid take an arrow in her throat. He heard his cousin's voice ringing across the hall, calling him outlaw, regicide, kinslayer. Banishing him from his home.

"We don't," he said. "We live and die by it."

"Brandr!" Gavfar boomed from across the hall, red-cheeked and merry. "Are you enjoying your food?"

"Of course," he said, turning to the man. "It's nice to not be eating my own cooking."

"My bride makes the best bread," the older man said

approvingly, patting his stomach as it shook with laughter. "Which I enjoy, perhaps a little too much."

"Nonsense husband," the matron said with a wry grin, "The world could always use more of you."

"Then you do the world a great service!" The man laughed again, the sound reverberating through the hall. "But tell me, Brandr. In seriousness. Do you have plans for tomorrow? Where were you heading?"

"I was heading to Gurrentown," Brandr said. "With some hides to sell."

"What kind?"

"Beaver. Some foxskins. Some Mertpeltr."

"The big forest fisher-cats? Those are rarer and rarer up here. We could use some of those. The fox, too. Not much time for trapping here. We'll take them off of you, and trade any supplies you need that we have... and more, if you can give my children some help on the ridge and around the farm. The onset of true winter requires many hands."

"Of course," Brandr found himself saying without thinking about it.

The old man smiled. His son glowered. Vriya gave Brandr a secret look.

"YOU'RE MEDDLING, HUSBAND."

"Am I, wife?"

"Yes. We left them so we could stop meddling. We swore, the five of us."

"But he's here."

"So he is. Just be careful. Vriya's eyes were on him tonight."

"Of course they are."

"You know what will happen."

"Of course I do."

"It is not his time yet."

"No. But he can find some rest here, at least. I hope."

A WOLF HOWLED in the night. Brandr stood alone in the woods, bare down to his linen trousers. There was a knife in his fist, and Grimr was stalking him. He knew it. His feet crunched over ice-bound snow and he ducked around the tree. It wouldn't help. He knew there was no escape from the Great Wolf. It would always find him; nothing could hide the blood of a Ulf-hadin, a wolf-warrior, from its scenting.

And nothing could save a Kinslayer from its jaws.

But that doom could be delayed. If Brandr could hold out just a little longer, till both moons had sunk below the horizon, he might just make it. All he had to do was make it a little longer. Heavy paws crushed through hard packed snow nearby, slowly getting closer. Brandr rose and fled toward another tree, one just over an embankment... but the wolf stood there, impossibly huge; its lambent eyes burning into him, its jaws dripping acid... it bounded toward him, leaping with lethal force, jaws big enough to consume all the light and hope in the world opening wide...

...and a bowstring sung.

Brandr snapped awake. He trembled, skin soaked in cold sweat, and felt something press against him. He opened his eyes; a gray and white elkhound pup lay beside him, gently pushing at him with its wet nose. The sound of the bowstring still echoed in his mind, but as the gentle light of breaking day streamed through the long hall's transom, the night's fear and worry were swept away until he could hardly remember what had happened. He reached up to scratch the dog's ear, and suddenly felt more refreshed then he had in months. He rose, trying to wipe away the remaining sleep. His head didn't hurt, either, despite all the strong drink. It was a miracle. "Strange blessings," he told the dog, scratching down to its neck. "But I'll not question them this morning."

"How'd you sleep?"

He turned and saw Veny, the middle brother. "Well enough," Brandr said. "It's long since I slept on a bench."

"Not your first time, though?"

Brandr smiled. "No," he said. "I've done it many many times. A large part of my life."

The boy. Young man? Nodded. "Good." he said. "It takes some getting used to."

"So what's the plan?"

"We ride up to the high meadows, we check on the herd, we make sure that their food is in order. We also check traps and board up some of the outbuildings against the snow. It really limits their use and make a mess when it thaws."

"Ride," Brandr said. "I didn't hear any horses. And this snow is a little much for them."

"They're not horses."

The lad gave him a honeycake. "Come on," he said. "The morning will soon grow long."

Brandr nodded and rose to his feet, taking a bite of the moist cake as he did. The soft crumb melted in his mouth, subtle and sweet. The dog rose with a small sound, and its pointed ears perked up.

"Aren't you a little young for this, Fraki?" The younger man asked.

The dog gave a pathetic whine. "Oh let him go," the mother said, passing by. "He's old enough. If he wants to range with you, let him."

The mounts were reindeer. Veny handed the red-leather reins of one to Brandr, grinned, and swung himself up into the saddle. The Skardr stared at the mount for a moment; it met his gaze with surprisingly intelligent eyes... and then it licked Brandr's forehead and tried to nibble his hair.

"Forward," Brandr laughed, and gently pushed the reindeer's head away. He put one big foot in a stirrup and heaved himself on top, and followed the three siblings out into the white.

They rode up Old Baldy on goat paths and across frozen brooks. The brothers rode together, cheerfully talking. Vriya rode with Brandr.

"It's incredible that there's a whole herd of reindeer up here and nobody knows about it. Or at least I don't. How long have you been here?"

"Long enough," she said as she rode, guiding her mount with just her knees and hips. A long unstrung bow of some dark, slender wood hung across her back, and a quiver of white-fletched arrows rode on her saddle. She turned and gave him a smile. "Longer than you."

"That's not hard," he said. "I haven't been here long."

"I thought so. You've got some of the world-bones in you now, but your eyes still look for the sea."

"Am I so easy to read?"

She laughed. "For me, maybe. I have a lot of experience reading men like you."

"Like me?"

She flashed him a grin and a wink, squeezed her reindeer's sides, and hurried on ahead.

It took all morning to break out from under the skeletal fingers of the winter forest; the sun was nearly at its zenith by the time they found open sky. A snow-covered meadow spread out in front of the riders. From here, they could look out and see most of the Northern Crown's snow-covered peaks and tree-clad slopes spread before them in seas of white that rose and fell. A hawk soared far overhead, circling wide in search of prey.

"A year trapping and hunting in these mountains," Brandr murmured. "And yet here I feel like I'm in another world. I never knew a place like this existed."

"Why would you?" Veny asked. "It's ours."

"As much as it is anyone's," Vrey laughed. "But there are many places in these hills that few human eyes have seen. Some that not even the elves have seen in their long years; this place has never been theirs."

Brandr drew himself up taller on his mount and gazed spellbound out onto the seemingly endless peaks. "It never seemed this vast before," he murmured, shaking his head.

"Perhaps you never took the time to see," Vriya said, stepping up beside him, her sharp eyes scanning the sky. "Goshawk," she said, suddenly, and the bird keened in the distance.

"Only your eyes, sister," Vrey said with a resigned smile. "Come on. Let's get to work."

THE SUN REACHED the top of its road through the sky and began to sink again, and they worked. They found the small sheds their father had talked about, brushed snow off their roofs and made sure they were secured against the cold and the snow. They cleared up fallen branches that had obscured some of the reindeer's paths, and moved fodder from hidden water-tight cellars into large mangers. Fraki played in the snow, stalking rabbits, and when he took one he merrily settled down by a snowbank to enjoy his feast.

"What beasts are these?" Brandr asked. "They're not like any reindeer I've ever seen."

"What do you mean?"

"Well, they're huge. Strong enough to bear grown men with ease. The snow doesn't seem to bother them; I can see their tracks, but they also seem to glide over it. I've never seen them so high up, either."

"These are a special breed," the older brother said with a shrug. "Unique to these mountains. An older kind I think than the herds farther West."

"Father calls them Mountain Reindeer," Veny said. "He's very creative."

"You seem to make a good living with them," Brandr said.

"They provide us with hides, and milk, and meat, and mouts, both for riders and labour. With the other bounties of the mountain, it is enough."

The sun had nearly sunk below the western slopes before they made their way back down the mountain to the warm hall hung 'round with ivy, holly, and mistletoe. Brandr feasted with the others, drinking well and eating his fill. Vriya sat across from him; he tried not to pay too much attention while she watched with her loch-dark eyes. After the food was finished, he sat and played with the grey-and-white elkhound puppy and its sibs, wrestling with them on the floor, laughing all the while.

When he closed his eyes to sleep, the grey puppy tucked in against his ribs, Vriya's gaze, blue and piercing, lingered in his thoughts until the dark took him.

❄

BRANDR SLEPT HARD. This time, he didn't remember his dreams, but the cold sweat clinging to his clammy skin told him they had been no easier. The song of a bow-shot still buzzed in his ear, yet he felt even more refreshed than the morning before all yesterday's hard work. .

"Do you often have guests here?" Brandr asked Vriya as they rode up the mountain paths with Fraki bounding happily along after them. His soul soared under the bright sky, unburdened by the miasa that had haunted him for months.

"Father takes them in, from time to time," she said, guiding her mount with relative ease.

"Do they stay long?"

"Long enough," she said.

The wind blew hard. Brandr watched the darkening sky. "Another storm's coming,"

Her eyes followed his gaze. "You're right," she said. "And this one will be savage. My brothers are on the ridge checking the traps. The herd is ours to push to safety. Come on," she said, squeezing her legs around her mount and rushing toward the herd.

"Where are we taking them?"

"The meadow is too exposed for a storm like that. There's a small valley not far from here. I'll show you the track."

They hurried the reindeer out of the high meadow. The gentle afternoon breeze gave way to the storm's rising gusts. Snow swirled all around them. They started on a narrow, slowly bending road. On one side, a steep hill covered in trees rose up to the mountain's heights. On the other, a steep ravine of sharp rocks and stony ledges fell away to the river below, its swift waters as yet unconquered by the omnipresent ice.

The sound of skittering stones and Fraki's sharp bark cut through the howling wind. Brandr turned and slid off his mount, fighting through the reindeer, to where Fraki stood

15

staring down. A juvenile reindeer had stumbled and fallen to a ledge a little below the path. Without thinking, Brandr went after her, sliding down the ridge fearlessly in a shower of small stones. The young bull reindeer cowered back, its eyes wide with fear. One of its front hooves moved badly, and it bleated pitiably. Brandr held a hand out to it, making a calming noise like he once would have with his father's horses. It shied again, looking at him like he was some monstrous predator. He knelt, lowering himself till he was smaller and unthreatening, and tried again. The reindeer stepped closer, still nervous, and sniffed at his hand. Brandr smiled, reaching into his pouch and digging out a morsel of honeycake left over from breakfast, and held it out with an open palm. The juvenile bull pushed it with its nose, and then ate. The reindeer's bleats became less frantic.

"It's hurt!" he called, stroking the side of the reindeer's head. "But I think it can still walk if I can get it up to the path."

"I've seen these beasts walk on three lame legs. But be careful!" she shouted. "They weigh more than they look."

"It's young," he said. "I don't need to push it far. But it's steep."

"Here," Vriya called back, tossing him a finely-woven grey rope. "Put it around him. I'll tie it to my saddle and see if we can assist."

The cold set in. Brandr's fingers hurt as he tied it in a loop around the reindeer's torso. "Are you ready?" He called up.

"Ready!"

He leaned in. The reindeer shrank away. Brandr got his weight under the poor thing and started pushing with all his might. Step by halting step, the reindeer moved up the slope. It neared the top then slipped and started sliding back down, its bleats rising in panic. Brandr moved his feet and gritted his teeth. His muscles screamed. The reindeer rose and a lashing hoof caught Brandr in the head. He plummeted backwards even as Vriya finished pulling the reindeer up. He didn't know how long he rolled down the side of the ravine or how far he fell. He remembered grabbing at some of the thin and scraggly underbrush on the hellishly steep slope, but it gave way under his weight. He fell again, and when his back and head struck a rock, the world went first red and then black.

Brandr stirred. The red slowly drained out of his vision, but the only thing to see around him was the hard, angry stone and the endlessly swirling stone. His head hurt. His back hurt. He tried to roll over to get on his feet but his left leg wouldn't support him. He almost fell farther toward the river snaking its way through the gorge below.

It was so cold.

Something warm touched Brandr, pushing at him in a familiar way. A worried grey face looked down at him; another sharp bark rang along the mountain path. He dimly saw a woman appear, calling him a fool, and she helped him to his feet. Her strength surprised him. He was not a small man.

"We are near Bluemist Gorge," he said, half-dreamily. The pain had receded now. He felt only cold and tiredness. "I know this place."

"You're right," she said. "You have a good eye for a damned fool. We need to get you out of here."

"What about the herd?"

"We're going to them," Vriya said. "Temoc is leading them. They will be fine."

"You need to go. You won't make it out of this gorge in time. You'll be caught in the snow."

"I would not insult my father's hospitality by leaving his guest to die in the cold."

"But…"

"They will be fine," she snapped. "We are going to them, but there is a place we can shelter on the way if it gets too cold. Now, let me get you back up this side and on your mount."

"How?"

She gave him a look as if he was dense as oak. "With the rope. As long as you have at least one foot and two arms, you will manage."

Vriya helped him up, and as she touched him again, a little clarity came back, then a little more, like he was waking up after a long dark sleep. Here in this place of ice and death, she seemed different, a fountain of color and life in a sea of white. A memory tugged at the edge of Brandr's thoughts, but it slipped away like a salmon in a mountain stream. He gritted his teeth. This was no time for mystery. The landscape required survival. Together, they worked up the rope, still steadied by Vriya's big mount. Brandr climbed until his arms burned and his good leg could hardly move, then he pulled himself onto the trail on his stomach. The moment on the road came back to him as the same chill sank into his bones.

Vriya followed up after him and helped him to the back of one of the reindeer, then she mounted her own. Once again her touch kept him going, and the cold fell back. They travelled down a hidden trail that Brandr would never have seen on his own. He was surprised the reindeer could find it; the trail curved around a steep mountain side and past the other, then the promised valley lay before them. Hidden and small, the valley was still large enough for the herd, protected from the worst of the wind and snow by the mountain-slopes and full of both trees and meadows.

"Good," she said, looking down over the herd. "Temok has gotten them here safely; they can spread out here and find refuge under the trees if needful." She looked over at Brandr, his face paler still even as he fought sleep. His knuckles were white around the saddlehorn. "There is a rutholm nearby. We will find shelter there."

"Rutholm? Root-home?"

"Just that. You will see."

She led him to a giant tree, an oak of the size that only grew in these mountains. "Here," she said. There was a small door among its roots, half-covered by the ivy that climbed its way up the ancient monarch. She turned to their reindeer, took off their saddles, and made a clicking noise; they ran off to join the herd, their hooves supernaturally light on the snow. She took him inside the tree; they both had to stoop, but within was surprisingly cozy. Fraki trotted in behind them, his tail wagging, and she shut the door against the growing storm. The hidden cottage wasn't very big, but there were shelves lined with dusty jars of food, and the door was stout, and while there was no fireplace, there was a small brazier for coals, and the stout wood walls kept the cold out well. Ropes of fresh holly and bundles of dried herbs hung just below the ceiling. There was a single bench for a bed. She went to a small closet and pulled out furs and blankets. "Wrap this around you. I am going to make a broth and then look at your injuries."

"I'm fine," he said. "I've taken worse."

"Brandr Aericson," she said severely. "I was not asking."

He conceded the point, and she worked on him after she lit the brazier. The smoke escaped up artfully hidden passages, and the sweet-smelling herbs and dried flowers she'd added made what smoke didn't escape at least more pleasant.

"Take off your cloak and your tunic," she said.

He stared at her, unmoving.

"Oh for... listen, Brandr. I have two brothers. And this can't be the first time a girl's seen your bare chest, and it's certainly not *my* first time. So strip and don't think anything of it."

He sighed. He undid the wolf's head silver brooch at his shoulder and took off the dark green cloak of river-sheep wool and tossed it on the floor. Then he reached to his shoulders, and pulled the rough brown tunic over his head and added it to the pile.

"Undertunic, too. Don't be impudent."

He sighed and pulled off the white linen undershirt, too, and added it to the rest.

She examined him. "There are a lot of wounds here, Skardr. You have been careless."

"I'm a warrior," he said, watching Fraki settle on the pile of his clothes in a contented heap.

"More than that," she said. "You're Ulf-hadr."

He looked away. "Is it that easy to tell?"

"Yes," she said simply. "It is. I assure you every member of my family knows."

"And you still let me into your home? Watch your flocks?"

"Of course," she said. "You would never violate hospitality, would you?"

"No, of course not."

"And you're not a werewolf yet," she observed.

"Not that, either," he said.

"Well there you go. I know the story, Brandr. An elite warrior-cult of Skardr born to specific bloodlines. Rituals are performed, granting the power of a mighty rage and mein in battle. You become stronger and faster and harder than many other mortals."

"But there's a cost," he murmured.

"Of course there is. No magic comes without cost, at any strength. The wolf spirit hunts you, and one day, it will claim you, and you will become a terrible, almost unstoppable monster. But you are not there yet, are you?"

He looked away.

"Regardless. Not even Ulfhednar are indestructible. Not until the end. And even then…"

"Certain weapons can still be used," Brandr agreed. He saw his brother again, or not his brother. A bipedal fur-covered thing that had once *been* his brother, eyes glowing lambent green as it stood over one of their shipmates with blood-soaked jaws. He felt their father's sword, their family's sword in his hand, the gold wire wrapped round the leathered hilt pressing into his palm, and felt the power humming in the silver-runed blade as he struck Aeric down. He took a deep breath and turned his head. "Certain swords."

She studied him. "Yes," she said, taking a jar of bluish paste off the shelf. She pushed the cork stopper out; the sharp smell of juniper mingled with the flower-scents from the fire. "They can." She sighed and started rubbing it into the wound on his back. It burned, but not badly; more like the comforting way whiskey burned down your throat. "You were lucky. Your back is hurt. This should deal with the worst of it, and some of my mother's tea should help heal the rest. I think you might need to let your head heal a little more before you sleep, but I can help with that. And your ankle isn't broken, it's just twist-ed." She ran her hand over his chest. "I can help with these scars a bit, if you want. Many of them are only half-healed."

He nodded. "If you like."

Vriya slowly worked with the paste, touching each wound in turn. She traced a knife-wound across his ribs. "Jealous lover?"

"Something like that."

She looked up and met his eyes with a small smile. "What was her name?"

"Sivrid," he said. He glanced away.

"Does she wait for you in some hidden farmstead?"

Brandr shook his head, and blonde locks fell over his face. "No," he said, pushing them back. "She does not."

"Fisher cat," he said as she spread the paste down claw-marks down his back. "Caught me unaware." Her fingers worked at a round scar on the bottom of his left arm. "Aethelede arrow during a raid. Drove right through my mail."

"As I said," she whispered as she closed up the small blue jar. "Careless."

"I lead a dangerous life."

"An excuse," Vriya answered. She placed the jar on the shelf. "And you have other, deeper wounds."

"Do I?" he asked, smiling at her. "I thought you'd got them all."

"I mean inside," she said quietly. "I see it in you Brandr Aericson. It festers in your heart."

His face went pale. "I never said Aericson."

"You didn't have to. I knew your father; the story of your blood is written across your face."

Brandr searched her eyes, then turned his head away. "I'll be alright."

"Fool of a man," she said, taking his head in hand and turning him back to meet her gaze. He felt the power behind her eyes, hot as fire, melting away his resistance. "How could you be all right when you refuse to air your wound? The heart will kill you in the end. Every time."

"I…" He closed his eyes. "I lost my brother to the wolf," he said at last. "We'd just heard that father'd been lost, but we were far from home, raiding another island. We heard the news, but we drew our swords and attacked anyway. It felt like the right way to honor his memory." His voice broke. "I don't know if it was the battle, or the grief, or what, but he lost his grip on the rage, and the next thing I knew…"

"He was changed," she murmured, still watching his face. "He was Grimr's."

He nodded. "He ripped through our enemies. Tore them apart." He closed his eyes and the scene played out on his face. "Then he turned on us."

Beldr. Sven. Hilde.

"He killed three of us before I took up his sword, our father's sword entrusted to his keeping, the sword father received as a prize for fighting the dragon in the high vale… I lifted it up and I took his head." His voice shuddered at the memory. "Kinslayers belong to the wolf."

She watched him across the small cottage but said no more.

The night grew colder. Fraki inched closer to the brazier, dragging the cloak and tunics with him. Vriya and Brandr ate some of the dried meat rations, and he made a little stew with dried vegetables and aromatics. He drank the tea Vriya made him while she took some woolen blankets out of a drawer.

"You should take the bed," he said as she carefully spread them over the bench. They might have been red once, long ago, but time had taken its toll.

"Nonsense," she replied. "We'll share it."

"But…"

She raised an eyebrow. "You can share the bed with me, Aeric's son, or you can share it with the dog. Your choice."

He gave in, and she smiled. She curled up against him under the thick blanket. "Good choice," she purred, running her nails down his bare chest, and when he looked into her eyes, they gleamed, gold-rimmed like a hawk's.

"THE WOLF HAS no hold on kinslayers," she said, later. "Only those who refuse to fight it."

"Mmm?" He asked, rolling over to sleepily meet her gaze. They seemed more human now, but there were golden glints in the flickering, pale light of the brazier's burning coals.

"He is not all-powerful. He was driven from his home, and he can be beaten."

He looked at her in confusion.

She ran her nails down his chest and pushed her palm right. "Remember, Brandr Aercison. You are more than your sins. He. Can. Be. Beaten."

The morning came, and with it a clear blue sky. The sun shone terribly bright on the white snow. Brandr squinted to see past the glare..

"How did you sleep?" She asked, looking past him, a blanket still wrapped around her.

"Better. Perfectly." He shook his head and looked over at her. "What did you do?"

"I helped heal your scars. Like I promised. Oh," she laughed at his disbelieving stare. "They're still there. But they have less power than they did, I think."

"Who... what are you?"

"Have you not guessed?"

Not long after that, they headed back down from the

valley, through the meadow and down towards Gavfar's hall. Brandr's ankle ached, but it could support his weight; Vriya summoned their reindeer with a high whistle and the uneventful ride passed soon enough.

They arrived at the hall, and happiness filled everyone's faces when they pushed through the heavy doors. The little children gave Brandr endless hugs, the old mother beamed, and the father and brothers clapped Brandr on the back. The man had another feast laid on and set Brandr to rest.

That night at feast, Gavfar rose. "It is always my way to give gifts at the dying of the year," he said. "But you, Brandr Aericson, my guest, have brought gifts to me instead; you have saved a young bull of my herd."

"But my host," he said. "You have many."

"So I do," he said. "But none more valuable than one so dearly paid for. What would you have of me?"

At that moment, the door burst open and the boys came in again, all talking with joy and mirth and merriment, and anything Brandr might have said was lost in the tumult.

Later he stood with Vriya near the back door. Mother had twisted mistletoe into the garlands decorating the hall. It would be Langennacht soon.

"I cannot stay," he said.

"Why not? Don't you like it here?"

"I do," he said, "So much. It is peaceful in a way I never expected to find."

"But?"

"But he is not ready for peace yet," Gavfar said, stepping out of the corner, a shadow across the side of his face so that only one twinkling eye could be seen. "This is not the place for him. You both know it."

Vriya looked at her father, then back at Brandr. Pain tightened the corners of her eyes. "There is nothing but sorrow out there for you, Brandr. Here there is nothing but mountains and trees and sky and the herds. Away from this hall... Grimr will find you."

"Wyrd will not be cheated," her father said.

Vriya gave her father a dirty look.

"Your father has the right of it," Brandr said. "I'm sorry, Vriya." Her eyes swiveled back to him. "Part of me will always be here," he added quietly.

"If you leave this place," she whispered to Brandr. "You can never come back while you still draw breath."

He nodded back. "I feared as much."

"But when you fall," she said, and her voice took on a hard edge. "I will come for you; and no wolf will ever come between us."

He smiled. "I had guessed who you are."

"It's about time. Clod."

"Your name is different."

Her own grin returned. "I have had many names."

Brandr packed what few things he had. He turned. Gavfar stood under the eaves, the shadows still playing across his face. He was dressed every bit as merrily as before, but there was something frightening and deathly about him, too. An unearthly sense of inevitably surrounded him.

"You make the right choice," the old man said. "This is not the hall for you. Not yet."

"Yet you took me in."

"I found a lost soul on a wooded path," the man replied. "It would have brought me nothing but shame to leave you there." He smiled. "Besides. Even Ulf-hadr need some respite, far from Grimnr's jaws."

Brandr looked away.

"I cannot change your fate," the man said gently. "You chose your road. Mother would not have it."

"Nor would I let you if you could," Brandr replied. "This is my burden to bear."

"Fatalistic Skardr," the older man said with a laugh. "Bound to carry whatever weight and not complain. My daughter's touched you now. And that will help. For a time. The wolf will not chance her arrows."

Brandr gave him a strange look, and then he shook his head and glanced down. "I don't belong here," he murmured. "And I never will."

"Oh, lad," the man said, his voice heavy with gentle, empathic grief. "You make the choices you must and do the best you can when the choice is before you. I see no stain on your soul."

Brandr looked away. "Yet I cannot rub it out. No matter how hard I scrub."

The man touched Brandr's shoulder. The shadow passed from his face, and two merry eyes crinkled at the corners in companionable sympathy.

Day passed into the longest night, and the holly-clad home feasted well in celebration. The large hall stood empty except for Gavfar and his family, yet Brandr felt like the hall was full and lively with many voices. A sense of community filled the long room, warming hearts just as the fire warmed their bodies. Brandr feasted on bread fresh-baked in iron pots, boar roasted on a spit over the fire and basted with a honey sauce, a rich creamy soup of reindeer's milk and autumn mushrooms. Vriya watched him, always, and when the shadows grew deep she disappeared. The hall quieted. The hearth was banked, and Brandr climbed onto one of the benches to go to sleep. Then he saw her standing before him. He rose halfway, but she put a finger on his lips and gently pushed him back down.

"Let us have this, at least," she said quietly, and she

leaned in and kissed him under the hanging holly and ivy. "Remember," she whispered, and pressed her lips against his. "When all grows cold, remember. A hearth burns here, hidden in the hills, and its light will always guide you home."

BRANDR WOKE. He was on the Low Road, surrounded by snow, nestled underneath a great tree. How long ago had he taken shelter here? The rising light of the sun shone bright on hard-packed snow. He shakily rose to his feet. He felt lighter than he had in ages. His pack weighed less, too. The hides he'd brought to sell in Gurretown were missing, and in their place was a length of finely-woven grey rope, a package of dried jerky, and a hunk of cheese wrapped in thin waxed cloth. Tucked beneath these was a small pouch of silver coins.

"Well," Brandr murmured. "Well-paid, I suppose."

There was a ruff, and a sharp bark, and he turned. A grey and white elkhound appeared with a loud, happy bark, diving into snow after a rabbit before turning to trot over to Brandr. It nuzzled his side and looked up into his face with pale eyes the colour of spring's first clear sky. Brandr smiled, and the sun shined brighter.

"Well," he said. "Hello, Fraki.

THE BOY WHO FELL OUT OF TIME

MILEVA ANASTASIADOU

*O*n Christmas eve, it always happens. Memories of that night fill my head wherever I may be, even tonight, even at this Christmas concert, memories don't care whether I'm among crowds or not, whether it's noisy or not; the Silent Night is always silent in my head, allowing room for magic.

A year ago before the magic started, we'd moved to the suburbs because dad had found a better job that allowed for an expensive rent. In the beginning, I didn't want to leave our old house. It had a small balcony from which I could see the playground across the street where my mother used to take me when I was little, yet I don't remember much from that season because I'd been too young to remember anything.

Dad looked happy with our new house. I liked it too. Not because it was large and comfortable, as the grown-ups say, but because it had a garden where they allowed me to play until it got dark and there was a wide street outside where cars rarely passed. I sat there alone most of the time, counting them, but sometimes my best friends were with me. I'd only known Gina and Dean, the twins, for a short time, but they kept me good company.

My older brother, Alex, was an excellent student. On the other hand, I was considered the problematic case of the family. My therapist claimed I had a vivid imagination for a boy my age, I was twelve already, yet I lacked in everything else. Dad said balance is the key, if one wishes to go ahead in life.

It was almost Christmas and Alex had left home two days ago and mom had been crying since then. I was more frightened than I had ever been in my whole life.

At midnight, I woke up to a strange noise on my window. It was the twins throwing pebbles at my window to wake me up. Gina looked excited as she gave me a piece of paper and asked me to read what was written on it.

"What's this?"

"Read it and you'll find out," she said without paying attention to my bad mood. The twins had always tried to lift my mood, yet sometimes they were tried too hard.

"I will come tonight, to take you on a strange trip. All I ask is for you to trust me. I promise this trip will be full of surprises," I read aloud.

Dean shrugged, looking at his sister.

"I told her that the paper must have slipped from someone. She doesn't listen."

"This message may be from a magic genie that promises to make your wishes come true. It can't be a coincidence. That your brother has just gone missing," said Gina in excitement.

I hadn't mentioned anything about Alex, yet news travels fast. Besides, the twins always knew all about me in a magical way. I suppose that's what happens with friends anyway.

"The handwriting seems familiar, yet I'm not certain," I said, feigning indifference, as my mind was exploring possible explanations. I was too old to believe in magic genies who fulfill wishes, although I thought that would be a nice and convenient explanation.

As if he read my mind, Dean shouted:

"We have no other option. We'll pretend it's a magic genie and we will ask for help to find Alex."

"How? There's no magic lamp around, as you may have noticed."

We sat in silence for a while to think of ways to make the genie appear without using a magic lamp.

"How long are we supposed to wait?" asked Gina, looking impatient and sleepy at the same time.

"Do you have anything better in mind?"

"We will think about it tomorrow."

I didn't feel like going to sleep. If the genie wanted to appear, it'd better come as soon as possible. The longer it took him to come, the more dangerous it was for Alex.

"What a brilliant idea," said Dean, clapping his hands ironically. With Dean's clapping, dust filled the room, much more dust than what's expected to be found in a kid's room that hasn't been cleaned for a couple of days. We soon realized that clapping must have ignited some strange dust-making machine or magic.

Instead of a genie, a man appeared out of the dust, in normal clothes, like the clothes dad and his friends wear. After taking a bow, the man revealed that his mission was rather concrete and his powers limited. He couldn't fulfill our wish, yet he intended to take us on a trip, in faraway places, to see and learn things we would never find in books.

I presented my objections. However nice that strange man seemed, I had been taught not to go far away, especially with strangers. Besides, I didn't want to cause any trouble. Mom was already unhappy enough with Alex missing.

"We will be back before anyone notices your absence because time counts differently when you travel to places like this. I promise you, this trip will be safe," the man promised to appease my fears and hesitation.

"How exactly will we travel?" asked Gina, who took a look around, but saw no vehicle.

"Magically," said the man, smiling. He took something that looked like a cell phone out of his pocket, which soon transformed into a big screen. The screen became brighter when the man pushed a button. He asked us to hold hands and he held on tightly to me.

"Off we go," he said and I felt as if I heard my father's voice.

We didn't go that far, yet it should have taken more than one step to go from my room to the living room. The screen behind us got dimmer until it disappeared.

The door opened and I watched Alex enter the house along with dad. I was ready to run and give my brother a hug. The man put his hand in front of me to stop me.

"We're not here to participate. We're only here to watch," he whispered in my ear. I found it hard to understand. Why shouldn't I participate in my family's joy?

"Alex is not found. He hasn't even disappeared yet," the man explained.

"Do you mean we're in the past?" asked Dean.

"Of course we're in the past. Even I have realized that," said Gina. Gina was not stupid. She was pretty smart, smarter than any other girl her age that I knew, but she liked to pretend she was stupid from time to time.

"I didn't expect such a low grade in physics. Do you

realize how disappointed your mother will be?" Dad said to Alex who bowed his head in shame.

"I can't understand what's wrong. Why didn't you study?"

"I did," Alex mumbled. Dad, as if he had expected that exact answer, went on, undaunted.

"Is this the best excuse you could think of? It's obvious you didn't study enough. You have a brilliant mind. I'm not going to allow you to waste it."

I saw my brother blush, holding back his tears, and I wished I could go there beside him and comfort him, and tell him that I know how hard he tried, yet the man gripped me firmly and didn't let me move at all.

We had all been expecting Alex's grades in agony, certain of his success once more. Just before he disappeared, my dad took the day off to go and get my brother's grades. Nobody mentioned anything about them during lunch that day because Alex had already gone missing, so we had more important things to keep us busy at that moment.

When I went downstairs for lunch, Alex had already gone and I found mom crying while dad mumbled incomprehensibly.

Gina sobbed beside me. Dean embraced her. The man let go of my shoulders, took that strange gadget off his pocket, pushed a button and the big bright screen appeared ahead of us once more.

We time-traveled to the school. I wished he hadn't taken us there. I didn't like this place at all.

"It's not as bad as you've described it," said Gina.

"Believe me, it's worse than you can imagine," I said without second thought.

The twins didn't go to school. I considered them lucky although Gina seemed to disagree.

"It's so nice to be among other children," she said, jumping with joy the moment the bell rang and all the kids rushed out of the classrooms and into the yard where we stood.

The other kids made me dislike school, and they were exactly why Gina liked the idea of school.

I saw myself walking out of the building, holding a book in my hand. I recall that day. It had been some days before school went out for summer. I couldn't really see the reason the man had brought us there.

Gina, on the other hand, seemed rather excited.

"Hey, you're here and there at the same time," she said.

I'd be excited watching myself from afar as well if I didn't already know what came next.

I saw myself walk as silently as possible. I remember I wanted to be invisible. I suspected that those kids were up to something and I wanted to hide, yet I knew well I wouldn't be able to escape if they decided to play another one of their tricks on me. Our teacher mentioned something about black holes in space. I found the subject interesting. The teacher talked about immense gravitational forces that don't even allow light to be seen. That seemed like a good way to be invisible, yet I hadn't really figured out how that might work. Instead, I only walked on the tips of my toes, as silently as I could, to escape their attention.

A tall boy came my way, teasing me. He wanted to grab my book.

"What a rude little boy," said Gina, watching the scene.

I couldn't fight him. I didn't want to make a spectacle of myself either. Pretending a fall was my only choice.

"Hey, I saw that, you fell down on purpose," cried Dean, like he'd just solved a big mystery of the universe.

"So what?" I asked him.

"Why did you do that?"

"Didn't you see him? He was coming my way, what else could I have done?"

The tall boy didn't want much trouble. He grabbed the book and left me alone on the ground.

"That wasn't nice, that wasn't nice at all," said Gina, who turned my way to see my reaction.

A bunch of kids watched from afar, laughing and mocking me and clapping in excitement.

The teacher had mentioned the possibility of time travel through those black holes. He didn't consider it possible or impossible. I'm pretty sure he didn't know much about black holes and time travel. They looked like difficult subjects to him, which intrigued me, considering adults usually pretend to know everything.

I remember wishing for time to stand still and for me to disappear into a black hole and never come back to school again. I only wanted to disappear completely, so that I would not hear the laughter of the kids around. I knew they laughed at me and that felt bad, really bad, like a knife piercing into my bones and tearing my heart in two.

The man held me by the shoulders as I began crying. Gina came near me and gently caressed my hair.

"Who's that little girl?" she asked when a freckled short girl approached shyly by my other self, who avoided her eyes and insisted on looking at the ground. I remembered her. Anna. Two seats behind me in class.

"Are you ok?" the girl asked, fixing the glasses on her nose. I hadn't seen that before. I only saw it from afar, watching the scene. I had preferred not to look at her. I had preferred to stare at the ground.

Yet Anna seemed worried. She seemed really caring, bowing down to give me a hand.

"Go away, I don't need your help," I told her.

I watched the girl walk away in sadness.

"I wish I could fall out of time and into a black hole," I told her, as she turned the other way and didn't look back until she reached the entrance of the building.

If I had lifted my eyes to see her, I would have realized her disappointment, yet I didn't.

"How rude of you," said Dean.

"I couldn't tell she was sad at the moment," I tried to defend myself.

"Enough with the past," said our leader, interrupting our conversation.

"Let us head towards the present now."

We didn't head anywhere. We only entered the big screen again.

This time, we landed on a roof. Looking down, I saw the playground I used to see from our old house and I jumped with joy.

I saw Alex lying in the corner. The sight of him made me immediately forget all about the incident with the book and Anna.

"Do not insist. I'm never going back."

"Do you plan to live on this roof forever?"

I recognized our old neighbor's son. He and Alex had been good friends, back when we lived here. They dreamed of having a band and playing music themselves. When Alex asked my father if he could have guitar lessons, my father refused. Dad considered guitars to be a waste of time, and he thought music lessons might distract Alex from studying.

Alex awkwardly pulled the strings of a guitar I had never seen before. I immediately excluded the possibility that dad had bought it for him.

My brother's awkward movements on the guitar turned

into a melody. We stayed there frozen, listening to him playing the guitar.

The man explained that Alex had been saving money for a long time until he managed to save enough to buy the guitar in secrecy.

"So, what are your plans now that you've left?" his friend asked when the music was over.

"I'm not sure yet. I've had enough of being the perfect student, though."

"I think you'd better go home and tell your parents what you're telling me."

"You can't understand a thing, can you? They won't listen to me. I'm nothing to them unless I'm perfect."

I was very angry at my parents right then. For making Alex feel like this over a stupid test. Gina cried beside me.

"What about the kid? Won't you miss him?"

Alex's friend obviously meant me.

"So," the man said, taking the strange gadget that looked like a cell phone out of his pocket, "now, we're supposed to take that scary trip into the future. That's what happens in stories like this one."

Gina nodded. She remained speechless though, probably paralyzed by fear. I realized that this thing with the man taking us here and there seemed like that old tale with the spirits that my mom used to read to us on Christmas Eve each year. Gina mentioned Alice in Wonderland, her own favorite story.

"We might have fallen into a rabbit hole," she whispered in my ear.

"That man doesn't look like a rabbit," I whispered back.

"There's no reason to be afraid," he explained. "I will only show you things you can change. You have all the time in the world ahead of you," he said, staring at me, so I realized this trip was all about me.

"If this trip doesn't concern me, can I not come?" Gina asked, trembling.

"You can discuss it if you want," answered the man, taking a look at his watch.

We formed a circle and talked in low voices.

"Do you really think it's wise to leave me alone on this important trip?"

Dean tried to defend his sister.

"You're old enough to handle this, aren't you?" he asked. The tone of his voice reminded me of mom when she tried to convince me that I was too old to behave like a child. My friends had stolen mother's trick and behaved in the exact same manner as her.

"He's not ready, don't you see?" he then told Gina. She shrugged.

"I like him a lot but it's a bit unkind to carry us around all the time, without even asking for our opinion."

"Stop pretending I'm not here," I said, a little louder than intended. It seemed that to the man who stood beside us, it sounded the same whether we talked in low voices or yelled.

"I'm asking you to consider joining me on this trip, please."

The twins exchanged glances. They often communicated like that, without even uttering a word.

"Ok," said Dean. "Remember you owe us one, though."

"Hurry, we're off in a little while," said the man who seemed fully aware we had just agreed, yet he preferred to feign ignorance.

Truth is, I hadn't really thought about my future. Seriously, I mean. However, what I came to see, once we stepped into the shiny screen and into the future, found me unprepared.

Across the room lay the older version of me, more than ten years older, perhaps even older than me now, on my bed which hadn't changed a bit and barely fit him. He pulled the blanket over his head. When Gina and Dean appeared at the window, he uncovered himself to welcome them. Mom called from downstairs, her voice hoarser than usual: "Dinner's ready. Come down here to eat with us. You might as well follow your father's advice and go out for a walk. You might make some friends at last."

The strangest part of this was that the future twins were exactly the same; they hadn't grown a day, while I looked like I belonged among the adults.

I looked at my friends who stood beside me, then at their future selves, then back at them.

"Why do you act surprised?" asked Gina.

"Because, as opposed to me, you haven't grown at all."

Dean was even more direct than his sister.

"You pretend you don't know," he said.

"Know what?"

"Imaginary creatures never grow old. They always remain at the age they have been created at."

"You mean I made you up? Is that what you're trying to tell me?"

"Don't flatter yourself, dear," said Gina giggling. "Your imagination is not that vivid to create a wonderful creature like me."

Dean burst into laughter.

"I have to confess we've had many friends before you, so you didn't imagine us first, as it seems."

The twins confused me more and more and the man's silence became irritating.

"You mean that if I don't do something about it, I will stay trapped in this room in the company of you two who will watch me grow while remaining children forever."

What an awful mess, the future. It didn't look that bright at all. Even my childish mind recognized the wrongness of my image in the future. I didn't want to end up being the boy who forgot to grow up. To grow into an adult who hides from reality. To be the boy who fell out of time and into a black hole in his brain and got stuck there forever.

"Child in time," said Gina. "I think I heard Alex sing about a child in time. Nice song, wasn't it?"

Dean, ignoring her remark, readied to speak, then hesitated. The man made a gesture, encouraging Dean to move on with what he'd intended to say.

"You owe us a favor, if you remember."

I nodded to show that I remembered.

Gina came close and embraced me. They communicated in glances again, without talking to each other.

"I think it's time you let us go after this trip ends."

"What on earth do you mean?" I asked, cold sweat on my back, making my shirt stick on my skin.

"You know what I mean. It's time we hang around with other kids that need us. You're not the loneliest kid in the world, you know."

I knew the twins were right. I should let them go, in case someone needed them more than I did.

It just hit me. I didn't see my brother anywhere in that future world, but I didn't have time to ask, since the man made it clear we should move on immediately.

I didn't recognize the place, but we were probably downtown because I saw lots of people waiting for the light to turn green so they could cross the street. As soon as the light changed color, the pavement got empty, ready to welcome the pedestrians coming from across the street, coming our way in a hurry. One of them fell on the ground, right in the middle of the street.

Some passersby gathered around him. We also got there, near the man who lay on the ground.

I exchanged glances with the twins.

"That man on the ground... he looks a lot like you, you know," said Gina.

The man took us back to the pavement.

"That man you saw on the ground is truly me," he said.

"Has something bad happened to you?"

"You could say that. I almost died there. But the ambulance came in time and doctors rescued me. Later on, people I didn't know took care of me and instilled some hope in my heart. Through their actions, they showed me to seek happiness. For what matters is not to be good at everything, as I had once thought, but to be good with people in need."

Gina was about to cry again. She would have started already if she hadn't panicked, having watched the tragic incident moments ago.

"You don't seem that old. Why did that happen to you? What did you almost die from?"

"Despair," said the man after some moments of pondering.

"You can't die from despair," said Dean. Dad used to say humans can handle a lot if they set their mind to it, so I tended to agree with Dean. Despair is not a disease. Despair is something you should fight against.

"Humans can handle a lot, until they no longer can," answered the man.

"People usually grow up without even realizing it: they move from childhood to puberty. Slowly, they stop playing. Little by little, they begin exploring things they like. They

41

may or may not study, yet they will eventually learn to do something useful, to ensure survival. And then they get serious. Not because they have to, but because they are tired of childish behaviour. They figure they have been childish long enough. Somehow, I had been born serious. I didn't play around as a kid, but I instead devoted myself to studying, and I became an excellent student."

"Just like Alex," Gina interrupted him.

"Just like Alex as you know him."

"What do you mean?" asked Dean in suspicion.

The man smiled.

"Alex was like that until he went to college. He changed there, though. The only thing he had on his mind was to play the guitar like he did earlier on the roof."

"Dad wouldn't allow that," I said.

"That's true. Only, nothing your father said could change Alex's mind. Alex finally finished his studies, although it took him more time than expected, despite everyone thinking he'd eventually give up. Then came the next stage. The stage of adjustment, as I prefer to call it. Alex decided that his father had always been right, that he had to find a job that wouldn't perhaps satisfy him that much, yet it would provide money for the family he would soon start. He got married and had a child. That child looks so much like you by the way..."

The man stared at me as I watched him talk, open-mouthed.

"...until he lost his job, after some years. Along with his job, he lost his wife. She took the child and moved away. Alex was all alone at that point. He went deep into despair. He wasn't used to not doing everything right, as you can already tell. And so came the last stage, that of self-pity and depression. He became strict with himself. Stricter than your father. He hadn't learned to enjoy life. And that's how we came down to this. To what you've just watched."

We were frozen. Time seemed still as we turned our heads to the side of the street, altogether at once, as if a magic wand had made us turn at the same exact time.

"So, that man on the ground is Alex?" asked Dean reluctantly.

The man nodded.

"Which means you're Alex," I said in hesitation, yet certain about the expected answer. My voice barely heard, lost and drowned between my sobs, yet even if the man couldn't hear it, he could definitely read my mind.

"I'm not only here for you, kid. I'm mostly here for me. I took a wrong turn somewhere along the way and I want you to help me see it. So that I don't waste so much time before I begin appreciating life. I trust you to save me, kid. I want to grow up the usual way. You will make sure I do, won't you?"

"I surely will Alex. I will do whatever it takes to save you," I thought while nodding.

I looked at my brother and felt like hugging him. When I went to approach him, as I opened up my arms and closed my eyes, attempting to show him all the love I intended to offer him in the future, the bright screen lighted up once more and pulled me inside like a whirlpool. Alex waved goodbye.

"See you soon, little brother," he said. "Don't get lost inside your head. There are people who need you out there," I heard him say, as I floated in time and space, before the screen spat me out and threw me at a place I hadn't seen before.

"Where on Earth am I?" I thought to myself.

A young woman stormed into the room holding a bunch of papers in her hands, heading to the sofa. I felt awkward having invaded her personal space and cringed in shame the moment she walked beside me. I then remembered I'd probably be invisible to her.

"You remind me of him," she said looking my way.

I turned around to check whether there was someone else in the room.

"Will you stop pretending that you don't hear me?" she asked.

"Can you see me?"

"I certainly can," she answered, giggling the way Gina giggled when she heard something funny.

"How's that possible?"

"It happens all the time," she said, feigning indifference. "You people come and go as you please. You don't appreciate my time. You don't understand that I have to concentrate and finish my book."

"Sorry, I didn't mean to interrupt you," I said as I wished Alex could be there with me to explain this.

I walked towards the door to leave, but the brightness of her face held me still before I opened the door.

"Oh, come on. You don't have to leave right now. You can sit here and help me write this book, perhaps."

I sat beside her on the sofa and watched her get lost in thought. The more I saw her, the more I liked her. I thought that was the kind of woman I wanted to fall in love with, once I grew up.

"I had a classmate once who looked exactly like you," she said, lifting her eyes from her papers, holding the pen in her mouth like a cigarette.

"He never noticed me though," she said and sighed. "I had to move on, you know? So I began imagining things. Little strange creatures to keep me company because I felt lonely."

"I'm different," I told her. "I do exist. I have a real life and I go to school like all children do and I have two parents and a brother, Alex, who loves me but he's gone missing now and I'm on a strange trip in time and space..."

"Really?" she interrupted me. "I haven't just imagined you then?"

"I'm afraid not."

"That's interesting. It hasn't happened before. A creature like you claiming to be real."

"I have imaginary friends too. I have Gina and Dean visiting me every now and then. Only now did I discover they're magical creatures."

"You know Gina and Dean too?"

I couldn't believe my ears. That woman knew my two best friends.

"You mean you have met them too?"

"Of course, I have. They came to me when I was much younger. They kept me company for a long time. Come to think of it, Gina had mentioned something about you. A little boy whose brother went missing. She came to me after you decided to let her go."

My mind started working fast to analyze the facts. If Gina visited her after me, then I was still in the future. That girl was older than me, yet in normal time we shared the same age.

"What's your name?" I asked reluctantly.

"I'm Anna," she said, confirming my suspicion.

"I can't believe it, Anna. You're so beautiful. I mean you're beautiful the way I know you too, yet now you're a woman and I'm still a little boy," I began rambling, realizing I don't make any sense.

"Blah, blah, blah, you're so talkative, will you be quiet for a while?"

Anna was my classmate. Two seats behind me in class.

She was the girl I was rude to when she came to give me a hand and help me stand up when the tall boy had stolen my book.

She lifted her eyes and threw the pen across the room. A tear or two appeared in the corner of her eyes, making their way on her cheek.

"You have no idea how it is," she said, wiping her face with the back of her hand. "To be alone on Christmas day. You're still so young."

"I'm sorry, Anna," I told her gently.

"You should be. You should have noticed me back then. We could have hung out together. We could have been best friends, yet you chose to ignore me."

"I will make it up to you," I promised and I truly meant it.

"It's too late now. I'm here alone, writing this stupid book about you, about the boy who fell out of time and never came back because you asked for a black hole to swallow you and I wanted revenge and that's unfair. You appear the moment I decide to trap you forever in that journey and you're such a sweet little boy..."

"Why would you do that, Anna?" I said, my heart pounding, my hands trembling, as she handed me the papers she had been holding all along.

"I like you too much to do that to you," she eventually said. "If I could turn back time, I would like you again."

"Hey, kid. Wake up." I felt a hand on my face.

"Alex," I yelled in excitement the moment I opened up my eyes. Alex was not as old as he had been a while ago, when he asked me to take care of him. I wondered if I'd come back home, if Anna had let me return to my time.

Bewildered, I looked around. The twins were not here. I made sure I was back in my room. I wanted to talk to Alex about all that had happened, but I preferred to keep my mouth shut. Not because he wouldn't understand. Alex would be the only one who might understand. He knew about the twins. He didn't make fun of me in general. I kept my mouth shut only because I felt so happy he'd returned, too. I only wanted to look at him, without speaking.

"You should do some cleaning up in here too. I haven't been away for long and you turned it into a dump."

I think what Alex meant was that he wanted me to do some cleaning inside my head. He mentioned our room because he was kinder than our parents, who didn't control their words if things didn't go their way.

"You were in my dream, Alex," I eventually told him.

"Really?"

"Yes, not the way you are now, you were much older and wiser. I didn't recognize you at all, despite the fact you looked a lot like dad and you took us with you, me and the twins, and we traveled in the past, the present, and into the future, like that story I can't recall the name of it. Gina knows it much better than me."

Alex grabbed me by the shoulders and shook me.

"Stop talking to me about the twins. You have to grow up, don't you see?"

I got away easily and ran to the window. Under similar circumstances, the twins always appeared to defend me, to stand by me. I didn't see them anywhere.

I put my hand in my pocket and the note was still there. I took a look. It bore his handwriting. I wondered how I hadn't recognized it from the start.

"Alex, the twins are gone. For good."

"It's about time," he said. He then regretted his words and approached me.

"How do you feel about it?"

"It's not a problem. I will make some real friends. That's

what mom says I should do, right? That I should find some friends and not spend that much time alone. I think I'm ready."

Instead of being happy for me, he looked at me, his face darkened with sadness.

"You mean Gina and Dean weren't real friends to you?"

"They weren't real, Alex. They were my imaginary friends, only I had not created them myself. If you can believe, I didn't imagine them. Someone else created them to keep company with lonely kids and..."

Alex interrupted me.

"That's not what I meant kid. The fact that they were imaginary doesn't make them unreal. They were there when you needed them. It's a good thing they left. But you have to keep them in your heart. You will never forget about them. You hear me?"

I thought about it before I nodded. They would remain as real as the journey had been. Whatever or whoever accompanies our hearts, even in our imagination, is real. Whatever we love, remains in our heart, even when it disappears.

"You should know Alex, you will become my best friend, and I won't let anything bad happen to you."

He smiled at me.

"We will be alright," he said eventually.

He came near me and fixed the pillow under my head.

"Merry Christmas, kiddo. Now go back to sleep, it's too early for presents," he said gently.

I closed my eyes and dreamt of the next year at school when I would meet Anna again. If I asked her kindly enough, she would perhaps say hello to my old friends for me, I thought. I never did, for Gina and Dean never visited her.

"Imaginary friends are personal," says Anna, holding my hand, swaying to the music, insisting I made them up in my mind. But even if it wasn't me who created them, they had no reason to visit her. She never became lonely.

"I had you, remember?" she asks, and I nod but she doesn't see me. She's already looking ahead at the stage where Alex and his band start playing Carol of the Bells. She's swept away, she's lost in Christmas magic, she sings along and sways, still holding my hand, and in her touch lies all happiness, all magic that started years ago when I fell out of time and into myself, into love.

A BLIZZARD AND CHRISTMAS
WREATHS

PERLA NASSER

*P*reparations for the annual Christmas fair had already started and it preoccupied the people of the town as they bustled through vendors of the market in search of the best ingredients. Lillith looked above at the sky purpled by dawn and its luminous halo of silver beckoning from beyond the horizon. She breathed in the rich scent of spices and pine and greeted the grinning vendors plying their wares through the now-muddy path. Salesmen coaxed her to taste their variety of cheeses, an assortment of nuts, and sweet dried fruits and she couldn't resist but get some to bring with her home.

Lillith got back home and the children's bubbly laughter could be heard from outside as they played with the freshly fallen addition of snow. She looked at herself in the mirror, her skin was darker than most, claiming some African blood in her ancestry. Other people would have hidden those roots, but she owned them with pride, attributing some romantic hot-bloodiness to them. The roundness of her face and the natural glow of her copper skin that she saw in the wash basin each morning, the black curls of her hair, the full lips, the thick eyebrows, the lazy gaze—every day she was more a lady. But she still had a youthful appearance about her, child-like and sweet.

"I heard Thomas was going to propose to her soon, he *loves* her—" she overheard her older sister, Alice, saying dreamily to her Mom.

"Lillith," said Alice, upon seeing her sister enter through the small kitchen doors, "we were just talking about you, I've heard great news!" she stopped kneading the dough for a moment to broadly smile at her sister, eyes gleaming in excitement.

"He's already talked to me, and I told him no." Lillith said and both her sister and mother let out small gasps and looked at each other, "I simply cannot see myself as his wife, loving him and bearing his children."

"Lillith you silly thing, you cannot say you haven't noticed his attention to you," Her mother said, "he's a good man and he loves you."

"Your cookies smell so great mama," exclaimed Lillith, complimenting her food and completely switching up the subject. She walked over to where her mother stood kneading the dough for the next batch of Christmas sweet bread and kissed her cheek.

From the corner of her eye, Lillith could see her older sister bustling loudly around the dim kitchen, lighting a few candles and making sure the windows were shut properly to keep the cold out.

"Are you going to be making those beautiful wreaths this year?" asked her mother with a kind smile that reached her eyes. "You know everybody loved those last year, and they looked so great with Thomas' garlands," she said while brushing the hairs that had escaped her small bun away from her face with the back of her hand.

Lillith remembered the handmade garlands that Thomas had made for the previous Christmas fair. She knew that he preoccupied himself to make those in an attempt to impress her and possibly spend more time with her. Even though it was sweet of him, she could not find it in her heart to love him back.

"Anything to make you and the town happy, ma," replied Lillith, grabbing a bite from the delicious gingerbread roll sitting on the counter.

The fair was held in the memory of Lady Catherine who loved preparing the most special Christmas treats with Lord Julian and offering them to the people all through-out December. But unfortunately, one gloomy winter, the fever was triumphant in her battle with the Influenza and took her from the people—and most heartbreakingly, from Lord Julian. His life had turned gray, and his favorite holiday with the company of people became a curse of self-seclusion. He refused to interact with anyone due to the pain the memories of the season would bring back.

"Lilly, Lilly, Lilly!" her little sister Danielle burst through the small kitchen doors in her adorable reindeer onesie and jumped into Lillith's arms who picked her up, hugging her tightly. Kissing her cheeks she looked up to see that she was followed by Thomas who smiled upon seeing her. She sweetly smiled back at him, but the gleam in his eyes was unmatched.

"I'll go down to the forest to collect what I'm going to be needing to make them," Lillith told her mother, setting her sister down who ran back into Thomas' arms.

"People talk of a snowstorm tonight, I don't think it's a good idea for you to go out today." Her mother said with concern in her eyes.

"Don't worry mama, I'll be back by dusk. I must go as I

won't have enough time to finish them." Lillith glanced back at the window. She was guilty of always leaving things for the last minute.There was still no sign of bad weather on the horizon, but uneasiness lingered at the back of her mind. *I have to quit my habit of postponing my tasks and responsibilities and leaving everything until the last minute.*

"Oh no, Lillith," Thomas' voice was heavy with weary scolding, "I will go with you, a lady like yourself mustn't go by herself in the forest," Thomas said and Lillith looked at her mother for help.

"Thomas dear, you can stay here and help me out with the baking, Lilly will be just fine." Thomas looked to Lillith and then back to her mother, slight disappointment in his eyes.

Ever since he'd confessed his feelings for her a couple of days ago, things between them had been awkward and uncomfortable. She didn't want to hurt him but at the same time, she valued her morals and refused to force herself to love someone she only saw as a friendly neighbor.

Thomas set Danielle down, and gathered up his cloak, hugging it to his chest. He followed her outside and got hold of her outstretched arm with one hand, his fingers encircling her wrist in an uncomfortable grip. He was watching her as though wishing it was she, and not the cloak, pressed against him, and he made an attempt to draw her nearer but she was quick to snatch her wrist out of his grip, "please let go, Thomas."

"Be careful and come back as soon as you can. I can't bear the thought of anything bad happening to you." He said, releasing her wrist. Lillith could say nothing, breath stuck in her throat, heart thrashing against her ribcage.

"I'll be back soon." *Just please leave me alone,* she thought.

With one last look at her house, she set off through the

silent, snowy forest, blood coursing past her ears. Though she'd slept little, energy flowed through her and drove her deeper into the forest.

JULIAN LOOKED at the love of his life. The warmth coming from the large fireplace caressed their bodies comfortingly and gave her plump cheeks a natural blush. He brushed her long fair hair that partially covered her naked torso, and let his fingertips glide across her soft skin. The sweet perfume that he loved on her was the only thing she was wearing and he closed his eyes as he breathed in her scent. The evergreen pine Christmas tree stood tall and dense in the center of the Great Hall; its invigorating and woody smell combined with the sweet smell of freshly baked cookies had traveled into the farthest corners of the palace, carrying with it the distinctive smell of Christmas. He averted his eyes away from the magnificent tree as she gently touched his chin.

"Look outside," she said and shifted to stare outside at the snowflakes dancing in the warm light that streamed out of the windows. The snow lay in deep drifts in the early-morning light, puffed up like a marshmallow and yet undotted by animal tracks. "Look at the beauty of this season, it's my favorite time of the year." She sighed and he hummed back quietly and pressed his lips onto her temple, tightening his grip around her waist.

"It wouldn't be the same without you," he whispered back to her, nuzzling his face into the nape of her neck. "you bring joy and light to my gloomiest days and darkest nights." His heartfelt whisper just louder than the sound of the crackling fire in the hearth.

"I cannot picture myself to be anywhere but here, with

you." she replied, kissing him slowly, "truly you have the whitest soul, as white as the newly drifted snow," her blue eyes gleamed under the warm light. "Merry Christmas my love." Shifting closer to her, she leaned her back against his warm chest and pulled the wool blanket higher over their bodies.

He closed his eyes and let his head rest back against the cushions of the comfortable chaise longue they were both laying on, hoping the memory of that perfect moment would last longer. Not too long after that, the familiar feeling of numbness started to settle in, and he could feel how he slowly and painfully lost her touch. The smell of her perfume started to fade and the vibrations of her symphonic laugh were gradually replaced by silence.

He opened his eyes and his heart sank once again as he came back to the darkness of reality. Death had already been chasing her, mercilessly snapping its jaws at her ankles, refusing to let her get away. Several times they thought she would outrun the fever, hollow-cheeked and panting from the chase, but on a cold winter night death had caught up to her and he was left with only a grieving memory. He still saw her everywhere: in the morning between market vendors where they shopped together for fresh vegetables and fruits, in their library where she used to sit comfortably on the window sill, lost within the pages of a novel, her fair hair swept behind her ears. Sometimes he saw her in the snowflakes dancing in the breeze on a quiet evening when the sunshine reflected on her hair, making it glow almost magically, and he saw her on his eyelids whenever his eyes fell closed.

Double glass windows covered in frost illuminated the library as he sulked there all afternoon, sunlight gilding across the crystal chandelier, throwing shadows along the hand-sewn tapestries and the velvet chairs his parents had once occupied. She felt closer here and he thought if he prayed hard enough, he might see her footprints in the snow, detect her scent in the breeze. But hope was lost and it had been for many years.

Life had cast loneliness upon his existence as a curse he found no end to, every day sinking deeper and deeper into the depth of insanity. The holidays were rolling around and he was stuck with the memory of her.

"Julian, my dear." He saw Mrs. Adley from the corner of his eyes and looked up at her. Her small dark eyes on her doughy pliable face held concern for the young man. "I made you some tea." She held a tray in her hands that carried honeyed biscuits, jam and sliced cheese, a pot of tea, and a pitcher of water. A small crock of half-melted butter sat beside the biscuits.

He felt grateful for having the sweet lady in his life, for she cared for him as her own son. He hated that she could read the pain in his eyes because he knew she would worry too much about him. She prayed for his happiness every night, prayed so his heart would open itself again for love.

THE SKY WAS GROWING DARKER, though the hour was too early for the sun to set. The clouds were thickening. *Perhaps there would be a storm after all.*

The day passed quickly, the morning turning to noon almost without her noticing. Lillith had found materials— leaves, evergreen twigs, mistletoe, and pine cones— except for holly. She stopped to rest just after noon, wishing she'd been thinking clearly enough to bring food for lunch. The snowflakes started tumbling through the air and her breath blew out in a cloud of steam. She knew had to start looking for her way back home but she was determined to find holly to bring back and hang up at the fair. Her brain didn't want to process the change but she couldn't deny the sudden frigid chill on her cheeks and the snowflakes collecting in her hair. When she turned around to head back, she noticed a little foxtail swinging side to side like a slow, gentle pendulum. Lillith eased herself into a more comfortable position and calmed her breathing, straining to listen to the forest over the wind. The snow fell and fell, dancing and curling like sparkling spindrifts, the white fresh and clean against the brown and gray of the forest. She watched the fox emerge from the bare, bony trees and trot belly deep in the cold powder, its russet coat like a stray flame in the snow. She observed as he stopped – nose pointed, one paw poised in the air like one of their old hunting dogs – detecting noise or smell. A mouse? A chipmunk? If he was lucky, a white-tailed rabbit? He looked thin and in need of that meal. She held her breath as he froze, waiting with him. Then he jumped away, darting off towards the forest, scared off by the horse approaching from the south and galloping towards her. Her eyes widened. The rider didn't seem to be aware of her sitting down in the snow and she screamed, quickly throwing herself into the snow a few feet away.

Her heart started pounding against her ribcage and dread settled in her chest as she had a feeling she knew exactly who it was. "Easy, easy there, boy.." She cursed at herself as she heard Lord Julian's voice whispering to his horse, confirming her suspicions. His voice was familiar to her as he used to speak to the people often, but to him she was just another face in the crowd. The horse neighed loudly, restless to get going on their journey back to the palace. *Please just ignore me and go, oh God this is embarrassing.*

"I'm so sorry we didn't see you in the snow," Lord Julian

apologized, getting down to help Lillith with her makeshift bag of rope and cloth. "We were chasing that little sly fox not expecting anybody to be out here on this part of the forest." He tried to explain himself as Lillith clumsily tried getting up on her own refusing his help.

"I'm okay, I'm alright," she assured, even as she tripped twice over her dress causing blood to rush to her face and ears.

"Are you sure you're alright?" He asked in concern, as he watched her pat herself, trying to get as much snow off herself as she could before it could fully soak through her coat.

After finally regaining both her balance and voice she said, "Yes, my Lord, I'm perfectly fine. I guess I wasn't expecting anyone to be out here either." She let out an awkward laugh, trying to forget her not-so-graceful head-first dive into the snow. She cringed as she felt her now wet hair sticking uncomfortably to her head and neck.

"Please call me Julian." She finally looked up at him and took in his elegant attire. He was wearing a white shirt under a high-collared blue coat accented with leather trim and detailed gold stitching. Gold buckles crossed his chest and a dagger was belted to his hip as well as a set of wooden bow and arrows slung across his back. When her eyes reached his face, she struggled to mask her admiration for he had one of the most beautiful faces she had ever seen: dark green eyes, a sharp nose, and high cheekbones framed with tousled, ink-black hair that was styled back except for a small strand that fell over his face.

"Julian.," she whispered under her breath as if in a daze and shook her head to quickly snap out of it before she embarrassed herself further. "..and I'm Lillith." She cleared her throat, "I'm Lillith." She repeated in a more confident tone. He smiled —and to make matters more challenging for her—the faint shadow of a dimple appeared on his cheek and she caught herself staring at his mouth.

He blushed deeply, suddenly very conscious of the fact that a woman was admiring his every feature so attentively. The dark stallion, as if feeling the tension between the two, pushed Julian's shoulder with its head causing him to bump into Lillith. "Nallbo!" Julian exclaimed in surprise, glaring at the horse in embarrassment. Quickly apologizing again, he grabbed the reins tighter patting the horse's neck, assuring the animal that they would get going soon.

"Please let me at least take you home," he said, breaking the silence, and quickly unfastened his cloak. He draped his warm cloak over her small and slightly shivering shoulders and she noticeably relaxed under his touch. She thanked him for his kind offer as more snow started to fall from the swarm of clouds that had filled the sky.

Julian straightened the reins, instructed her to grab the pommel, and helped her up the saddle. He followed, grace-fully getting his body behind her. They cantered along a silent path when the wind suddenly picked up. In another time and weather, he would be glad to be riding double in the snow, the weight of a girl against his chest but he couldn't deny the worry in his heart when he felt her shiver. "I think it would be a better idea to get back to the palace," he broke the silence, " I worry that you might catch a cold if we don't get you warm and dry soon." She thought the offer to be a very kind gesture. For some reason, his worry for her made her cheeks blush and his firm arms on either side of her waist weren't of help.

Silence enveloped them, broken only by Nallbo's hooves rhythmically sinking into the freshly fallen snow. Snow dusted across Julian's hands, collecting in the stallion's mane.

She looked behind them. The trail was equally coated in snow. Large flakes filtered down through the trees.

The trees started to thin gradually before giving way to the open fields where the beautiful palace stood on top of a hill. They kept along the well-trodden path lined with high trees, their snow-covered branches intertwined and glistened above their heads. Lillith stared up in awe at the serene surroundings and listened closely to the whispering of the cold breeze and silence of the fresh snow. The palace was a lavish three-story high architectural beauty of sand-colored stone, heavily curtained windows, and tall column pillars. Lillith straightened her back as Julian pulled the horse to a stop and let go of her waist. They had formed a cocoon of warmth, and his cloak—fur-lined leather— smelled like oranges and cloves. As soon as they got off of Nallbo, a stocky man with a bushy grey mustache greeted them both and took the horse back to the warmth of the stables.

"Let me get this for you, Miss, "said the man, referring to her makeshift bag holding her twigs, "I'll bring it for you inside." She let go of it, thanking the kind man in return.

Julian led Lillith up to the grand doors of the palace and held them open for her. The growing wind was blowing straight through the fibers of her unlined coat, and she felt chilled to her core. She shivered appreciatively and hurried inside, rubbing her hands together and blowing her hot breath into them.

A woman she had met before twice in a market greeted them. She had eyes like currants, dark and small, and set in a doughy, pliable face. She was tall for a woman of her generation – five foot nine or so – and her white hair was fastened in a bun just beginning to come undone at the sides. She was wearing a half-apron over a tweed skirt and what appeared to be a hand-knitted Aran cardigan, and there were simple black shoes on her feet.

A half-beat passed before realization dawned on the old woman's face "My dear!" the woman exclaimed upon seeing Lillith, "I cannot believe my eyes!" she looked at Julian with a bright grin that reached her eyes and then back at Lillith, straightening the red apron at her waist. "I apologize for my bold excitement it's just that these walls hadn't had the pleasure to enjoy the company of another woman besides myself ever—"

"Mrs. Adley please!" Julian's voice cut off her rant, his cheeks flaming in embarrassment. Lillith stared up at Mrs. Adley's kind brown eyes, noticing how her smile reached the faint creases of her eyelids.

She ushered them inside before quickly shutting the big ebony doors, locking the biting cold outside.

"We need to help Miss Lillith get warm and dry," He rambled. "I mean you Mrs. Adley, not me, of course." He took a step before them and led the way through the corridor and into the spacious lobby toward the grand staircase.

"May I ask what you were doing out alone in this weather?" Mrs.Adley asked the question Julian had been meaning to ask Lillith since the moment he'd met her.

"I was looking for Holly to decorate the wreaths," she replied, but continued when she saw the confusion on her face, "for the annual Christmas Fair." She trailed off when she noticed Julian's shoulder hunch slightly at the mention of Christmas.

"Ah! We have those in our garden! We can go and get you some in the morning," Mrs. Adley clapped her hands as they took a turn into a hall with double doors and ceiling-high windows that looked outside. The sun was hidden beneath a constant swarm of clouds.

"The morning? I cannot stay here overnight, I must get back home." Lillith said, suddenly remembering her mother and how she'd fall sick with worry if she didn't return home by nightfall.

"I'll send a carrier pigeon to the central post office to have someone send the news to your family about your whereabouts and well-being," Julian assured her without hesitation. Deep down he knew he enjoyed her unexpected company and did not want to see her leave that soon.

Julian excused himself to go change, leaving Mrs. Adley to lead Lillith into the guest room where, Mrs. Adley instructed, Lillith would find everything that she needed. "Dinner will be ready in a couple of hours dear, and if you need anything else please don't hesitate to come and find me, I'll be downstairs in the kitchen." Thanking her, Lillith walked into the room, closing the white door behind her.

Lillith surveyed the large bedchamber with its pale-pink walls delicately sketched with rose-gold patterns that matched the moldings. Beautiful ivory-striped upholstery decorated the room. Lillith ran her hand over the tasseled cushions, along the frame of the sofa, and across the bed as her feet sank into a plush rug.

She stepped into the bathing chamber and smiled in excitement upon seeing the tub sunk into the marble floor. She sank her toes into the lukewarm water and added more coals to the chute, to keep the water warm for hours on end. Lillith had never experienced such luxury—even at the height of her family's wealth, she had often shivered her way through the bath.

A couple of hours later, as the sun had started to set, Lillith heard a knock on the bedroom door. She set down the hair brush in front of the vanity mirror and straightened the beautiful long-sleeved dress she had found in the dresser.

Opening the door, she was met with Julian's handsome face. He wore a long dark coat with an immaculate white cravat tied at his neck and golden cuffs at his wrist. He didn't even try to hide his admiration for the beautiful woman standing before him.

"The color suits you very well," he said and stared at her, mesmerized by her curly dark hair that curled around the graceful turn of her neck. The beautiful silk dress of darkest blue complimented her distinctive features and copper skin.

"May I escort you around the palace?" he asked kindly, offering his arm to her.

"Yes, of course," She said, placing her arm in the crook of his elbow. He gave her a dimpled smile and motioned them forward down the hall.

They walked in silence along with the beautifully decorated galleries, her eyes admiring all the beautiful artwork illuminated in the hallway. She could sense Lord Julian watching her, and she tried to fight the blush rising to her face.

Julian led Lillith to their dinner in the great hall. A colonnade ran down either side; she looked on her left at the vast wall of stained glass. There were no pictures in the glass, only an intricate swirl of many-colored diamond panes that she imagined would cast a rainbow of glimmers over the white tablecloth on a sunny day. At the far end of the hall, a great empty arch looked out on the western sky which raged in a white snowstorm. Chandeliers hung from the ceiling and cast a warm, flickering light over the grand table.

Lillith said down and traced the tip of her finger over the silver-lined swirls of the dishes before her, and laughed at her upside down reflection in the grand baroque silverware.

"I am ravenous," said Lillith at the sight of the food, the delicious smell made her stomach growl.

"Do eat up my dear!" Mrs. Adley was nothing if not indulgent, especially when it came to feeding Julian and his guests. Lillith and Julian both enjoyed their food with glee and complimented Mrs. Adley a couple of times.

She insisted on helping the staff to clean up, as it seemed absurd to her to let anyone else clean up after her. "Tomorrow we'll go pick Holly from the garden as we agreed," said Mrs. Adley. "You should go to bed and rest darling, your eyes are glistening like a dove's." she laughed, pinching Lillith's cheek. She excused herself after bidding the staff and Mrs. Adley good night. The hallways were dimly lit and quiet, except for the wind whistling outside. As she turned the corner she bumped into Julian's hard chest and her hand shot up to grab his shoulder. He was quick to catch her by the waist and help her regain her balance.

"I'm so sorry," she let out a small embarrassed laugh and looked up to realize that his face was inches away from hers.

He held her gaze and his eyes traveled to her lips, "No, I wasn't looking where I was going, again." He smiled in amusement. She could feel his hot breath against her lips, and the mere thought of their lips touching had her stomach almost exploding in butterflies. Her heart beat erratically against her ribcage and she wondered if he could feel it too with her chest pressed up tightly to his.

"Good night, Julian," She whispered before slowly removing her hand from his shoulder.

"Good night, Lillith," He replied, creating some distance between them. She left and entered the guest room without turning back to look at him. Her knees gave out and she crashed into the fresh cushions of the bed. She took in deep slow breaths to calm her frantic breathing.

Oh my goodness, he almost kissed me! A voice screamed in her head as she broke into a heartful giggle.

That night she dreamt of the beautiful Lord with the saddest green eyes and a soul as white as the newly drifted snow.

AFTER A LONG NIGHT of the ruthless storm, warm sunshine shone over snow-coated trees. Julian braced himself for frigid air, but that morning the winter weather felt more temperate. The wind did not weave through the trees, and instead, the sun beat down, causing a constant *drip-drip-drip* around them. Lillith's joyous laugh filled the morning air as both she and Mrs. Adley chattered while picking and cutting branches of Holly. For some reason, hearing Lillith's laughter warmed his heart up and he could almost hear it thump loudly in his chest.

Julian stared out to the horizon, the wind in his face as though blowing breath into him, bringing him back to life. He closed his eyes and breathed in the biting cold air. The feeling of someone approaching him caught his attention, and he looked around to find Lillith making her way towards him through the thick snow. Though the wind played with her hair like a kitten after string and her cheeks were rosy from the bitter winter air, she moved with ease and grace. Her frame was slight and thin under her open wool coat but there was nothing fragile about her. She looked strong and resolute. He caught himself staring at her for longer than a gentleman should've and cleared his throat, snapping himself out of the daze.

"Let's go bake some cookies!" she exclaimed with a gleeful smile, holding the holly she'd picked up, Mrs.Adley hot on her heels. "I have a couple of recipes that I think you'd love." Lillith told Julian, sending him a playful wink. He laughed at her contagious excitement and picked a small twig that got stuck in her hair. "Beautiful." He whispered his thoughts out loud and she gave him a small smile as she walked past him, back towards the palace.

LILLITH BUSIED herself fetching spices down from the racks —cinnamon, star anise, cloves, ginger, sage, and nutmeg— crumbling them between her fingers and breathing in the scent. The seasoning had been her job when she was too little to knead the cookie dough and she knew the best combinations by heart. They spent all evening sifting and whisking ingredients for various cookie recipes. Mrs. Adley rolled the dough into thin layers and Lillith, together with Julian, cut the dough with various cookie cutters. Although he was hesitant at first, he had to admit that he'd missed these holiday traditions. Lillith wrapped the dough that she had prepared— following her mother's twisted sweet bread recipe—and tucked it close to the hearth to rise. She pulled out the risen dough for cinnamon rolls she had prepared a couple of hours before and both women started shaping the small buns, generously adding sugar and cinnamon. After placing the cinnamon rolls into the tray, Lillith carefully slid it into the oven.

Hours filled with good chatter and laughs had passed by, and every now and then Julian would steal admiring glances at Lillith. He could barely remember the last time he'd had so much fun around Christmas time and loved every moment that he spent with Lillith. Finishing off, they washed their hands in the basin, pulling their aprons off, chattering.

❄

MORE HOURS HAD PASSED without Lillith noticing and dinner time rolled around sooner than she thought. She thought of her mother and hoped that she had gotten her message. Lillith complimented Mrs. Adley for the delicious food making her blush and laugh. "We would absolutely love to have you more often for dinner, right Julian?" Mrs. Adley asked, nudging Julian who momentarily choked on his sip of wine.

He cleared his throat a couple of times, visibly embarrassed, and said "Yes, definitely. Your company is lovely," and rubbed his sweaty hands on his dark trousers.

After dinner, Lillith went to see the library that Julian had told her about, and as she scanned the walls, each one lined with shelves and each one full of leather-bound books, at least a hundred books, more than she knew existed in one place, she felt her heart might burst. Lillith had always loved to be read to, and though she could read the words herself, there was a magic in having them spoken aloud to her, She could close her eyes and simply listen, and weave images in her mind as the stories unfurled. She could hear the crackle of the fire burning brightly in the hearth and watched the flames swirl and dance as the comfortable warm atmosphere engulfed her.

Later, she felt the need to breathe in fresh air so she threw on her coat—that had finally dried—and stepped out onto the balcony, a glass of wine in her hand. Darkness had fallen but the moon hung huge and white, turning the wide, unbroken drifts into a winter wonderland. She could hear the cool breeze as it whispered beneath the silent moon and she shivered slightly as it tugged her hair and coat. She watched snow crystals as they gleamed under the light of the bright round moon slightly hidden behind sailing clouds.

"I hope I'm not intruding," Lillith turned around to see Julian behind her, holding a bottle and a glass of wine for himself, "such a beautiful season, but unfortunately I can't stand the cold." He said letting out a small laugh and shivering slightly. Lillith offered to go back inside but he protested, "no, it's refreshing. Catherine would always make me go out in the snow." He chuckled and told her how they used to go horseback riding in the snow almost every morning, and that despite the biting cold he cherished every moment as long as she was there to warm his heart.

"I'm so sorry for your loss," Lillith whispered. She couldn't imagine the heartbreaking pain of losing the love of your life.

"It's been almost three years already, I know she would want me to move on." He slightly shrugged his shoulder, watching the wine as he twirled it in the glass. "And it was only yesterday that I had decided to finally try and give the snow another chance," he joked and looked over the railing at the glistening snow, but she couldn't take her eyes off of him.

"And how did you like it?" she asked, a smile playing at her lips.

"I didn't like it much until I saw the fox that led me to you." He looked at her, moonlight casting shadows across his handsome face. A warm feeling bloomed inside her and she felt her heartbeat quicken.

"I do not know if it was meant to be but I'm glad that you're here, even if it's just for a while." He said, a glint of sadness in his eyes at the thought of her leaving. He didn't understand how a stranger could confuse him the way she did. Julian had almost forgotten what it felt like to crave someone's company, to long for their presence and touch.

"I did not expect the events of yesterday to turn the way that they have," she replied. "Thank you for taking care of me, I would've caught a really bad cold if it weren't for you. I don't even know how I even ended up on that field." She laughed and cursed at herself for thinking that it was a good idea to sit down in the snow.

"It was my pleasure," he genuinely said, smiling at her. Then a bitter thought that he had been pushing to the back of his mind since his eyes met her on the field crossed his mind. "Do you," he paused, rethinking his words, blaming the wine for making him speak up, "do you have *someone* waiting for you back home?"

Lillith blushed. She understood his question and what he meant by *someone* and for a moment she thought of Thomas who claimed to love her but quickly pushed that thought away. *That would never work out, he's not the one for me.*

"I'm sorry if I'm being bold with my words, it's really none of my business." He said nervously, running his free hand through his hair.

"No, no! It's nothing of the sort!" she burst out, realizing that she took too long to reply and he thought the contrary, "My heart does not belong to anyone, *yet.*"

Lillith's answer brought Julian comfort, and he let out a breath that he had been holding, relieved to know that he might have a chance to claim the love of the enchanting stranger.

THE NEXT MORNING AT BREAKFAST, Mrs. Adley barged into the dining hall with a worried look on her face, "I'm sorry Lord, but there's a man demanding to see Miss Lillith. I told him that he must wait but he won't listen!" hearing her alarming words, Lillith's heart sank.

She put down her cup of tea and frantically looked

towards the door where she saw Thomas appear, shouting, "I must see her at once!"

The moment Thomas stepped into the room, Julian shot up from his seat and protectively pushed Lillith behind his back. "And who will you be? And how dare you enter my palace in such a manner!"

Julian's tone that sent chills down Lillith's back.

Thomas' raging eyes traveled to Julian's extended arm that kept him at a distance from Lillith and said, "What is the meaning of this? I have been worried sick about you, I couldn't sleep at night and you're here having a tea party with *him*."

Julian threw a confused and pained glance at Lillith who could silently read the pained questions in his eyes. *Why haven't you told me about him? Who is he to you? Why am I angry at the thought that you might never be mine?*

Lillith could feel her pulse in her throat and she gulped down before turning to Thomas, "go home Thomas, I owe you no explanation about my whereabouts," She stepped next to Julian, "I thought I made it clear for you when I told you that I had no intention of marrying you. My heart does not belong to you, never has, and never will. I'm sorry Thomas." Her heart ached as she saw the pain in his eyes, but she couldn't lie to herself and pretend she would ever be happy with him.

"Your feelings are just confused, you must love me—" Thomas began but Julian interrupted him and signaled to the guard to take him out as he started to show signs of violence. Thomas shouted after Lillith who broke into tears, feeling horrible for breaking Thomas's heart, as she sank into Julian's arms.

"I feel horrible, he's not a bad person," she cried, her heart aching.

"You shouldn't darling, he's a boy that can't handle rejection. He should understand that no means *no*," he said, placing a kiss on the top of her head, "I'll take you home whenever you want. Please don't let him ruin our morning." He smiled down at her, gently wiping her tears.

LEAVING a kiss on Nallbo's head, Lillith pulled her coat tighter around her body but it couldn't compare to the warmth of Julian's chest pressing against her back. "Thank you for bringing me home," she smiled at him and he couldn't take his eyes off of her face. He wanted to grab her face and gently kiss her but he feared that she wouldn't want that, and stopped himself.

Seeing his obvious hesitation she raised herself on her toes and left a warm kiss on the corner of his mouth. "I hope to see you at the fair next week." She whispered to him, giving him a branch of mistletoe from her bag of materials that she thankfully hadn't forgotten about.

THE CHILDREN'S angelic voices singing in the choir, the smell of freshly baked goods, and the Christmas tree standing tall by the ice rink, adorned in the most beautiful and colorful toys, brought joy and glee to everyone in the town. Lillith stood in awe at the entrance, gasping at the beauty of the fair, aglow with dozens of fairy lights, the walls of the cabins hung with endless boughs of evergreen and holly, mistletoe too.

The whole day she kept watching the entrance, hoping that Julian would show up. Thomas hadn't bothered her since the last time she saw him at the palace and she was relieved. Nightfall rolled around, and the place had become more crowded, some eager to meet Santa in his cabin, others waiting in line to get into the ice rink, and still others enjoying the Christmas goods that were offered—Lillith among them of course, savoring her mother's gingerbreads.

"Glad to see that pile of sticks turn into such beautiful wreaths," Lillith head shot up upon hearing Julian's joking voice and quickly brushed off the crumbles from the gingerbread off her face and skirt.

"Julian! Mrs. Adley!"Lillith greeted them in excitement, rising to give them each a hug. She noticed that his other staff were with them and gleefully greeted them all.

"Lord Julian! Such an honor to see you here," her mother came from behind her extending her hand to greet him, "so glad you could make it this year." She added while shortly shaking his hand. Her sisters shyly waved at the guests and looked at Lillith in confusion. Alice cocked her head to the side and shot a grin at her sister, *When did this happen?* Lillith read in her older sisters' eyes and laughed.

"Please call me Julian, and your amazing daughter convinced me to come," he looked at Lillith in adoration, "your cinnamon roll recipe is to die for!" He complimented Lillith's mother and she laughed, swatting his arm as she blushed.

No one is immune to his charms.

After a small chatter, the pair excused themselves to go and have a small tour of the place.

"You folks have done an amazing job, Catherine would've loved this," He said looking around at the crowd. His warm hand found her cold one and intertwined his fingers with hers before bringing it to his lips, placing a kiss on the back of her hand. Her heart fluttered and she stepped closer to him as he continued, "it's time for my heart to love again, and I choose you Lillith." He whispered, pressing his forehead onto hers, weaving his fingers in her dark hair, caressing her cheek with his thumb. "I know it's sudden and very unexpected but what I feel for you right now is—" she cut him off by finally pressing her lips against his.

She gave up trying to understand her feelings and just kissed him, there in the freshly lain snow. And though she wasn't sure where her future was headed, the kiss was, for that moment, everything she wanted.

THE BEST IS YET TO COME

H.R.SCHWARTZ

*T*he sky is always gray this time of year. Tiny white flakes drift down from the thick clouds. They are preparing to split open and drop their contents over the entire city, but not yet. Right now, they wait, as I wait.

The city is quiet. I'm out well past curfew, but it's worth the risk. Worth sneaking up on the hilltop that overlooks the city to be alone with the person I care most about in the world. Even if he doesn't know it yet. Or maybe he does and doesn't feel the same. Being near is enough for me for now, even if I'm early. He's not here yet.

I sit on the icy ground, watching my breath come out in little frozen puffs. Below, the city is lit up with Christmas lights and decorations as it is every year. It's beautiful, and no view beats this one. I had to be careful coming up here-getting caught could lead to a whirlwind of trouble. If it snows much harder we will have to cover our tracks on our way back home.

Behind me, I can hear the gentle crunching of the ground.

"You're late," I say without looking behind me.

"Yeah, yeah," James says as he moves closer. "Guards

were patrolling the street." He sits down next to me and play-fully shoves his shoulder into mine. "They probably saw you sneaking out and set out a search party." He laughs and tilts his head backwards looking up at the sky.

"You're just not as good as me. Admit it."

"Oh mighty Lila," he says dramatically, "who could ever compare to your cunning and stealth?"

I laugh and we fall into an easy silence.

This is our tradition. Every day, starting on December first through Christmas eve, we meet at the top of the hill after curfew. I don't really remember how or why the tradi-tion started, but it has been held every year for the last five years. Sometimes I will bring hot chocolate or muffins from the bakery I work at, but I was off today so I came empty handed.

"Here," James says, handing me a canteen. "I figured you wouldn't have anything for us today, so I took the liberty of bringing something."

I eye the canteen warily. "What is it?" It's not that I don't trust James. I just don't trust his *taste* in drinks.

He laughs. "Just try it. You'll like it, I promise."

Slowly, I open the cap and tip some of the contents into my mouth. The liquid is warm and sweet. It tastes like salted caramel and chocolate. It's delicious. I close my eyes in bliss.

"That is so good! Where did you get it?" I hand him the canteen and he lifts it to his lips. I watch the way his lips press against the opening, wishing that if only for a moment, I could *be* the canteen.

"My Nan made it," he says, closing the lid again. "She even filled up the canteen and told me that it was for our 'secret rendezvous'." He smiles at me, "Apparently our secret meetup isn't as secret as we had thought."

"If she keeps supplying us with drinks like this, I don't care what she knows!"

James sighs contentedly. "Beautiful tonight." The snowflakes catch in his lashes as he tilts his head to the side to look at me. "Might be hard to meet tomorrow if those clouds open up."

"We'll figure it out." There hasn't been a single storm that has stopped us yet. Even if we only stay for half a minute to look at the city, we always make it.

"What are you doing tomorrow?"

"I have to work. I'm training a new girl, so I'll be pretty busy all day."

He nods. "I might swing by to say hello after I meet up with the boys. Eric is wanting to go to the Dance Hall. Apparently, there's a recital there and he's anxious to see the girls dressed up in their tight costumes." He huffs a laugh and rolls his eyes. "I think he's hoping that if he's smooth enough, he will be able to walk out with one of them on his arm."

I burst out laughing. "No girl in their right mind would go out with him! He's too…"

"Ugly? Obnoxious? Loud? Gross?"

"I was going to say pushy," I laugh. "He's not ugly, just a bit different." I'm trying to be nice. Eric really isn't good looking at all, and instead of making up for it with charm, he's overbearing, annoying and pushy. I get along with him well enough, but his advances get tiring, so I try to avoid him most days.

"Different," James says almost to himself. "That's one word for it." He takes another drink from the canteen and hands it to me. I accept it and drink deeply, wondering what it would feel like to have his lips on mine. Drinking from the same cups is as close as we have ever gotten. "Ready to go yet? I think my butt has gone numb."

I smile and nod. "Mine too."

James stands and helps me to my feet. Together, we work our way carefully down the hill. Going up and down isn't even the tricky part. The tricky part is getting back home without being caught. Still, we have a five-year streak, so I'd say we are pretty good at it.

We run quickly and quietly down the back alleys of the city, hiding behind dumpsters or in tight spaces when needed. At the final intersection, James darts right and I go left. I wave to him as we both disappear in the shadows of the night.

My house is dark when I get home. I make my way around the back and quietly lift the window to my room as I do every night in December. I have to be careful to take my shoes off before I touch the carpet, or the dirty, wet footprints could give me away. I quickly and silently slip back into my room and slide the window shut. I am still for a moment to see if anyone is awake in the house. There are no other sounds. I breathe a sigh of relief.

I get ready for bed and slip under the covers, ridding myself of the chill in my bones. I fall asleep easily and dream of snow and secret meetings in the dark.

"LILA! You're going to be late!" My mother's voice rings through the house.

I bolt up in bed. I overslept! I must have forgotten to set my alarm last night! I can't be late. Not today. Not for my first official day training someone. It's a huge step in responsibility. I can't afford to mess it up already.

I barely glance at myself in the mirror as I get ready. Luckily, I always lay out my work clothes the day before, so I am able to throw them on in no time and bolt out the door. I can hear my mother yelling something about breakfast, but I'll eat once I'm at work. There are plenty of muffins left over from the day before that I can snack on. I won't starve.

I missed the bus which means I'm going to have to walk across town. I don't have the time to wait for the next one. I hunch my shoulders against the cold and walk briskly. I'd like to run, but I'm not confident that I won't slip and crack my head on the pavement. Besides, the guards would get suspicious of someone running and then I'd be late *for sure.*

A horn sounds beside me and I glance at the car that has pulled up next to me.

"Hey beautiful," Eric says smoothly. "How about you and I go get something to eat, and I can bring you back to my place for some... dessert."

I roll my eyes. "I'm almost late for work, Eric. I can't talk."

His face changes from predator to friend. "Hop in," he says. "I'll drive you there."

I hesitate a moment, then sigh and slide into the passenger side. "Thank you."

"No problem," he says. "I know you're James's best girl. If he knew I let you *walk* to work, he would find a shallow grave to bury me in."

We both laugh, but I can't help the warmth that flows through me and the little smile that continues to tug at my lips. His "best girl." I like the sound of that.

Eric pulls up to the bakery and I hop out. "Thanks again," I say as I wave to him and hurry inside. I glance at the clock. I have five minutes to spare. I breathe a sigh of relief. I'm not late.

The new girl is already waiting for me as I hang up my coat.

"You must be Amanda," I say. She nods shyly, looking

uncertain and out of place. She has a sweet face, with gentle brown eyes and short blonde hair. "I'm Lila. I'll be the one training you today. Did you receive your badge yet?"

She nods again, "It's right here," she says holding it out to me.

"Perfect. Let's get you clocked in."

Once Amanda warms up, she is friendly and talkative. I already like her. I think we are going to be fast friends, which would be nice because I don't have many girl friends around here. My typical crowd is James and the guys, plus the two or three girls I've kept in touch with from school.

Amanda does fairly well. She has a hard time piping frosting onto the cupcakes, but that's to be expected, and her coffee froth designs are atrocious, but that's normal. Otherwise, she catches on quickly.

The door chimes and James strides in coming straight to the counter. I can't help the stupid smile that plasters onto my face at the sight of him. He rakes his hand through his dark hair, trying to tame it after removing his hat, but it's adorably messy. His mouth quirks into a smile when he sees me, and he shrugs.

"You've seen worse," he says with a laugh.

"That's true."

Amanda stands beside me, a blush already creeping into her cheeks. I glance back at James and I see him looking at her. My heart sinks a little.

"James, this is Amanda. She's the new trainee. Amanda, this is my best friend, James."

"Nice to meet you," she says, ducking her head a little.

"Likewise." He watches her a bit longer, then turns back to me. "So, listen, the boys and I are going to see a movie tonight. Do you want to come? Amanda and the girls can come too if you want. We can have a big group outing." His smile is easy. He knows I'm going to say yes.

"I'd love that!" Amanda's smile is brighter than the sun and I realize that her face is more than simply 'sweet,' it's beautiful. Especially when she smiles.

"Great! Then I'll see you ladies later." He winks at us and heads back out the door.

Amanda turns to me, her smile so bright and genuine I can hardly stand it. "He is so cute!" she exclaims. "Do you think he might have thought the same?"

"Probably," I say flatly.

"I can't wait for tonight. I've never been out in a big group like that. Maybe I could sit by James." She looks at me and hesitates. "You don't mind, do you? I know you said he's your best friend, but there's nothing romantic there, is there? I don't want to interfere."

I force myself to smile at her. "Go for it," I say enthusiastically. "There's definitely nothing romantic between us. We are just friends." Just friends...

I drown out her giddy chatter and try to push aside my possessive jealousy. He only saw her for two minutes. That doesn't mean that he is interested in her. Though, he *did* invite her to the movie... But, it's for a casual outing with all our friends and he didn't want her to feel left out. Then again, his eyes lingered on her longer than necessary. I know that look. It's one he has never given me, but one I've longed for. He's interested in her, and I've set myself up to be pushed out of the picture.

The day drags by. My thoughts wander off every few minutes. I'm killing myself over the 'what-ifs' between James and Amanda. By the time we clock out, I'm ready to go home. The movie won't start for a few hours, so I have time to clean up and get ready to go.

I say good-bye to Amanda and take the bus back home. I have a couple chocolate muffins for James and me later tonight when we meet up on the hill. Until then, I'll keep them sealed in their bags. Maybe he will bring some of his Nan's hot chocolate again.

My phone rings and Emily's name pops up.

"Hey babe," she says the moment I answer the phone. "I heard we are all going out tonight."

James must have told her. "Yeah. James wanted to see a movie and thought it might be fun." I'm still on the bus, but I'm close to home. My parents will still be at work when I get back. That will give me some time to get ready for tonight.

"Good," she says. "I've had my eye on that cute little friend of his. What's his name? Josh?"

I roll my eyes. "Of course, you do. Be nice to him, he's not as forward as you."

Emily laughs. "More fun that way. Alright babe, I'll see you tonight then."

"See you later." We hang up as the bus pulls up to my stop. I hop off and hunch my shoulders against the cold. It's a short walk back to the house, but the temperature has dropped a lot already.

I shake my coat out when I get inside and hang it up in the closet. Then I make my way upstairs to take a shower. I want to be as fresh as possible. I've never really thought about getting dressed up for James, but the way he looked at Amanda today has me reconsidering. I want to look pretty. I want him to notice me the same way he noticed her.

I quickly shower and blow dry my hair. It has a natural wave to it that is pretty on its own when I blow it out. I brush it to give it more shine, then leave it down. It's long, hitting the middle of my back and a rich chocolate brown. I typically leave it up because it's easier to deal with, but not tonight. I want James to really see me tonight.

His favorite color is red, so I pick out a vibrant red sweater and pull it over my head. I pair it with a cute headband that serves as an ear warmer and hair accessory. I swipe on some mascara and eyeliner, and a light coat of lip gloss, then give myself a once-over in the mirror. I look pretty cute, if I do say so myself.

My phone rings and I pick it up. James' name flashes on the screen. I look at myself once more in the mirror, feeling a boost of confidence I didn't know I had.

"Hey!" I say cheerfully.

"Hey, you ready to go? I can pick you up in a few minutes."

"Yeah. I just need to grab my coat and I'll be ready."

"Okay," he says. "See you in a few."

I hang up and can't get downstairs fast enough. What will he say when he sees me? Will he acknowledge how I look? Will he ignore it? Did I go overboard? Maybe I shouldn't have put on the lip gloss. I never wear lip gloss.

I grab my jacket back out of the closet and anxiously wait for his arrival. I know it's not a date because he's my best friend and we are going with a big group of people, but I so badly want it to be one. I don't know why the thought of him with Amanda has me acting so crazy.

I feel my phone vibrate in my pocket. I was hoping he would come to the door. Instead I receive a text message that reads "*Here.*" I sigh and throw on my jacket, covering my cute outfit as I head out the door.

His car is pulled in front of my house and he gives a little wave when he sees me. I smile brightly and open the passenger door, quickly sliding into the seat and closing out the cold outside.

He looks at me and cocks his head to the side. "You look nice," he says. "Who are you trying to impress?" He laughs and looks out the window to the left so he can safely pull away from my house. I can feel the blush creep in and feel the disappointment. Looking *nice* isn't what I was going for. I guess it's better than no comment at all.

"I just felt like dressing up a little," I say off-handedly. "I don't do it often and thought it might be fun. Besides, you never know who you might see at the theatre!" My high pitch is making me cringe. I see him glance at me and raise his eyebrow, but he doesn't comment. Why does he have to be so perfect?

We pull up to the theatre and see our group waiting for us just inside the doors. I see Amanda standing awkwardly off to the side. I do feel a bit bad for her. She doesn't know anyone besides me and James. Not that she really knows us either. She's only met James once and I only worked with her for one shift. Even so, a huge smile breaks across her face when she sees us. Her eyes immediately lock onto James.

"Did you guys buy your tickets yet?" James asks as we push through the doors.

"Yup," Eric replies, "just waiting on you guys."

James looks at me, "I'll get yours this time. Next time it's your turn." He winks and walks up to the counter.

Amanda is standing next to me looking nervous. "Do I look okay?" she asks quietly as the group chats and waits for James.

I look at her and sigh inside. "You look beautiful," I say. She's wearing a sparkly black shirt that hugs all the right places. The minimal makeup accentuates her naturally pretty face. I'm honestly jealous.

Emily walks up beside me and links her arm through mine. "Hey babe!"

"Hey, Em."

"You look smokin' hot," she says pushing me out to take in my outfit. "You trying to snag a guy?" She wags her eyebrows at me, and I laugh.

I roll my eyes at her. "I'm allowed to dress up from time to time," I say.

"Mmm-hmmm," she smirks at me.

"Tickets acquired," James says, showing off the two tickets in his hand. I no longer have my jacket on, and he can see my entire outfit. I see him give me the once-over before handing me my ticket, but he doesn't comment.

He and Amanda lock eyes. She smiles shyly and dips her head. I try to suppress my frown, but it's not easy. Emily glances at me as we all head into the theatre and take our seats. She doesn't say anything, but I suspect she is suspicious.

James sits between me and Amanda. I hear them whispering back and forth throughout the movie. I don't even know what's happening in the film. My mind is elsewhere.

Emily nudges my arm and mouths, "Are you okay?"

I nod. Then shrug.

She stands and begins to slide past me but grabs my hand as she does and tows me with her. James looks at me curiously but moves his feet for me to pass him. Emily drags me out into the hallway away from the theatre rooms.

"Spill it," she says, crossing her arms over her chest.

"What do you mean?"

"You're in love with him," she whispers accusingly.

I look down. I can't deny it. She will see right through me.

"Why haven't you told him yet?"

"Because he's my best friend," I say. "I don't want to ruin things between us if he doesn't feel the same."

"But if you don't tell him, how will you ever know?"

I shrug.

She sighs. "So, this Amanda chick..."

"Yeah?"

"She going after him?"

"I think so," I say. "She asked me if it was okay and I told her yes."

"Why would you do that?" She nearly shouts.

"I don't know," I say miserably. "I'm not sure how to handle all of this."

Emily watches me for a moment, then comes over and gives me a hug. "If you need to talk or cry or vent, I'm always around."

I want to cry and vent, but now isn't the time. I hug her back. "Thanks."

"Let's get back in there before they start asking questions."

I nod and allow her to tow me back into the theatre. The rest of the movie goes by in a blur. I zone out as we walk out, smiling when the others laugh, nodding when I think I'm supposed to. Amanda and James are talking animatedly with each other and it's nearly more than I can take.

James and I say good-bye to our friends and head back to his car. Finally, I can be alone with him for a minute. The snow is falling harder now, and it has piled up on his windshield.

"Are you alright?" he asks as he pulls out of the parking space. "You've been a little quiet."

"I'm fine," I say. "Just a little tired is all."

"Not too tired for tonight, I hope," he replies with a smile.

That lifts my mood a bit. "Never." I smile in relief. He's still my best friend. He's still James. I'm working myself up over nothing. Even if he does end up with Amanda, things won't change between us.

"So, Amanda seems pretty nice," he says casually.

"Yeah, a bit shy though." I really don't have anything bad to say about her. I honestly like her. She's sweet and sincere. I wish I could *not* like her, but the only reason I wouldn't is because she likes James, and that's not fair.

"I'm sure we can break her out of that," he says with a laugh.

I huff a laugh. It sounds forced even to my own ears. "Yeah, I bet we can."

We fall silent as he drives me home.

"See you in a few hours," I say as I hop out of the car. "Bring your Nan's hot chocolate if there's any left."

He smiles a bit. "You got it."

THE CLIMB up the hill is a bit harder tonight. The snow isn't thick enough to get a good grip under my boots and the wet ground is slick. I have the two muffins tucked away in my jacket. If I fall, I'll smash them. They will still be edible, but not as pretty as I'd like. We've had smashed muffins from time to time. James always teases me about my fall but has never once complained about the mangled muffins.

When I get to the top, he's already waiting for me. The lights below look magical tonight. Maybe it's just me. Maybe I'm feeling a little romantic.

"You beat me here," I say in surprise. "That's a first."

"I wanted to make sure you didn't take the best spot," he jokes. "You got the goods?"

I whip out the bag of muffins. "Right here. And you?"

He holds out the canteen and shakes it. I can hear the liquid swish inside.

I take a seat next to him and hand him a muffin. These are my favorite. Dark chocolate with milk chocolate chips. Not overly sweet, but the perfect pairing with his Nan's hot chocolate.

"So," he says, dragging out the word. "What did you think of the movie?"

I freeze. I don't remember any of it. "Um, yeah, it was good."

"You're a terrible liar, you know," he says with a smirk. "I know you were zoning out through most of it."

"Oh yeah? You think so?" How did he know that? He was talking to Amanda the entire time.

"I see more than you realize," he says. "Like I know you weren't just tired tonight. And when you went out of the theatre with Emily, I know you were upset. What I don't know is why."

I shrug. "Just a lot on my mind. Nothing in particular, just overwhelmed with work and stuff."

"And stuff," he says quietly. He doesn't press me anymore. He knows me well enough to know when I'm done talking about something. But I know him well enough to know that it bothers him anyhow.

We don't stay there for long. It's too cold out. Once we finish our muffins and hot chocolate, we head back down the hill and to our own homes. I think one of the guards sees me this time, but he ignores it. Either he is too cold to care, or he's feeling charitable since it's Christmas time. Whatever the case, I'm not complaining, and I'll never tell James. If I do, I'll never hear the end of it.

When I arrive at work the next morning, Amanda is waiting. She looks too cheerful for this time of morning.

"Hey," she says the moment I walk in. "I had tons of fun last night."

I nod and walk past her to clock in and grab my apron.

"James is so sweet. He asked to take me out for dinner tonight. Isn't that great?"

He didn't tell me that.

"I think we really hit it off last night. We talked through nearly the entire movie. I felt a little bad because we missed the movie, but maybe that can be our second date."

"Sounds great," I say with a forced smile. "I'm glad you guys are hitting it off. He's a great guy."

She just keeps talking and gushing and daydreaming. My stomach is in knots. Why can't I be this candid with him? Why can't I tell him how I feel? If I don't, it's going to tear me up inside watching her come in everyday gushing about their dates and romance. I don't think I can handle that.

"Are you okay, Lila?" Amanda asks suddenly.

I realize I've been zoning out. I snap myself out of it. "Yeah, I'm great! Just a little tired is all." That excuse is beginning to wear out. I wish I was a better liar.

"Oh, okay. If you're sure that's all…" she watches me for a moment. I simply smile and nod.

James comes in to say hello before his shift starts at his father's store. He and Amanda flirt over coffee and muffins. She gives him a blueberry muffin for free which he graciously accepts. He hates blueberries. He winks at me before he leaves and dangles the bag. I love blueberry. That means we only need one muffin for tonight.

When our shift ends, I practically run out the door. I can't handle hearing more of her gushing about James. *My* James.

When I meet James on the hill, he doesn't mention their date at all, and I don't ask. We simply talk about our days, our friends, the lights. He hands me the blueberry muffin and all I can think is... why can't you see?

Sleep doesn't find me easily. I'm restless. How many dates will they go on before I go crazy? How much of Amanda's gushing will I be able to handle? In truth, not much more.

Waking up in the morning feels like a train hit me. I'm exhausted physically from the climb and lack of sleep, and mentally from thinking of James.

Amanda is at work early again when I arrive, but she's quieter today. She smiles at me when I come in, but she's not talking about her date with James. Not pouring over the details that I'm so curious about, but also don't want to know. Instead, she's quietly reserved. Polite, but not overly friendly.

When I clock in, I know I should ask her about how it went. It's the "friend" thing to do. I sigh deeply within myself and plaster on my best smile. "So, how did your date go last night?"

Instead of answering me, she says, "Why didn't you tell me?"

"What?"

"You should have just told me you had feelings for him," she says gently. "I never would have pursued him the way I did."

"I don't know what you're-"

She holds up a hand and smiles. "Lila. I can see by the way you look at him when he comes in. It's *more* than just friendship that you feel for him. The way that you were so quiet at the theatre and the looks you got when you saw us together. I may be new around here, but I'm not blind. You should have told me. I thought something was off when I told you about our date last night. You were really quiet. I couldn't stop thinking about it."

I inhale deeply. I didn't realize it was so obvious to her. "I'm sorry," I say. "I didn't think it would bother me as much as it has. I know he doesn't feel the same."

"You don't know that," she says gently. "Guys can be really thick sometimes. You should just let him know."

"Maybe I will," I say. She walks away seemingly satisfied as I mull over the idea of letting James know how I feel. I just don't want to ruin our friendship.

Christmas Eve is tonight. It's the one night that James and I do something a little different on our trip up the hill. We exchange our gifts while looking out over the lights. It makes the presents feel that much more magical and special- even if they are normally gag gifts. But still, it's the moments together that make it so special.

The shift flies by and before I know it, it's time to clock out. I've been mulling over what I am going to say to James. It's Christmas Eve- what better time to tell him how I feel? And if he doesn't reciprocate my feelings, I'll just have to live with that. As long as it doesn't damage our friendship. Honestly, I think if I knew for sure how he felt, I would be able to move on. Not knowing is the hardest.

I tuck some leftover apple streusel muffins into my jacket as I head out the door. The snow is really coming down hard. I can hardly see the ground as I walk to the bus. The streets are jammed with cars rushing about doing their last-minute shopping before everything shuts down for the holiday. I like the quiet of Christmas day. Everyone with their families. That's how it should be.

The bus drops me at my stop, and I trudge through the snow and into my house. My mom is baking, and it smells heavenly. Apple pie, pumpkin bread, chocolate chip cookies. She goes a little nuts with the food, but we all enjoy it, so I never complain.

Maybe I can sneak a cookie or two for James. I know he loves my mom's baking.

"Lila, is that you?" her voice comes from the kitchen.

"Yeah, mom," I call back. "Everything smells amazing!"

Her head pops around the corner. "Thanks honey," she says with a smile. Flour is smeared across her face and her apron, but she is still beautiful as ever. "Your dad had to run out really quick to pick up some more eggs. The family are all coming over early tomorrow, so I need to make sure we have enough snacks to last the entire day." She rolls her eyes and laughs. I know she loves hosting our get togethers, especially when she can show off her cooking skills.

"Sounds good. I'm going to head upstairs and take a quick shower. I'll be down in a bit."

"Okay, take your time."

I pull off my boots and coat and head upstairs. My mind is still mulling over what I am going to say to James. "I know you may not feel the same, but I'm in love with you." Nope, too cheesy. "I think I've fallen in love with you. It's okay if you don't feel the same, but I needed to tell you." I cringe. This is going to be hard.

I take a quick shower, then go downstairs and help my mom store all the things she's baked. The kitchen is a wreck, so I help her clean that too before my dad gets home. We have our silly little Christmas Eve traditions that I love and look forward to every year. My mom makes hot chocolate with extra marshmallows, then we all sit around the television and watch a Christmas movie or two and just before we all head off to bed, my dad reads *'Twas the night before Christmas.*

I say goodnight to my parents and look at our beautifully decorated house. So full of lights and magic. The Christmas tree is sparkling with ornaments and colored bulbs. I hope that this magic will stay with me when I meet James.

Everything is quiet in the house and the lights are dark. My parents are no longer talking. It's time to meet my best friend. I grab my jacket and boots, the muffins, cookies I snagged, and his gift, shove them all in a small backpack and climb out the window.

The snow is thick. I'm going to have to brush aside my steps as I make my way to the hill. I grab a long stick and walk slowly, brushing away my footprints as I go. It takes a lot more time than I would have liked, but I make it to the bottom of the hill without any issues. I didn't actually see any guards out tonight anyhow. Maybe they were given the day off because of the snowfall. No one in their right mind would come out with the snow coming down like this. I'm not really sure what that says about the two of us.

My feet sink into the snow as I trudge up the hill. It's already up to my ankles. I have no doubt that it will be up to my knees tomorrow morning. I'm out of breath by the time I make it to the top. The view is incredible. The lights from the shops are glowing against the white of the snowfall. It looks like one of those Christmas villages that people set up on display. So beautiful.

James is standing under a tree with a large canopy. It's keeping the snow from falling on him. His arms are crossed as he stares out at the city. Even silhouetted against the snow, and bundled in thick clothes, I can see how handsome he is.

He doesn't hear me approach and jumps when I join him under the tree.

"Jeez," he says dramatically, dropping his arms to the side. "You almost gave me a heart attack."

"I told you I was stealthy," I smirk.

He turns back to the city. "Beautiful tonight." He seems distant. Like something is on his mind. I know the feeling.

"It is," I agree.

"Can I ask you something?"

"Go for it," I say, digging the muffins and cookies out of my bag. I start to pull them out, but freeze...

"Why didn't you ask me about my date with Amanda?"

I don't really know what to say. Because I couldn't bear the thought of hearing details of you with another girl? I shrug and hand him the goodies. "Apple streusel from the bakery and chocolate chip cookies from my mom."

He takes the bags but doesn't open them. He just waits.

I sigh. "Because..." I can feel my body getting all jittery. This is James. He's my *best friend.* I've talked to him every day about anything and everything. So why am I finding this so hard? "Because..." I look up at him, "I didn't want to hear about it."

James frowns. That came out wrong.

"Amanda told me something that night," he says, looking straight ahead at the city lights, "and I wanted to be sure that it was true, so I didn't mention the date. And when you didn't ask about it, I guess it kind of confirmed it."

"Confirmed... what, exactly?" My heart rate is picking up. What did Amanda tell him?

He shakes his head. "I'm sorry."

"What?" That's not what I expected.

"Lila, I am so unbelievably, overwhelmingly, impossibly in love with you that it actually hurts. Your smile and laugh get me through each day. The way you wrinkle your nose when something bothers you. The way your face lights up when I come visit you at the bakery. The way you always make sure that you're the first to the top of this hill. And you know that I hate blueberries and love apple. I tried so hard to not love you, but you make it damn near impossible." He laughs. I'm crying. He moves closer to me, pulls the gloves off his hands and wipes away my tears. "I'm so sorry that I didn't see how hurt you were when I was talking to Amanda. She was only a distraction from you. From someone I thought I couldn't have."

I can't speak. My heart is so full I think it might burst. "I love you too," I whisper. It's all I can manage, but the smile on his face tells me it's enough. He lowers his mouth to mine and claims it as his own. His lips are warm and soft, familiar from knowing how they look when he speaks and laughs, but new and unexpected in ways too perfect to describe.

He pulls back slightly to look into my eyes. They are still streaming with tears. He brushes them away. "I have your Christmas present," he says with a smile.

"That wasn't it?" I laugh through the crying.

He shakes his head. "Here."

"I have yours too," I say. I reach into the bag and pull out a small package. We exchange our gifts and burst out laughing at the same moment. He pulls my gift from the wrapping and I pull out his. We have bought each other the same hideous hat.

"I think we have really bad taste," he says.

I nod. "We must," I reply. "We chose each other."

His smile is brighter than the lights below. "I'll never regret choosing you," he whispers. He wraps his arm around me as we sit under the tree and watch the snow fall. Somewhere in the distance, we hear a clock tower chiming midnight. It's Christmas day.

"Merry Christmas, Lila," he says kissing me on the top of the head.

"Merry Christmas, James."

IT DOESN'T FEEL LIKE CHRISTMAS

KATIE KENT

"*W*here are the decorations? This place is usually lit up like a firework at Christmas."

I heard Lauren's voice before I saw her. I rolled up my sleeves as warmth spread over me. As I glanced in their direction, she walked into the room with my brother, Matt. Seeing me looking over, she raised a hand. "Hey, Ems."

"Hi." I turned back to the TV as I felt my cheeks heat up, and tried to focus on the programme, but I could only think about how much I wanted to put my arms around Lauren, run my hands through her long, dark hair and kiss her.

"Emily didn't want us to put any decorations up this year." Matt's voice now.

"What, are you kidding?! It's Christmas! Ours were up as soon as Thanksgiving was over." Lauren came to my side. I hadn't seen her in weeks because she and Matt wanted to give Mom some space. Or that's what they said.

"It doesn't really feel very much like Christmas this year." I sighed, turning the remote around in my hands. "It feels wrong to celebrate when Mom is so ill."

"Your Mom will be okay." She sat down on the sofa next

to me. "Trust me. I have a feeling. She's going to make it through this."

"You don't know that." I felt tears spring to my eyes, and had to concentrate really hard to stop them spilling down my face. "She's at the hospital now, having chemo. It's not like she just has the flu, or something. This is the c-word. It's a big deal. And I don't really feel much like getting into the Christmas spirit right now."

She gave me a sympathetic smile. "I'm sorry, Ems. But your Mom is a fighter. If anyone can beat this, she can."

"We need to stay positive. You're talking like she's already dead." Stood next to where Lauren was sat, Matt clenched and unclenched his fists. "Maybe Lauren is right," he said. "Maybe we should put up decorations. Make it nice for her."

I shook my head. "It just doesn't feel right."

"But…"

"Leave it, Matt." Lauren squeezed his arm, and jealousy flooded through me.

I JUMPED at the sound of the door opening.. "Mom!" I sprang up off the sofa as Dad helped her inside, and winced. I'd been sitting there for so long that my legs had gone to sleep.

Her face looked pale, but smiled when she saw me. "I'm sorry I woke you."

"I wasn't asleep," I began to protest.

She eased herself onto the sofa as Dad headed off into the kitchen, and I sat back down next to her.

"I'm glad you had a nap. I know you haven't been sleeping that well lately."

"I've been sleeping fine," I said, but she stopped me again.

"I hear you at night, tossing and turning. And crying. It breaks my heart. You know you don't have to hide your feelings from me."

The tears came to my eyes again, and I sniffed as I brushed them away with my fingers. "I'm sorry, I thought I was being quiet. I'll be okay."

"As will I." She smiled again. "I'm feeling positive about this, Emily. You're not getting rid of me that easily."

A sob broke out from my mouth, and I tried to cover it up with a cough. "How are you feeling?" I asked.

"I'm alright." She leant back against the sofa. "Tired and nauseated, but otherwise okay."

Dad came over with a glass of water. Handing it to Mom he asked me, "Where's Matt?"

I shrugged. "He's upstairs with Lauren, I think. I'm sure I would have woken up if they'd come down."

"Lauren is such a nice girl." Mom took a sip of the water. "I know she's been staying away to give me space. I'm so glad that she and Matt are together."

"We don't know that they are." I fiddled with my phone, not wanting my expression to give my feelings away. "Matt denied it when you asked him."

Dad laughed as he opened the newspaper. "Come on, they're inseparable. He's always at her house or here with her or out with her. I think it's pretty unlikely that they're just friends. I've seen the way they look at each other."

I felt the bile rise up in the back of my throat. I hoped to God that they were wrong. Having designs on my big brother's best friend would be one thing, but having a crush on his girlfriend would be another thing entirely.

❄

"So, how's your Mom doing?" my best friend Alex asked me at school the next day.

"She said she's doing okay." I unwrapped my sandwiches from the aluminium foil. "But I'm not sure I believe her. I know the chemotherapy is knocking her for six. She always looks so ill when she gets back from a treatment. She must be scared. I think she's putting on a brave face for me."

"Like mother, like daughter." Alex pulled the zip on her can of Coke and took a gulp.

"What do you mean?"

"Aren't you trying to put on a brave face for her?"

I thought for a moment. "I guess so. But she doesn't need me falling apart on top of everything."

"Perhaps not. But there are other people looking out for you. Me, for a start. Or Matt. You can be honest with us."

I gave her a smile. "Thank you, I appreciate that. But I don't really feel like I can talk to Matt about this."

She frowned. "Why not? He's your brother. He's probably feeling scared too."

I fiddled with my ring. "'Coz of Lauren. My parents seem convinced that they're dating. Every time I see Matt, I think of them together, and I feel really guilty."

"Ems." She reached across and squeezed my hand. "You can't help how you feel."

"She came over yesterday," I said.

"Ah." Alex nodded knowingly. "So that's why you're feeling like this. You had an encounter with her."

I rolled my eyes. "You make it sound so clandestine. I should be so lucky."

"Haven't the feelings lessened at all? You hadn't mentioned her for a couple of weeks."

"That's because I hadn't seen her in a while. I only had to hear her voice and I felt like I was in an inferno." I took a bite from my sandwich.

"Oh dear, you have got it bad. Do you really think they're dating?"

"I dunno." I unscrewed the lid of my water bottle and took a sip. "I mean, it makes sense. They do spend all their time together, and why wouldn't he? She's hot."

Alex laughed. "Just because you think she's hot doesn't mean that Matt thinks the same. They've been friends for years, right? It could be purely platonic. "

"Dad said there's no way they can be friends. He said he'd seen the way they look at each other." I raised my sandwich to my mouth again, but then put it back down; my stomach was churning.

"Oh," Alex said. "What way?"

"I don't know. Like they want to rip each other's clothes off, I guess. Good job Dad hasn't noticed me looking at her like that too."

"Well, have you noticed them looking at each other like that?" she asked.

"No. But then I haven't really been looking out for it. I spend half the time I'm around them unable to take my eyes off her, and the other half trying to avoid looking at her so no one notices how I feel about her."

"Didn't you say your Dad asked him and he said they weren't together?" Alex opened a packet of potato chips and offered them to me.

"No thanks." I nodded. "He might be lying though."

"Why would he? What possible reason would he have to keep a relationship with her a secret? It's not like it would be anything scandalous. Unless..." she trailed off.

"Unless what?"

She gave me a sympathetic look. "Unless he knows how you feel about her, and is trying to spare your feelings."

I groaned. "If he knows, that means she knows. Oh God, how embarrassing." I put my head in my hands.

I felt her hand on my back. "Don't stress. I'm probably wrong."

AS THE DAYS of December rolled past, the school began to resemble the inside of Santa's Grotto. Why on earth did they need multiple Christmas trees? One would have been enough. The whole thing just irritated me. Mom could be dying, I had a thing for my brother's possible girlfriend, and I did not care about Christmas one bit.

Waking one Monday morning, I pulled the curtains back.

Snow had fallen overnight, covering the ground like a blanket. As I looked out of the window, a robin perched on top of the mailbox.

"You've got to be kidding me," I said out loud to myself, as I took in the Christmas card scene. So much for trying to ignoreChristmas this year. We hadn't had snow in December for years. I felt like the universe was playing a trick on me.

I pulled the curtains back across and lay back on the bed in the dark. I suddenly felt exhausted, like even getting up would be too much effort.

"Not going to school today x." I texted to Alex. "Not feeling up to it. See you tomorrow. x."

The reply came immediately. "Take it easy x."

I heard the bustle of sounds below me; Dad shutting the door behind him as he went off to work, Matt making his breakfast and then leaving the house himself. Then it all went quiet.

I must have fallen back asleep, because a knock on the door woke me. "Emily?" Mom's voice came through the door.

"Come in."

The door opened as I glanced at the clock. How had it gotten to 10am?

Mom sat down on the edge of the bed. "No school today?"

"No." I sat up against the pillows. "Didn't feel up to it."

She nodded. "That's okay. But have you seen outside? It's snowed! Looks real Christmassy."

"I don't want to be reminded of Christmas right now," I said.

She frowned. "Emily, you love Christmas! I remember when you were little you used to insist on staying up all night so you could get a glimpse of Santa."

I couldn't help but laugh. "I've grown up a bit since then, Mom."

"We always used to be exhausted on Christmas Day," she continued. "Because we couldn't go to bed until you'd eventually fallen asleep, so we could put the presents in your stocking. Each year you stayed up later and later, and we got more and more tired."

"It doesn't really feel like Christmas this year." I looked down at the bed, not wanting to meet Mom's eyes.

She sighed. "But it *is* Christmas. I may be sick, but Christmas is still coming. Once I'm better you'll regret having missed it."

"All I want is for you to be better," I said. "I don't want any presents this year."

"Is that really all you want, honey?" She looked intently at my face.

Does she know about Lauren?

I swallowed. "Well I could always do with some new shoes." If Mom hadn't been sick I'd probably have told her about my feelings for Lauren- I didn't think me being gay would be a big deal to her- but she didn't need this right now.

ABOUT A WEEK LATER, I came home from school to find Matt and Lauren decorating the lounge. A bare Christmas tree stood by the TV, and gold tinsel draped over the paintings. Matt untangled the tree lights from the box when I walked in. *Baby, It's Cold Outside* played from a speaker on the sideboard.

"What are you doing?" I felt anxiety rush through me as I took in the scene. This felt so wrong.

Lauren turned around. She looked especially beautiful today, wearing a white jumper with the outline of a large snowflake in silver on it. The colour looked good against her hair.

"We're just putting up the decorations." Matt finished untangling the lights and started to wind them around the tree.

I felt like steam whistled from my ears. "I told you I didn't want decorations," I said. "This is disrespectful to Mom."

Lauren came over and stood next to me. The scent of her perfume wafted across my nose. "Don't blame him. This was my idea. I wanted to do it. I didn't give him much choice in the matter, actually." She gave an apologetic laugh.

"She can be very scary sometimes." Matt had finished draping the lights and started to straighten them out.

My anger dissipated slightly as I addressed Lauren. "It was your idea? Why?"

She shrugged. "I wanted you guys to have a nice Christmas. I know you've got other things going on, but it's Christmas. I'm sure your Mom just wants things to be like normal. I know she's too ill to do it, and your Dad has been busy ferrying her to appointments. But we can do this for her. I think she'll really like it, don't you?"

I hesitated. I'd been so against wanting to celebrate anything to do with Christmas that I hadn't even given a thought to how Mom would feel about it.

"I think you could be right." I felt slightly choked up. "Thank you."

"It's nothing. I care about you guys."

She cares about me? She's probably just being polite, I reasoned. She did this for Matt. She must really like him to go to all this effort to give him a nice Christmas. I suddenly started to feel a little bit sick.

"Do you want to help?" Lauren picked up the gold star from one of the boxes and passed it to me.

"Okay." I wanted to just get out of there—I felt like a third wheel—but it seemed a bit rude. I walked over to the tree. It towered above me, so I went to the dining table and took one of the chairs. I dragged it over to the tree and stood on it. I still had to stand on tiptoes to reach the top of the tree. I managed to reach over and put it on the top of the tree, but as I did so I lost my footing and began to topple off the chair.

Lauren came running over and caught me as I fell.

"Thanks," I said, when she'd put me back on the ground. My face flushed again. I liked the feeling of being in her arms; for a moment I had felt safer than I had done in months.

Matt had a slight smile upon his face as he arranged the tinsel around the tree.

Does he know I like her?

I shook my head as I picked up a box of purple baubles. I

couldn't ask him if he knew I had a crush on his girl. "Shall I start hanging these?"

"Go for it." Matt picked up a box of silver icicles and Lauren took the gold snowflakes and for the next few minutes we were quiet as we hung the decorations from the branches, the only noise the Christmas songs from the speaker.

"There." Lauren put down her empty box and Matt and I finished ours a few seconds later. She stood back and looked at the tree. "Good job, guys! It looks great."

I went and stood next to her. She was right- the room looked so festive now.

"Time for the finishing touch." Matt went over to the plug and switched on the lights. Immediately the tree started to twinkle as the lights flashed on and off.

"Wow, look at that." Mom stood at the bottom of the stairs, gripping the banister. "It's Christmas after all." A single tear made its way down her face.

"Mom!" I rushed over and put my arms around her.

She smiled. "It's okay, Emily. I'm just happy. This is all I wanted, a proper Christmas with my family."

"I'm sorry." Guilt immediately rushed through me. "I was so caught up in it feeling wrong for me to celebrate Christmas when you were ill that I didn't really stop to think about how you must be feeling about it all."

"Don't be sorry, I understand. And the tree is up now. It looks amazing."

"Well you can thank Lauren, it was her idea."

Lauren waved it off. "It was nothing, honestly. I just want you all to enjoy Christmas, as much as you can."

❄

THE DAYS TICKED BY. I had tried to get into the Christmas spirit as much as possible, helping Mom write her cards and buying presents, but it still didn't feel like a normal Christmas.

As I came down for breakfast on 23rd December, Mom and Dad were on their way out the door, off for another treatment of chemotherapy. I hated these days, hated the thought of that stuff going into her. I knew doctors meant for it to help, but she always came back tired and one time she couldn't stop throwing up. I felt tears spring to my eyes, it was so close to Christmas.

I headed off to the kitchen and made myself a bowl of cereal and a glass of juice, then took it back to the lounge and started eating it in front of the TV.

The doorbell rang and made me jump. Lauren stood on the doorstep when I opened the door.

"Hi," she greeted me.

"Hey." I wrapped my arms around my body, embarrassed to have her see me in my pyjamas. "Sorry, lazy morning."

She giggled. "Cute pyjamas." I flushed. "Can I come in?"

"Oh yeah, sorry." I moved aside and she came into the house. She had a blue rucksack on, which she put on the floor whilst she took off her coat.

"I think Matt is still in bed," I said.

"I didn't come to see Matt." She looked into my eyes as she spoke. "I'm here for you."

I swallowed. "Me?"

She nodded, then picked up her rucksack, walked over to me and unzipped it. I peered in. It was full of food- I could make out a bag of flour, a bag of sultanas, a bottle of something, some oranges, butter, sugar, eggs, and a bunch of other things.

"What's this for?" I asked.

"We're going to make a Christmas cake."

"You what?"

"It's not Christmas without a cake. I know your Mom is usually the one to make them. And I'm not sure I would trust Matt in the kitchen. But you, that's a different matter. Those flapjacks you made a few months ago were delicious."

"You remember those?"

"Of course. I was touched you kept one for me."

I bit my lip. "I made a lot of them," I mumbled.

She put the rucksack back on her back and I followed her into the kitchen. As she started to put the ingredients on the kitchen table, I said, "You know we have some of these things in the cupboard?"

She smiled. "Well yeah, I suspected you did, but I didn't know which ones and I wanted this to be a surprise so I thought I'd just bring everything."

"Alright." I stood next to her as she continued unpacking.

As she took the oranges out, she said, "Why don't you go and get dressed whilst I finish unpacking?"

"Oh yeah." I'd kind of forgotten I was in my pajamas. "See you in ten."

When I came back down, all the ingredients were neatly arranged on the kitchen table, and she'd also taken some bowls and a cake tin out of the cupboards. She smiled as I approached. "Shall we do this?"

"Go for it." I felt a glimmer of excitement. Mom would love the fact we had made a cake, and the idea of doing this with Lauren made the surprise even better.

"Usually you'd make a cake a couple of months ahead of Christmas." Lauren was scrolling through her phone, presumably looking at the recipe. "But I'm sure it will be fine."

"Thanks for doing this."

"My pleasure." She looked up, and our eyes met. I had to

force myself to keep breathing. "I know your Mom has chemo today. I thought this might take your mind off that, even for just a bit."

"That's sweet." The words were out of my mouth before I had a chance to think about them, and I cursed myself in my head.

Talk about being obvious. I gripped onto the edge of the worktop.

"You okay?" she asked, softly.

"Just tired." I forced a smile.

"I'm not surprised." She put her hand on my arm. "You guys are going through a lot. Matt said he was having trouble sleeping."

"Matt's having trouble sleeping?" My brother always seemed so together.

She nodded. "He's more sensitive than he seems, you know. He's struggling."

"At least he has you."

I looked at her, waiting for her to confirm or deny a relationship with him, but she just smiled. "As do you. Now, let's get started on this cake."

She poured sultanas and dried cherries into a bowl and opened the lid of the bottle of brandy, soaking the fruit. After she finished, she held the bottle of brandy out to me. "Fancy a tipple?"

I hesitated. "Are you having one?"

"You bet." She took a large swig from the bottle and passed it to me.

I took a tentative sip. My eyes watered, and Lauren giggled. "Your face!"

She asked me to line the cake tin with greaseproof paper, whilst she started to weigh out the butter, sugar, flour and some spices and tip them all into another bowl.

"What can I do now?" I asked.

She nodded towards the egg carton. "Break me four eggs into the bowl, please."

I opened the carton and took an egg out, cracked it against the side of the bowl, and threw the shell in the bin. Once I was done with the other three eggs, she picked up a spoon. "We need to mix it all together, and then it's ready to put in the oven. Do you want to switch it on?"

I went over to the oven and turned it on, then set the timer for five minutes, as she began to stir the mixture.

I hovered over her. "Lauren..." My heart pounded as I spoke. Our faces were so close, I could have easily leaned over and kissed her right then.

"Yeah?"

I swallowed. "Are you and my brother dating? He says you're not, but Mom and Dad seem pretty sure he's lying."

The corners of her face turned up. "And what do you think?" she said.

I shrugged. "I dunno."

She burst into laughter. "I'm sorry, Ems, but that's too funny. I'm not dating Matt. I'm not into him. In fact I'm not into guys, period."

My breath caught in my throat. "You're not?"

"Nope." She rested the spoon against the bowl and fixed her eyes upon my face. I felt like I was burning under her gaze. "I thought you might know that."

My throat felt dry. "Why's that?" I asked.

"Why do you think?" She licked her lips, not taking her eyes off my face.

I felt like I was going to pass out. Slowly, I leant towards her. She didn't flinch, even when my lips met hers. Her lips were soft and warm and tasted of brandy. Heat spread through me as she kissed me.

When we finally pulled apart, I felt giddy.

"Good answer." She grinned at me. "I've been waiting months for that."

"Bet I've been waiting longer." I let out the breath I'd been holding. "Did you know?"

"I suspected." Her face looked slightly flushed. "At least that you were into girls. My gaydar is pretty reliable."

"Why didn't you say anything?"

"Your mom's sick. I didn't think it was the right time to make a pass at you."

"It might have taken my mind off it." We both jumped as the oven timer went off. I went over and switched it off.

"Well, at least now you know how I feel about you."

"What about Matt?" I asked her.

"What about him?"

"He might be jealous."

She laughed again. "Ems, your brother and I have been best friends for years. Don't you think we know everything about each other?"

I raised my eyebrows. "He knew?" I felt myself cringe.

She picked up the spoon and resumed stirring the mixture. "Yep. Even if I hadn't told him directly, I think the seven million times I mentioned you might have been a bit of a giveaway."

"What did he say?"

"Not a lot. Mainly he just rolled his eyes." She giggled. "It was probably a bit weird, his best friend having the hots for his younger sister."

"And he doesn't like you that way?"

"I told you, we're best friends. I know everything about him. I don't think he'd be able to hide something like that from me." She let go of the spoon again, stuck one finger into the cake mixture and waved her finger in front of my mouth. "It's ready to go in the oven. Give it a try."

I blushed.

"Come on," she urged. "It smells good."

It did smell good. *What the hell.* I opened my mouth and sucked the mixture off her finger. It tasted rich and sweet.

"Ahem."

I released her finger as Matt cleared his throat. I hadn't even heard him come down the stairs.

"Busted." Lauren smirked at him.

"Is this what it looks like?"

"We may have just kissed." She looked happy, and I felt a sudden jolt of happiness myself. My life may have been tough at the moment, but the girl I liked liked me back. That was worth a lot.

Matt scratched his head, a slightly awkward expression on his face. "That's great."

Before I had a chance to say anything, I heard the key turn in the front door lock, and Mom and Dad walked in.

"What's going on here?" Mom asked, walking over to the kitchen table, pulling out a chair and taking a seat. She looked exhausted.

I shot Matt a warning look. "Lauren was helping me make a Christmas cake."

Her eyes lit up. "Oh Emily, that's great. It smells delicious." She turned to Matt. "She's a keeper, this one."

"Mrs Anderson…" Lauren began.

I shook my head at her.

"How many times have I told you to call me Cheryl?" Mom's eyes twinkled.

"Okay, Cheryl. I feel I should tell you that I don't want to be with your son."

I focused on a spot on the wall above Mom's head.

"Oh, right." Mom looked embarrassed. "Sorry, I just assumed. You two are inseparable."

"I want to be with your daughter."

I squeezed my eyes tightly shut. You could have heard a pin drop.

"Emily?"

I opened my eyes. "Yes, Mom?"

"Do you want to be with Lauren too?"

"I...." I hesitated- this wasn't how I had planned to come out- but then I noticed that Mom had a smile upon her face. "Yes," I said. "I do."

"I'm glad. I like her."

I finally allowed myself to relax. "That's good. Because I kinda like her too."

"HAPPY CHRISTMAS." Lauren gave me a peck on the cheek.

"Happy Christmas to you too." I gave her a kiss back. "New coat?"

She was wearing a bright red coat with a black faux fur trim.

"Yep. Present from my folks."

"It looks good on you."

"Thanks. It's nice and warm too." She took the coat off and hung it on the peg, putting her tote bag on the floor first.

"Lauren, I thought we told you not to bring anything." Mom tutted when she saw Lauren's bag.

"You did. But I couldn't come empty-handed. Besides, I had to get something for my girlfriend."

My girlfriend. I still couldn't quite get used to that.

"I think she was happy enough just to be with you. We

haven't been able to wipe the smile off her face for two days."

I blushed. "Come on, Mom."

"It's nice to see you happy," she said.

She was wrong- I *was* happy to be with Lauren, but I *had* stopped smiling, last night.

"You okay?" Lauren asked me in a whisper, when Mom had gone back to sit down. "You look tired."

I shrugged. "Barely had any sleep. It suddenly hit me that this could be Mom's last Christmas." My voice wavered, but I couldn't cry now.

"Oh, Ems. You can't think like that." She reached for my hand and gave it a squeeze. "Just concentrate on today. Give her a nice Christmas."

Dad's voice came from the kitchen. "Would someone mind peeling the potatoes for me?"

Mom got to her feet.

I immediately went over to her. "What do you think you're doing?" I asked her. "You're banned from the kitchen."

"I think your Dad could do with some help."

"That's what we're here for, Cheryl. Leave it to us." Lauren took my hand again and led me into the kitchen.

"Okay, if you're sure." Mom sat down again. "Careful, I could get used to this."

We peeled and cut the potatoes and carrots, cut the ends off the green beans and prepared the stuffing. "What's next?" I asked Dad.

"It's all done." He wiped his hands on the apron and smiled. "Thanks for all your help."

"What about the washing up?" There was a pile of dirty cutlery and chopping boards next to the sink.

"Oh." He turned to the pile as if he hadn't noticed it

before. "Well if you don't mind, then that would be a great help, thank you. I need to baste the turkey."

I yawned as I walked towards the sink, and Lauren grabbed my elbow. "You're dead on your feet," she said. "Why don't you go and have a nap?"

"But what about the washing up?"

She leaned in and gave me a quick kiss on the lips. "Babe, I've got this."

"WAKEY WAKEY." The feel of lips on mine woke me up.

My eyes opened slowly. "Hey."

Lauren sat on the side of the bed. "How're you feeling?" she asked.

"I'm okay." I sat up against the pillow. "The sleep really helped. Thank you."

"My pleasure." She leaned over and kissed me, slowly and deeply. "I've been wanting to do that all morning," she said, once we'd finally pulled apart.

"Tell me about it." I grinned. "What time is it?"

She looked at her watch. "1:35pm."

I pulled the covers off quickly. "1:35?! I've been asleep for ages. You should have woken me earlier."

She shook her head. "You needed it. Anyway, dinner's ready so we'd better go down."

The thought that this could be Mom's last Christmas dinner hit me again as I saw her sat at the table, but I managed to push it down. As I piled the turkey on my plate, Lauren put her hand on my arm and smiled at me. She seemed to have such a knack for knowing when I was feeling sad. I decided to just concentrate on the food, and it was delicious. We were all stuffed when we'd finished. Mom didn't eat as much as usual, but she gave it a fair go.

"Who would have thought Dad would be such a good cook?" I put down my fork and held my stomach. "I feel like I'm about to burst."

He took a sip from his glass of bubbly. "Well, I didn't do it alone. You and Lauren were a great help. Which is more than I can say for some people." He made a point of glaring at Matt.

Matt shrugged. "Someone had to look after Mom."

"Yeah." I rolled my eyes. "She looked like she was really enjoying watching you fly that drone around the lounge."

"At least I didn't go upstairs and nap for hours."

"Matt, don't. She needed that sleep." Lauren lay back in her chair.

I shot her a warning look, but Mom said, "Emily, don't think I didn't notice that you looked like you had barely slept a wink. I've told you before, you don't need to hide it from me that you're struggling. Same goes for you, Matt."

"It's Christmas." I swallowed a lump in my throat as Matt looked away. "I didn't want to spoil it."

"It's been the best Christmas ever." Mom looked at each of us in turn. "But I'm sure next Christmas will be even better."

I really wished I could be as optimistic as she was.

"It's not over yet," Lauren said. "I haven't given you my gifts." She went back into the lounge and came back with the tote bag slung over her shoulder. She sat back in her chair and put the bag on her lap, then began to pull parcels from it. Each was wrapped in silver paper adorned with gold and white snowflakes and had a name scrawled on them in black marker pen.

"Matt," she said, handing him a parcel. "Happy Christmas and thanks for being the best friend I could ever hope for."

"Thanks." Matt took the parcel, looking embarrassed. He tore the paper off. It was a Lego Star Wars kit.

His eyes went wide. "Woah, nice one. Thanks, Lauren."

She smiled as she reached into the bag for the next parcel. "Cheryl, this is for you." She passed it to me and I handed it to Mom. "Thanks for welcoming me over for Christmas dinner when you're going through such a lot."

Mom unwrapped it slowly, revealing a bath set, with bubble bath, soap, body lotion and a bath bomb. The brand was a pretty expensive one. "Thank you," she said, unscrewing the lid from the body lotion and giving it a sniff. "It smells great."

Dad's gift came next, and he held up a bottle-shaped parcel. "I wonder what this could be," he said, shaking the bottle and winking at Lauren. I rolled my eyes as he unwrapped it. "My favourite whiskey." His eyes lit up. "I'll look forward to that later. Thanks, Lauren."

"Emily may have helped me out with that one. Thanks so much for the great meal. It was delicious." Her hand went into the bag once more as she brought out the last present.She handed me a small box. "Here you go, Ems. Thanks for being my girl."

I took the paper off and opened the box, finding a silver heart-shaped pendant on a thick silver chain. "It's lovely." I took the necklace out of the box and undid the clasp.

"I'll help you put it on." Lauren took it from my hand, held my hair out of the way and fastened the necklace around my neck. "Now you have my heart, both figuratively and literally."

Matt mimed sticking his fingers down his throat. "Get a room."

"Come and show me the necklace," Mom said.

I went over to the other side of the table and Mom took the pendant in one hand and inspected it. "It's beautiful. You're a very lucky girl."

"I am. And I have something for you, too." I turned to Lauren. "I'll just run upstairs and get it."

"I didn't realise we were doing presents." Matt dropped his head. "I didn't get you anything, sorry."

"Matt!" I shook my head. "She's your best friend and you didn't get her a single thing?"

"It's cool." Lauren smiled at him. "Just being here with you guys is all I need."

"Doesn't let you off the hook," I said to Matt, as I ran up the stairs. I came back with her present and handed it to her. "Happy Christmas."

"Thank you." She took the paper off carefully, revealing a silver charm bracelet. There was one charm already on it, a small silver heart.

"Snap!" I said, and she grinned.

"I love it." She was already fastening it around her wrist.

"You have my heart too."

TWO DAYS LATER, Mom told me that they were off to the hospital to meet with the consultant and find out whether the chemotherapy had been working. Lauren came round to keep me company and try and take my mind off it.

She, Matt and I sat on the sofa together watching Home Alone, my favourite Christmas movie, when we heard the key turn in the front door. Immediately, all our heads swivelled to the side.

"Home Alone again?" Dad dropped his car keys in the

bowl on the sideboard. "I would have thought you'd be sick of this movie by now."

"It's Christmas." I looked at my parents, trying to determine whether they looked happy or sad. I both wanted them to get to the point as soon as possible, and to never tell me.

"Anyway." Matt pressed pause on the remote. "Do you have news?"

My heart started beating fast again. This was the moment of truth. What if it was bad news? What if Mom only had a few weeks left to live or something?

"Let me sit down." Mom headed to the armchair.

Lauren pulled on my sleeve. "I should probably go. This is a family moment."

"No." I took hold of her hand, linking her fingers with mine. "Stay. Please."

She hesitated, looking at Mom.

"Please do stay," Mom said.

"Okay." Lauren squeezed my hand.

Once Dad had sat down in the other armchair, Mom started to talk. "I won't prolong this. It's good news. The treatment has been working. The cancer is shrinking. There will be some more sessions, and monitoring, but I should make a full recovery."

I felt tears in my eyes. "Really? You're serious?"

"I wouldn't make this up, Emily." She looked across to our clasped hands, and smiled. "Looks like it's been a good Christmas for all of us."

A TOAST TO UNEXPECTED COLLISIONS

CJ MATTISON

You're an idiot, Gregory Buffett. Stuck in the snow with a broken heart...

... in a ditch in the woods in the Ohio countryside at nine o'clock at night, when he'd believed he would be attending a holiday party with Monica, his girlfriend of two years. Who'd just broken up with him.

"You're too passive, Greg," she'd said. "You don't take charge often enough, and I feel like I have to take the lead in everything."

Bah, humbug.

He slouched in the driver's seat with the engine and heater and defroster running, fidgeting to classical music on the satellite radio, waiting on the wrecker. Powdery snow continued to flutter down like feathers. There was just enough moonlight filtering through the clouds to cast the woods in a pleasant, silvery glow. Under different circumstances it would have been beautiful, in the afterglow of a wonderful dinner and an evening with your love interest and close friends. Even with the BMW's yellow hazard lights flashing against the perfect white snowbank.

OK, loser, stop feeling sorry for yourself. Life's good even if it doesn't feel like it right now.

But it didn't feel good. He felt lost. Where was that someone who appreciated him for who he was, and not who they wanted him to be? Was it so hard to fit into someone's version of a suitable man?

Be tough. Play sports, real sports, like hockey, not figure skating. Play the drums or lead guitar, not the harp or flute or even the cello.

Yet stay in touch with your feminine side, but not too much. Hang in the den with the guys talking football and not in the kitchen with the women discussing the latest bestseller.

Bah, Humbug.

A few cars passed on the two-lane country club road as he waited. Most of those cruised by, barely slowing down, until one silver minivan stopped and a thin Indian man rolled down the window to inquire about him. He was fine, just waiting on a tow. Fine. Yes, thanks for stopping, I'm just fine.

I'm fine.

Finally, lights came up behind and slowed, blinding headlights set very high and far apart, like the lights on a ski patrol vehicle. Like those you see when you've been shamed into taking a slope too advanced for you and you hyper-extend your left knee and it still bothers you on cold nights like this one.

The wrecker pulled by slowly, one of the newer ones with the tilting bed and not the old hook type. Bold red and black script spelled "Horachek and Sons" on the otherwise spotless wrecker's white door. The driver raised one hand in acknowledgement as he passed, pulled in front of the car, and backed up. Greg shut off the engine and climbed out, pulling his black leather coat tighter around his middle. His bad knee twinged when he hoisted himself from the low seat onto the slippery shoulder. The air was fresh and chill and piney. He shivered when it cut through his pale green nurse's scrubs. He probably looked like he was wearing pajamas.

Under the shadows of the wrecker's flashing lights, the short wrecker driver in beige winter coveralls pushed himself from the wrecker's high seat, and eased to the icy blacktop. The driver was stocky and walked with their feet wide apart like a high school wrestler. They stopped to eye the car for a moment, shook their head, then walked out from under the light's umbrella. Their face wasn't that of a former high school athlete; cheeks too round, skin too smooth, eyes large and fiery blue, lips too thick and peachy.

It was a young woman, early twenties-ish, about Greg's age. Her hair, dark as espresso, was pulled back under a festive red and white stocking cap.

"Good evening." she said in the gruff voice of a high school wrestler.

Greg caught himself staring at her lips, which were full and warm orange and out of place on the face of someone wearing a work jumper.

"Thanks for coming," he said, shivering again. "I had a little trouble."

"Bad night to be on the road," she said, "if you don't know what you're doing. Level Four snow emergency."

"It happened pretty fast."

"All wheel drive, too."

"I got something in my eye."

She cocked her head. "Really? What was that?"

Tears.

"I don't know. Allergies, I think. Look, I need to get home-"

"Sure. So do I."

She shook her head again and turned toward the truck's cab.

"That'll be one-fifty," she said over her shoulder. "I have a credit card reader in the truck."

"One-fifty? That seems—"

"Look," she said, stopping at the truck's rear bumper. "I can leave it there, if you want. I got three more calls. Too many people who don't need to be out tonight. Can't miss a party, right?"

"Okay, Okay. Pull it out, please."

She nodded, went back to the truck. Fifteen minutes passed like an hour, with the woman hooking up straps to the car's front end. She grunted often, dropped a few well-placed curse words, around loud whining noises from the truck hoist. Greg shivered with snow trickling down his neck and feeling totally inadequate. Eventually the car crawled from the ditch and onto the truck's tilting bed. The driver leveled the bed, then went to the truck's cab and returned not with one of those aluminum writing boxes where they usually stored all their papers, but with a tablet computer.

Greg asked, "Could I drive it home?"

She took his card without looking at him, shook her head. "Nah, you damaged the front end. I assume you want me to take it to the BMW dealership in Dublin."

"My sister's going to be very upset." She looked up from her tablet then, her sapphire eyes glinting under the front of her cap. Her orange lips drew a tight line.

He imagined how he looked, dark hair everywhere, brown eyes red around the rims, skin pale and drawn by the cold, dressed in pale green scrubs, black work shoes, half-wrapped in a black leather coat. When they were dating, Monica had called him a younger and better-looking Warren Beatty. It was bull. He had no illusions about his looks. But now, for sure, he was quite the impressive picture. But why was he worried about it, with only this woman to see him?

He said, "I borrowed the car. For a party I was supposed to be going to."

She looked back down at her tablet without comment. She tapped the screen, then offered it to him.

"Sign here, please."

He wiggled his fingertip across the screen.

She examined his signature, handed his card back. "I... uh, can give you a ride home after we drop this thing off."

Where did he have to go, really? He'd traded the emergency call duty with his work partner, Janet, to have the evening and night free. And now he suddenly and unexpectedly had no plans.

A bar maybe? White wine? No, a lemon drop martini. No, bourbon. A double, dammit.

"Thanks," he said, meaning it.

He twisted his knee and nearly fell climbing into the rumbling, vibrating truck, but managed to struggle into the passenger's seat. The vehicle was huge on the inside, dark gray interior, well-laid out with comfortable, heated seats, dash controls and entertainment system better than the Beemer. Room enough for a card party.

The stereo was on and the sound was deep and mellow. He'd expected rancorous classic rock or head-banger music, but it was jazz. Real jazz, not smooth. The smell of vanilla spice covered the persistent odor of diesel fuel, the sweet fragrance emanating from one of those air fresheners they give you at a drive-through car wash, hanging from the rearview. He always declined them.

The driver climbed into the truck's arena-like interior, looking like a child in the driver's seat. She engaged gears, checked her mirrors, then steered the truck onto the pavement. The headlights lit the woods and the falling flakes in blazing white light, like the pursuer's headlights on a police reality TV show.

They drove in silence for several minutes, with the voices of Miles Davis and Don Evans accompanied by the rumble of the engine, the surround-sound shoosh of the tires, and the clunk and squeak of the windshield wipers. His own disturbed headspace weighed on him in the tense cabin, until he spoke just to distract his thoughts.

"I'm Greg, by the way."

She glanced at him with a look that said not another talker. But she humored him.

"I'm Sheila."

"You a mechanic?"

She eyed him again.

"That a problem?"

"No. My girlfriend was a mechanic. For a race team. For a while."

"Something happened to her?"

"Happen to her?"

"Yes. You said she 'was' a mechanic. Sounds like something happened to her."

He should have left the silence alone.

"No. Except that she dumped me tonight. I guess I should say my *ex*-girlfriend *is* a mechanic."

Was Monica really dead to him already? From her tone when she'd dismissed him, she hadn't left any hopes for a reconciliation. Probably better for him, merciful really. Let him off the hook so he wouldn't find himself hanging on, waiting for a voicemail telling him it was all a big mistake and he could come back. But it made him angry that she was handling their breakup with such maturity, such class. His breakups had always been disastrous and emotionally scarring.

Sheila said, "You don't seem too torn up about it."

"Well, I've had plenty of time to get over the shock sitting in the car for two hours."

"Hmph. And you'd still be there if I hadn't filled in tonight. AAA calls always get low priority because the tow companies get paid less."

"One-fifty is less? I'd hate to see the regular charge."

They'd come to a stop sign and Sheila gave the brakes an extra bite so Greg was shoved forward against his shoulder belt.

"Look," she said. "I can turn this thing around and drop you right back where I found you. Just say the word."

What was he doing? Chill.

"Sorry."

She lingered at the sign long enough to emphasize her point. When she finally guided them onward, he occupied himself by looking out the window.

The world was a real winter wonderland. The pristine white blanket coated the woods and fields and fences and street signs like sparkling fondant. The sticky white stuff piling up had not yet been sculpted by school kids into awkward snowy denizens, with tri-sectional bodies that tapered from paunch to head. Nor had the snow been carved by the tracks of animals or hunters. It would be whisper quiet out there after the tow truck passed, a quiet that was timeless and pastoral. Standing alone in a field, or with a dog or a god, there would come a gentle holiday feeling, a euphoria of spirit one tried to bottle in snow globes and family photo albums and old holiday movies.

He said, "I'm sorry for acting like a jerk. I guess I'm more upset than I thought."

She glanced at him again. "I'm not your ex-girlfriend."

"But you're kind of like her. Tough. Strong. Able to do things. You curse with competence and without reservation. And you're a mechanic like she is. I couldn't compete with her. She said I was too sensitive. I sniffle a little at weddings and sad movies. Big deal, does that hurt anyone? I grow hybrid roses in the summer and I know how to make macarons that melt in your mouth and my coq au vin is better than sex. And my favorite opera is Madame Butterfly. Too sensitive and too passive, she said. Bah. Not manly enough, she meant. Why does a man have to fit her image? Geez, Sheila, stop me before I hurt myself."

What sense was it ever to try to fit anyone else's image? Because he enjoyed colored vodka cocktails and nice china didn't make him less of a man. An attractive woman in a little black dress and strappy heels still got his blood going.

He sat panting in the suddenly too-warm cab, watching snow fall, listening to the tires whisper a lullaby and the wipers beat with metronomic persistence.

Sheila broke his reverie. "I didn't say I was a mechanic."

"Pardon?"

"You said I was a mechanic. I never told you that."

He finally caught his breath. "Have you...uh, been doing this, towing I mean, for a long time?"

She sighed, nodded.

"Yeah. But not anymore. I'm just filling in tonight. Dad came down with the flu, and my one brother's in Florida visiting his wife's family."

"Oh, that's..." He was thinking "That's unfortunate." But what he decided to say was, "That sucks."

She glanced at him again, frowned. "Yeah, I guess. My plans got cancelled anyway."

"Really? What were they?"

"Going to a party. With my boyfriend. Ex-boyfriend, after tonight."

"I'm sorry." In the pause before she spoke again, he realized he meant it.

"This isn't your car, huh?" she asked.

"No. I drive a Subaru."

"My ex – Robert — is a lawyer. He drives a BMW 7-Series. When you climbed out, you kind of reminded me of him. I thought you were just another German-car jerk. Especially when you got nervy about the charges. He makes more than one-fifty in half an hour, but he still counts pennies like a miser."

"Well, I can assure you, I don't make that much."

She went on, undaunted. "I like wine. I can tell the difference between a cabernet and a merlot. Still, he said I was too rough. Silently smoldering and aggressive. That sounds a bit hypocritical coming from a lawyer, doesn't it?"

Quiet listening seemed the thing to do. Sheila swung her hands over each other to turn the truck from the old country two-lane onto I-33 out of Marysville, a rural four lane road with a median. They would be in Dublin in minutes, and that saddened him. There was more to this woman wheeling the big truck like an expert than her high cheekbones, sapphire eyes and puffy orange lips, although those things were certainly charming. Beneath the sardonic, rough and tumble exterior was an intriguing, mysterious personality.

Outside, the snow continued to fall, no longer in fine, dainty dove feathers, but in heavy palm-sized chunks that could cover a highway in minutes. Only a few miles to the dealership. He wished for a traffic delay to give him more time with I'm-Not-A-Mechanic Sheila, the tow truck driver.

She must have felt him looking at her face, because she returned his look, before refocusing on her driving, which seemed to take intense concentration. He'd seen emergency room interns working with less intensity.

"What does your ex do now?" she asked.

"Oh, Monica, the former speed track mechanic, is now a personal trainer slash make-up artist slash tri-athlete. How's that for pressure?"

Sheila made a face. "How did someone like you end up with her?"

She was baiting him, but it didn't seem mean. "I told you, I can cook. She dug my coq au vin."

Sheila chuckled, this time with real disdain in her laugh.

He said, "You see? No respect. You women want men who check off every box. A macho street fighter one day. Then a guy who loves gardening and bathroom remodeling the next, and then who can recite love poetry from memory."

She smirked. "Right. And you men want women who can balance a checkbook, clean fish, rock the bed on Saturday night, and then drive a golf ball on Sunday morning, but never farther than you."

It was his turn to laugh.

"What's this?" he asked, pointing to a black garment bag hanging behind her seat.

She glared at it over her shoulder, eyes flashing. "Dress. I wasn't kidding when I told you I was supposed to be at a party tonight."

"May I look?"

"Are you kidding? No."

"Oh, c'mon. You'll never see me again. It's not like I'm going to trash your look to your friends."

She shrugged. "Fine."

He reached behind her and pulled the plastic-wrapped garment carefully into his lap. The protective sheath hid a black party dress, sequined on the upper half and silk pleats in the skirt. Black rhinestones decorated the décolletage and the cuffs, which would hit a petite woman like Sheila about mid forearm. His mind went there, imagining her walking toward him with the pleated skirt kicking at her thighs, how her fit shoulders would look above the neckline, how it would form to her waist. He liked the warming effect the image gave him.

He whistled quietly between his teeth. "Very nice. I'll bet it looks good on."

She shrugged again. There was pain hidden in the simplicity of that gesture. She was afraid of showing too much, afraid she'd spill it out like he had.

She said, "I only tried it on once."

"Special evening planned?"

She acted like she needed her full attention to driving. When she responded, her voice was all hard edges.

"I thought he was going to propose. Stupid of me."

He was suddenly stunned, like a deer in the headlights in a whirling emotional blizzard, as if the inside of the truck had become an upholstered snow globe caught in a rumbling, bouncing earthquake. He felt if he emitted the wrong tone at just the right volume, the glass might shatter and all manner of unpleasantness and painful shards might blizzard in on them.

He was jarred from his emotional paralysis by his cell phone vibrating in his coat pocket, at the same time an alarm sounded to his left, from the truck's dash. As he pulled out his phone, in the corner of his eye, he caught her punching at a device in a dash sling.

An emergency text message burned bright red on his phone's screen. Sheila stared at her dash device and read out loud, as if looking over his shoulder and reading from his screen.

"Major accident I-33 at Loop 270 near Dublin. All inbound traffic advised to divert to I-42.'"

She shook her head. "I'm not on call, but I may need to respond to that if it's bad."

He said, "Really? As a tow driver?"

"No. I'm an EMT. But I'm working on my PA license." She smiled, just a hint of a smile, as if relieved to let a secret out, as if there was shame in seeking something beyond one's current situation. "I told you I wasn't a mechanic like my three brothers, although my pop would have been fine with that."

He studied her as she called into her dispatcher, speaking in the concise and practiced language of a seasoned emergency worker. Damn, she was smart too. Another Monica, excellent at everything? How was a guy supposed to step up and take charge with a woman who was so strong and capable?

After breaking the call, she shook her head.

"Sorry, Greg, but I have to go immediately to the crash site. Police and Fire are having trouble getting through the stalled traffic. No time to drop you and your car."

"Let's go. I might be able to help."

She cast a disapproving side-eye at him, then down to his green-clad legs. Her eyebrows rose about a millimeter. Her eyes continued to gauge him until, without looking at the controls, she flipped on the lights and sirens.

The truck's engine growl pitched up a half octave, and they accelerated into the left lane. She leaned into the truck's wheel and controls and drove as if she'd been born in the seat. She seemed to have an almost intuitive sense of when other cars were going to move into their path, where to guide the heavy vehicle. When traffic bottled up in a sea of red lights ahead, she veered right onto the shoulder and steered like a snowmobile racer through the snow ruts there. She used an exit interchange to pass the traffic snarl then sped back onto the highway beyond the jam. Watching her thrilled him, and sparked thoughts he didn't need when he was about to need all his focus. She didn't speak except to ask him to get her medic kit from behind his seat.

They powered to the wreck site in less than five minutes. Once there, Sheila steered the big truck off the road and around in front of the wreckage. There appeared to be at least five cars involved, in various levels of damage, parked at angles on the shoulder and right lane. None of the car damage looked fatal. Traffic was crawling by in the left lane.

One of the vehicles parked crooked on the shoulder was the minivan that had stopped to help him. He recognized the plates – pink with the curved ribbon for breast cancer awareness. The passenger side was dented all down its length and both windows were broken out. A short man and two women were standing near the vehicle, lit up by the headlights from the cars backed-up behind them.

Sheila swung the truck back up into the pavement at an angle and parked, killed the siren, but left the lights on and the engine running.

She said, "It will be better if you stay here."

"No. I've got this."

She frowned but said nothing more. She grabbed the medic satchel he handed her and bailed out.

When he opened the door, a blast of chilling, snowy air blew through the truck, powdering the seats with puffy white speckles. He slid from the high seat into shin-deep snow. Three steps toward the minivan, his foot found black ice and skidded. He landed firmly on his backside.

He grumbled a curse word and picked himself up. With a

jab of sharp pain, his left knee nearly buckled. Cold wetness seeped through his scrubs and underwear to his butt.

Sheila was running toward the van, and hadn't seen him fall.

When he reached the van, the passengers were milling, stunned into inaction. The driver was the man he remembered, an older, thin, dark-skinned man with thick black mustache and brows. He was trying to assist a younger woman in a gray knee-length coat and bright scarf, daughter possibly, who was hunched over and holding her right arm. An older woman, probably the man's wife, held a frizzle-haired baby in a pink swaddling blanket. Her own dark coat was pulled open revealing a bright blue traditional gown – a sari? She held the baby close to her, trying to cover it with her coat against the cold wind.

Only the man spoke fluent English, but was able to translate through his chattering teeth. The young woman, indeed his daughter, may have broken her arm on the window pillar. He and his wife were not seriously hurt, but obviously close to shock.

As Sheila examined the young woman's arm, Greg broke out his best nurse smile, and went to work. The car was full of glass, but through the broken window, he was able to recover a knitted bag with the baby supplies, including another blanket. Greg gave this to Sheila, who used it to tie a temporary sling under the younger woman's arm. The elder woman spoke to the husband, who translated that the baby had soiled its diaper.

With the van full of glass, there was no convenient place to change the diaper, so Greg peeled off his long black leather coat and laid it fur-side up on the icy pavement. He laid the baby on it and changed its diaper with a fresh one from the supply bag, surrendering his monogrammed handkerchief in the clean-up process, while the grandfather used an umbrella to shield them from the wind and snow. When Greg had finished sealing the fresh diaper and snapping the child's romper, he caught Sheila watching him. Was he scoring points with her?

By then, a Franklin County sheriff's deputy had arrived, and Sheila and Greg assisted the family to the safety and warmth of the deputy's cruiser. His coat smelled vaguely of baby poop, so he opted to be cold and wet rather than malodorous, and carried the coat over his shoulder.

Next, they assisted an elder African-American woman in a small silver SUV. The woman appeared to have whiplash. With Greg assisting, Sheila comforted her and used inflatable supports from her medic kit to immobilize the woman's head. The woman was very upset, late for her family's annual present-giving party, something she looked forward to every year. Sheila had a way, a gift of voice that she hadn't shown in the truck. She assured the woman her family would wait for her, and Sheila would make sure to contact them as soon as more help arrived.

Soon the local fire and EMT drove up in a circus of lights and sirens and roaring engines. Sheila and Greg briefed the command leader on the status of those they had assisted. The adrenaline wore off, and Greg began to shiver. His bottom felt numb. He wanted a hot bath and hot soup.

They didn't talk as they walked back to the tow truck. The numbness in Greg's bottom had spread to his whole body. He was exhausted, wet, cold, and suddenly hungry, but the cab's warmth did much to help him recover. Better yet, all the action, the helping of others in need, had done much to help his mind and soul recover from the break-up humiliation he'd been nurturing.

Back in the driver's seat, Sheila zipped up the medic kit and stowed it behind his seat.

"You've done this before," she said.

At her questioning look, he said, "Emergency room nurse Greg Buffett, at your service."

"Ahh."

They drove mostly in silence. She found a holiday jazz station and let the soft tones fill the snow globe of the truck's cab. The snow continued to fall and pile up and snowplows passed with regular succession. He watched her drive, admired the purpose and efficiency of her movements, the flex of muscles in her cheeks when she clenched her teeth, the hard focus in her eyes. The more he watched her, the more intrigued he felt.

She worked the truck through the snowy Ohio mid-December Saturday night traffic to the closed BMW dealer, and dropped the car in an empty spot near the service area in the back of the main building. He felt his insides deflate. It was too early for the night to end, a night that had somehow become oddly special despite the harsh beginning.

The parking lot was in its own way a kind of wonderland, with shiny expensive toys for the well-to-do. The stuff of TV commercials with men and women surprised with new BMW's and Audi's and Mercedes by their significant others. Upper Middle-Class fantasy.

She asked, "Where to?"

He wasn't cold, but he was still tired, dirty, and hungry. But in that instant, he remembered he'd left a garment bag in the BMW with a pair of dress slacks, sport jacket, shirt and tie, chosen for a specific Christmas celebration.

He said, "What's your favorite holiday movie?"

She looked at him, puzzled. "'Home for the Holidays' with Holly Hunter." She examined his face. "Yours?"

"It's a Wonderful Life. Your favorite holiday drink?"

"Hot chocolate with peppermint Schnapps."

"Mine's a turtledove martini."

She asked, "You like the Nutcracker ballet?"

"Hate it."

"Me too."

He said, "I have some party clothes in the car. I'd hate for them to go to waste."

"I know where there's a party tonight. You want to go?"

He started to agree, but then a little mental hazard alarm sounded in his head. Take charge, it warned. Women don't want passive men. They want men who act like "*men*."

"Maybe," he said. "But I know a guy who knows a guy who owns the Seven Spoons Bistro. I'm pretty sure I can get us a table near the jazz band."

She gazed out the windshield into the swirling whiteness, then dropped the truck into gear.

She drove them to the Seven Spoons, an intimate club decked in mahogany and brick, unpretentious, a place that felt more real and authentic than he'd felt in many months. They carried their garment bags into the restrooms, and he tried to make himself look like someone going on a date. The pink shirt and gray wool jacket and slacks had not wrinkled, and hung from his tall rangy frame like they were on a hanger. His skin was still a bit raw, but his brown eyes were clear with no sign of red. He kept his thick brown hair just long enough to comb, and he wetted it and combed it straight back. Warren Beatty, he wasn't, but this was who he was, and it would have to do.

They emerged from the restrooms at almost exactly the same time, even though she'd warned she may be awhile getting ready.

Her look had not suffered from her hurry. Her black hair,

thick and shiny, hung down to her shoulders and framed her fair, heart-shaped face. The LBD framed her athletically-fit body perfectly, hitting just above the knee, the off-the-shoulder neckline flattering but not risqué, twinkling sequins above the waist and sparkles hidden in the silk skirt. Strappy black heels. All classy, alluring. He felt the temperature rise.

He said, "I was right. That dress does look good on."

She smiled at his jacket and slacks, his face, his hair which he'd combed back. "You clean up pretty well yourself."

They took their coats and bags to the coat check booth, then he offered his arm.

"May I buy the first drink? Schnapps, was it?"

She looped her arm through his. "No, I think I'm in the mood for a turtledove martini."

He led her through glass doors into the club room, a dark den where holiday jazz notes swirled like snow in the breeze. As they entered, they were greeted by Greg's friend and club manager, a great bear of a man named Willy Jones, former second-string lineman for the Ohio State Buckeyes football team and now a policeman in the Dublin force.

Willy was all smiles as he kissed Sheila's hand and led them to an intimate table near the back of the club, away from the kitchen and restroom, where the sweet sounds of the four-person jazz ensemble weren't loud enough to smother conversation. The guy had a knack for reading situations.

For the first few minutes, they just sat looking at each other. Greg didn't feel the need for talk. He felt drained by all that had taken place in the last five hours. Sheila seemed equally at ease with just sitting in the ambience of the dark club, letting the earthy, sensual music wash over her. She smiled at him and brushed a lock of hair from her temple with one finger. Her liquid-blue eyes drew him like silent promises.

She had been attractive in an athletic, business-like manner while she drove and worked the accident scene, but the baggy work overalls and hat had done her no justice. She was stunning, with perfect features and eyes almost too wide and bright for her narrow face. She'd found time in the club restroom to accentuate her look with makeup, not heavy but in an ethereal lightness, a bit of powder, a touch of blush, and a hint of lavender shimmer to her eyelids. The tiny birthmark on her cheek was untouched, and her lips were slightly brighter pink, maybe lipstick or just a trick of the intentionally warm lighting. Her look all added up to more fantasies filling his weary mind.

She was genuine and authentic, with the look of someone who was comfortable with themselves and didn't feel they needed adornment. He felt at once humbled by her inner and outer beauty, and emboldened by it. She had, after all, dressed up for him. And in a manner that held no pretense, that revealed the person that she'd so far kept hidden. Did his taking charge in choosing the venue release her vulnerability? Could he respond in kind? Was there any way to make this evening just the first of many with both of them still stinging from recent break-ups?

The waitress brought their turtledoves in tall, wide, frosted martini glasses. The stem chilled his fingers, revealing how warm they'd become, a heat that seemed to fill him from within. He raised his glass in a toast.

"To...new beginnings?" he said.

"To unexpected collisions," she said. He could remember nothing ever as subtle and yet disturbing as the smile she gave him. They sipped and he couldn't tear his eyes from the tip of her tongue sweeping the sheen of tan liquid from her lips.

"What's your perfect way to start a relationship?" he said.

She smirked. "I don't think I've found it yet."

"Me either. But maybe this is it."

"I usually jump into things and see what happens. Does that scare you?"

He thought about that a moment. So odd for him, being crushed by a break-up, from a relationship that seemed perfect at first. But now he was unexpectedly with another woman and such an intriguing, complex woman at that, and his time with Monica seemed destined to fail. Should he have seen it at the time? And this stunning, empowered woman sitting across from him seemed suddenly so right. But how would he know? Was there any way to avoid another loss, another tragedy of the heart?

"Yes. No. I don't know," he said. "It's too early to think about another broken heart. Doesn't it feel that way to you, Sheila?" He tasted her name for the first time, and his mind filled in flavors he could only fantasize about.

For an instant she moved far away again, a tragedy, like she'd drifted away when she'd talked about her misreading of her boyfriend's intentions. With one stupid question, Greg had sent her on her own emotional journey, and now he wanted to comfort her, to pull her close, to press her against him, to protect her from the pain.

But there was that other darker, more lurid part of him that couldn't look at her without dreaming of holding her in another way, touching her in other ways that would allow her to forget.

He shifted uncomfortably in his chair.

Her eyes drifted back from infinity and found his again. She smiled, shrugged.

"For me, it's like driving in the snow," she said. "Sometimes you have to just commit to a path and hit the accelerator." Her blue eyes danced. "By the way, this coq au vin you make – you said it was how good?"

They talked. He tried not to stare at her face and her lips and failed badly. She invited him to dance and he found she had skills, moving with a gentle grace to the soft rhythms, dipping and rising again as if riding ocean waves, her attention on him as she moved. He could hardly pull his eyes from her, the way her little black dress clung to her frame, how her legs flexed beneath the hem, the way her short hair bobbed when she shimmied.

As if reading his mind, the band slid into a slow number and without hesitation she took his hand and slid into his arms as they slowly spun. Her sapphire eyes were inches from his, and a faint scent of flowers, daisies, inflamed him further. He could feel the tension growing within. And the longer the slow dance went on, the more closely she clung to him, letting her hand caress the small of his back.

The number ended, and they stood holding each other, eyes locked. It felt like a pivotal moment, when this new thing they were doing might make or break in how he handled it.

Take charge, Greg.

He bent his head down to her upturned face and laid his lips gently on hers. She didn't pull away, or resist, or hesitate. She met his lips with hers and closed her eyes, and for a paused moment in time, they were together in body and that most intimate of things, the first kiss. He felt they were the only two people in the wonderland of the dark room, with the smells of holly and her perfume and the distant noises of people moving around them.

This was a kiss that should last forever.

But it couldn't. When he pulled back her eyes opened with a blue-as-blue twinkle that told him all he needed to know.

She requested a break, and he kept her hand in his and led her toward a break in the tightly packed tables. As he led her back to their table in the back of the bar, a man sitting along the aisle slid his chair out slightly, blocking them. It took a moment for Greg to recognize the man, and with recognition came distaste. Dirk Collier, Dublin, Ohio beat cop. Across from him at the small round table sat Terry Spell, another cop Greg dealt with regularly, one with whom he counted the minutes until their interactions were over.

"Well, if it isn't Nurse Jane," said Collier.

Greg felt heat rise to his face, and it wasn't with arousal.

"Dirk."

"Shouldn't you be back in your little sanctum at the ER?" His sneering eyes moved from Greg to Sheila, who stepped back instinctively. "Well, who have we got here? I'm Officer Collier, miss, and I'm damned glad to see you. What's your name?"

Something hard and dark moved inside Greg, a dangerous tension he hadn't felt often and didn't like.

"Good to see you two officers," said Greg and began to lead Sheila around Collier's chair.

But the off-duty cop was not going to let them by. When Sheila tried to pass, he gripped her wrist.

"No hurry, there, honey. Jane, you go on back to your table and the lady can join us here."

The dark thing within him, the man thing, pushed through Greg's defenses and he found himself moving before he could stop. He gripped the hair on the back of Collier's head and before the cop could react, slammed his face into the table, spilling the cops' beers and creating a loud crash that killed the music and turned all the eyes in the club on them.

Greg pulled Collier's head back so he was looking awkwardly upward.

"Release the lady's hand," Greg said in a hard voice he didn't recognize.

Sheila wrenched her wrist free. Across the table, Spell rose from his seat.

Greg felt a large presence behind him and a wide hand pressed his shoulder.

Willy spoke behind Greg's ear, "Sit down, Terry."

Spell looked over Greg's shoulder at the huge man and lowered himself back to his seat.

"Let him go, Greg," said Willy. Greg released his grip on Collier's hair and the glaring punk shook himself and straightened. "Time for you to apologize to the lady, Dirk."

Collier said, "I think it's time for me and Nurse Jane to step outside and sort this out."

"Ain't happenin,' not at my club. One of two things are going to happen here, Dirk. Either you're going to apologize to the lady and mind your own business for the rest of the night, or you're going to find yourself ass-first out in the snow and there will be an incident report on your supervisor's desk by noon tomorrow. Your choice."

Collier's sneer deepened, and his clenched eye ticked. The place was dead quiet, except for the muffled sound of traffic passing on the street.

Then Collier chuckled. "You're right, Willy. I've been an ass. I do apologize, miss. You all go back to enjoying your evening."

Willy said, "Good choice." He nodded at Greg and Sheila to return to their table. To the enraptured crowd, he said, "Show's over, folks."

As if on cue, the drummer tapped his sticks three times and the band eased into a mellow version of "Satin Doll."

They returned to their table and sat quietly. Sheila looked at the table and silently fumed. Greg thought her anger was directed at the two asshole cops who'd spoiled their first evening together, but it became obvious she was angry at him. But why?

Finally, after two songs worth of torturous silence, he asked, "Do you want to go?"

Her lips pulsed but she still didn't look at him. "Yes."

They gathered their coats and clothing bags from the coat check desk, then he followed her toward where the tow truck waited at the far end of the lot. The snow had stopped and the sky had cleared, so cold it was almost difficult to breathe. The stars burned and glittered, and the half-moon lit the parking lot in cold, blue twilight.

He glanced around to see if Collier was waiting for him, hoping for it, wishing the idiot hadn't let the grudge go. He wanted to pay the asshole back for ruining what was the most promising evening and new beginning Greg had felt in a long time, perhaps ever. But Collier was a no-show, probably best for both of them.

The truck was cold, but soon warmed as Sheila wheeled the big noisy machine around the lot and out onto the road. They drove in silence, until she unexpectedly pulled the rig into the lot of the BMW dealer. She pulled the truck around the building to the back lot where his car was parked. She dropped him at his car and he felt like his heart was dying in the prison of his chest. She parked in a spot between shiny new sedans and SUVs. When she cut the engine, the building blocked almost all the noise from the few vehicles passing by the front of the dealership. Behind the building, they were nearly as isolated as they'd been on the country road where he'd been stuck.

They sat in silence for a few minutes, with Sheila taking big breaths and blowing them out in great sighs. He waited for the eruption that would be the end of their short, amazing, fantasy-inducing time together. At last, after several minutes in the warm cabin, she pushed her coat from her shoulders and let her fingers ride up and around the huge gray steering wheel.

"Look," she said. "I'm sorry I got upset, but I need you to understand something. I've got three older brothers and all my life they've tried to protect me and keep me from doing anything dangerous and coming to my rescue and smothering me. I don't need that. I don't need another smothering brother, and I don't need someone to stand up for me. I can take care of that myself. I can take care of myself."

She hadn't ordered him out. He needed to understand her? Was there hope? He struggled over words.

"I'm sorry," he said. "Maybe I shouldn't have stepped in, but I…did it without thinking. Something clicked and I just wanted to rub that rude asshole's face into the wood."

"Well, you can't do that again. And it's not about you," she said. "It's about me, what I let happen to me with Robert. I can see now that I got in too deep with him. I got too far away from who I was. And then when he told me tonight that it was over, I had to suddenly grab ahold of me and take charge again, to take charge of me. All of me. And it wasn't until you slammed that guy that I realized why I was feeling so relieved tonight, and it was so easy with you."

"It won't happen again, I promise. I understand where you're coming from."

She shook her head. "Do you? Do you really understand what I need? I don't think you really do."

In a smooth gymnast's move, she pushed from her seat, rolled over the wide gray console, and landed on her knees straddling his lap, her warm hands pinning his arms to the armrests. Her face was just above his, inches away, her blue eyes burning into his. Her daisy perfume filled his nose.

"I don't think you really do, Greg. I'm in charge of me. I...control what I do. I can take care of *all* my needs."

Without hesitation, she pressed her lips to his, firmly, her mouth finding his, opening, her tongue seeking his and finding it. He felt she was a succubus, taking the very life from him, a life he found he was suddenly glad to give.

After a very long time, she pulled back, her eyes alive and wild, her mouth wicked and smiling.

They breathed against each other, his arms pleasantly and sweetly holding her, pressing her to him as he'd longed for all evening. Finally catching her breath, she laid her forehead on his shoulder.

Muffled against him, she said, "Do you understand what I was saying now, Greg...about me taking care of my own needs."

"I think I understand what you meant...about choosing a path and then stepping on the accelerator."

She giggled.

"And I think I'm going to love your coq au vin," she said.

Eventually, she returned to her seat, started the engine and gazed at him with a mad twinkle in her eye. The fantasy had faded to reality and with it an ache that he couldn't remember ever feeling before.

"Where to?" she asked for the second time that evening.

"Well, I've got nowhere to go and no way to get there. So I guess you're still in charge."

Her eyes narrowed and her smile widened.

"I think you finally understand. Only one of us can drive.

Maybe we'll take turns. But right now, I'm behind the wheel."

She guided the wrecker around the building and out onto the divided highway, and then she stepped on the accelerator. He watched her drive and let the fantasies fill his head again.

WALLS BETWEEN US

BREANNA BRIGHT

*B*lair knocked on the apartment door. She stood in the hallway, holding a suitcase and wearing a heavy winter coat as if she were at a bus station instead of a friend's apartment - stranded and left someplace unfamiliar. Gretchen answered the door, ushering Blair inside quickly. She ran back to the living room, trying to get things packed into several large suitcases.

Blair stood awkwardly in the entryway, still holding her own bag, surveying her temporary home. The apartment was surprisingly spacious with lots of natural light.

"Sorry, I'm running late," Gretchen explained as she sat on her bag to zip it shut. "I'm so glad you're here. I was really worried you might bail on me," Gretchen forced the teeth of the zipper together. "No offense."

"I mean, I need a place to stay, I'm not exactly selfless in this." Blair said, shuffling her feet as she stood awkwardly in the living room.

"True. Okay, so I stocked up on food, mostly the basics like milk and bread, so if you want certain snacks you'll have to get those yourself. There's plenty of cat food, so

Tchaikovsky is all set . . . I really, really appreciate you watching him for me."

"No problem. Again, you're helping me more than I'm helping you," Blair said. "I've got four weeks of freedom and nowhere to live."

Gretchen looked at her sympathetically. "Yeah, I'm sorry about you and Caleb. How are you doing?"

"It's . . . weird. After five years together it's like I've been thrust into a different life, you know? Cat sitting has saved me."

Tchaikovsky suddenly appeared and approached Blair to sniff her feet. Before Blair could pet him he turned away, uninterested.

"You sure you're going to be okay by yourself though?" Gretchen asked as she grabbed a rolling suitcase. "I hate the idea of you alone during the holidays."

Blair's stomach clenched at the reminder that she wouldn't get to see her family this year. With Caleb out of the picture she needed to save every penny so she could get a new place to live. No warm atole or homemade tamales. Just her. Alone.

"It'll be okay." Blair said, "I could use some quiet."

"If you're sure . . ." Gretchen seemed unconvinced, her expression riddled with sympathy. "Okay . . . I guess that's everything." Gretchen sighed stressfully and gave Tchaikovsky a quick ear-rub and forehead kiss before heading out the door.

Blair stood in the silent apartment, then stared down at the cat. He regarded her with the same uncertainty that she felt. The silence sank in.

She gave Tchaikovsky a forced smile. "It'll be fine. Alone time is good, right?" She felt like the happy part of her brain was trying to shove the sad part into a suitcase, sitting on top of it and yelling, 'we're fine! Everything's good here!'

She just wanted to relax, to get over Caleb, and to get through Christmas.

Trying to distract herself, Blair turned on Netflix. Tchaikovsky warmed up to her quickly, settling down in her lap. Blair smiled and stroked his ears. Soft light fell through the sliding glass door which led outside onto a small patio. Hiding out in her friend's dorm for three weeks hadn't been easy - she had to avoid the RA and sleep on the floor, so having space to herself was a relief.

"This isn't so bad, everything will be okay," she told the cat.

Her cell phone rang.

Blair's stomach flipped when she saw Caleb's name on the caller I.D. What did he want? What more could there possibly be to scream and argue about?

Did he want her back?

Did she want *him* back?

Heaving a deep sigh she declined the call. She couldn't do it. Not right now.

Large tears welled up in her eyes and rolled down her cheeks, dripping down onto her hands as she began to sob.. She threw her phone on the floor in a fit of rage. Tchaikovsky darted away to hide, frightened by her sudden wailing. Blair stood up and stomped out onto the patio.

The icy, December air hit her bare feet and face harshly. The cold air refreshed Blair and gave her the jolt she needed.

The patio overlooked a small but private lawn area with some young naked trees whose branches shivered in the winter air. Blair breathed deep as hot tears rolled down her cheeks.

Her face crumpled up like paper as she realized that it was

really over. Five years down the drain. Another sob burst out, and she put her face on her knees.

Below her feet, Blair heard the slide and shut of another glass door, reminding her that someone lived downstairs. She heard the distinct *click* of a lighter, then a puff of grey smoke floated up past the balcony. Blair looked down, trying to get a look between the boards, but could only make out a sliver of brown hair.

She heard a voice below her, "Lady, I swear by all flowers, don't cry."

Blair froze, not knowing what to do. Was that from a poem? It sounded familiar. A cloud of grey smoke drifted up past the balcony and disappeared. She felt embarrassed; apartments were notoriously thin-walled, he must have heard everything.

"Sorry," Blair murmured.

"Don't be sorry." The voice drifted up with the cigarette smoke, relaxed and casual. "Here." Something flew into the air and arched, landing on the patio. It was a chocolate Christmas tree covered in a festive wrapper. Blair cupped it in her palm and smiled.

"Th-thank you."

"Go relax," the stranger advised, "you'll be fine."

Blair heard the scrunch of a boot grinding concrete then the slide and click of the door as it opened and closed.

BLAIR FROWNED, opening her eyes to the dark bedroom. She couldn't figure out what woke her, but then she heard a *ding* from her cell phone, and then another. Text messages.

A *lot* of texts, it turned out. She squinted at the too-bright screen, it was 1 a.m., and Caleb had sent her five messages, all huge walls of text. Blair sighed and immediately deleted them without reading any. She found his contact and hit the block button.

Tchaikovsky yawned and uncurled himself from the nook he had made in the crook of her knees and stood up. Blair followed suit and turned on the lights. Deciding she needed a blast of cold air, she wrapped herself in a bathrobe she found hanging on the door, and stepped out onto the porch.

She liked how the icy wood felt on her bare feet. It grounded her and kept her mind from drifting into dark places with thoughts of being homeless and alone forever.

Below her feet she noticed the glow of a cigarette, and then a voice drifted up from the dark.

"Can't sleep?"

Blair blinked in surprise.

"N-no."

"Me neither. I'm a night owl."

"I'm . . . just under a lot of stress."

"You don't actually live here, do you?"

"No, I'm house sitting for my friend."

"Ah, I knew Gretchen lived up there by herself, so I was just curious."

Blair shifted her feet, which felt numb. Her teeth chattered. "Thank you again for the candy."

"Was it good?"

"Yeah."

"Good."

She heard the scrape of a boot. In the dark she couldn't see his cigarette smoke, but could smell it.

"You'd better go in, it's freezing out here."

"Do you think it will snow?" Blair wondered, glancing up at the starless sky.

"Not tonight, but soon," the voice answered. She heard

the slide of the glass door, and opened her own, heading back into the cozy apartment. She raced back to bed, where Tchaikovsky had already taken over. Blair jumped under the covers. Her frozen feet made the warm bed that much sweeter.

IN THE MORNING Blair went shopping. The crowds at the strip mall weren't too bad since it was a weekday, so she was able to find parking and go to her favorite thrift store.

The best part of the store was the huge bookshelf that lined the back wall. The books filled the air with the smell of aged paper. Blair took her time, reading jacket copies and first pages. A battered Christmas romance caught her eye and she carried it with her as she browsed the rest of the eclectic selection.

Blair wandered over to the side room which was filled with clothing. She browsed the clothing racks, getting a chuckle out of some of the more audacious outfits.

After the break-up, Blair sold or gave away most of her possessions because she simply had no place to keep them. Aside from the suitcase of essentials, and her backpack of school supplies, she lived sparsely.

As her mind wandered, sifting through the clothes and listening to the swish of the hangers on the bar, Blair's gaze caught something shiny - a glittering red dress the shape of an hourglass. The sleeves came off the shoulders, and the hem ended at the top of the thighs. There was even a display of matching heels next to the rack, also red and very high.

Blair pulled it off the rack and held it against herself, captivated by the shimmer.

Her desire for the dress surprised her, it was the kind of

garment worn by a woman with lipstick and flawless mascara, who stood tall and proud no matter what her body looked like.

Blair had met Caleb when she first started college. She never had the chance to be that woman who dressed up and went out on the town. Granted, she had always been content staying in, reading books and cuddling, but now she wanted to be the woman she pictured in that dress, and take back the time she had given to Caleb.

Blair plucked it off the hanger and went to the fitting room, bringing the heels as well. The dress clung to her body, hugging against all her curves accentuating her shape rather than making it unflattering. With the heels on, Blair stood tall, she felt powerful and sexy staring at herself in the full-length mirror, dress glittering.

She undressed and added it to her collection. Her love of thrift stores saved her a lot of money, and the dress boosted her confidence in a way she really needed. It was worth the price to feel as good as it made her feel.

"Oh, I'm glad you found this," the cashier said, folding the dress up into a bag. "Got big plans?" She winked.

"Haha, maybe . . ." Blair said. Did she have plans? Where could she even wear a dress like this? She didn't care, there would be something.

Buying the dress meant she couldn't eat out for lunch, so Blair returned to the apartment. Tchaikovsky greeted her with enthusiasm. She reached into the bag and showed him her purchase.

"What do you think?"

Tchaikovsky's pupils widened a bit to take in the sparkling fabric, and he gave it a quick sniff.

"Thanks, I thought it was pretty."

Blair put the dress away in the bedroom, hanging it on the

bathroom door, then returned to the kitchen for lunch. She had nothing else planned for the day, so she ate and settled in to relax.

Even with the distractions, Blair's mind still nudged her with the problem of her living situation. She worried that she might have to leave school so that she could work full time. She couldn't afford a dormitory. She could barely afford an apartment, even with a roommate.

Blair sighed. Tchaikovsky seemed to sense her tenseness and hopped off, padding away with his tail curved into a question mark in the air. Blair stood up as well and headed for the sliding glass door, she found herself almost hoping that her faceless friend would give her some company, but there was no cigarette smoke greeting her that afternoon. Blair suspected her below-deck neighbor was working.

BLAIR WORKED THE NEXT DAY, and she felt happy to get out of the apartment for her shift. Blair worked in the uptown mall, in a clothing store called Gallery Rouge. It was a smaller store with inexpensive clothes aimed toward young adults. That afternoon, shoppers filled the store. Blair hung up her coat in the break room and put herself behind the counter, relieving the opening manager, Rita, who looked at her gratefully.

"No time like the holidays, right?" Rita muttered sarcastically. Blair opened her mouth to answer, but a customer placed a pile of clothes on the counter in front of her. She worked quickly, avoiding small talk to get through the line. Rita patrolled the floor, tidying up the ever-collapsing piles of folded shirts.

Blair liked Rita, a tall, athletic woman in her thirties who had worked in retail too long to enjoy things like Christmas, or weekends, or people in general. They had worked together for about a year and became good friends in that time.

"You okay? You're really quiet." Rita pointed out.

"Just tired," Blair said. *What else can I say? Can't confess everything to my boss in the middle of a work day.* By the end of her shift, clouds filled the sky, turning it gray and overcast. She wondered if it would snow. The thought filled her with hope.

Blair quickly got into her car and turned up the heat, sitting and rubbing her hands together while it warmed up. An unwelcome thought drifted into her mind, that if she ever became homeless she would sleep here. The thought immediately brought her to tears, and Blair sobbed into the console, trembling from the cold and the stress.

Sniffing and hiccupping, Blair pulled out of the parking lot and headed straight for Gretchen's apartment. She went to the bathroom and scrubbed her face in the sink, blowing her nose, and letting the warm water bring life back into her fingertips. She stared at her red, swollen face in the mirror, and felt the weight of everything come crumbling down on her.

Fresh tears came as she left the bathroom, bringing a wad of tissues with her. She started to look around for Tchaikovsky, but something else caught her eye, a cloud of grey smoke floating by the window like a misshapen balloon.

Blair stepped out onto the patio and sat down, wiping at her eyes.

"How's it going up there?" the disembodied voice asked.

Fine, I'm just tired.

"Horrible."

"Want to talk about it?"

No.

"Only if you want to hear it."

"Lay it on me."

"I just . . . I don't know what to do," her voice cracked and Blair started crying again. She heard the click of a lighter as her companion lit another cigarette. "M-my boyfriend broke up with me, and I don't have a place to live, and I'll have to quit school, and- and its stupid Christmas, and it's all stupid."

"Stupid Christmas is my favorite, much better than regular Christmas."

Blair coughed up a slobbery laugh.

"I bet if you asked around you could find some room-mates to help you out."

"It's that or quit school."

"Nothing wrong with taking a break if you need it." She heard him take a deep inhale of his cigarette.

Blair sighed and set her tissues aside. "I feel stuck. Every-thing is so hard and tiring, no decision sounds right."

"Well, I tell you what . . ." Grey smoke floated up. She found the smell oddly relaxing. "Don't make any decisions. In four weeks if the world hasn't given you a solution just come knock on my door and stay in my spare room until you figure things out."

Blair smirked. "Thanks."

"I'm being serious," the voice said, "it's like you said, it's supposed to be Christmas, you're on winter break, right? You shouldn't be spending this time wondering if you're going to be homeless, so don't. In four weeks you'll have a place to live downstairs. I've got an air mattress, you'll be fine. But I bet an answer will come."

"Yeah?"

"You'd be surprised how these things work themselves out one way or another."

"You know this from experience?"

"Oh yeah," he laughed a little, "plenty of that. You're going to be just fine, I promise."

"So, four weeks, no worrying. The answer will come or I'll come live with you?"

"It's a deal."

"I don't even know your name," Blair said, finally relaxed enough to smile.

"It's Cole."

"I'm Blair."

"No more worrying, okay, Blair?"

"Okay." Blair took a deep breath and leaned her head back, devoting herself to the idea. Four weeks. No more planning, no more anxiety. The clouds swirled above her. They looked heavy and white. "Do you think it'll snow?"

"No," Cole answered confidently.

"You sound very sure."

"I always know when it's going to snow. It's coming, but not here yet."

"Will you let me know?"

"Sure thing."

Blair realized how chilly it was. She trembled and her fingers felt numb. She knocked on the patio floor, a two-tap goodbye, then retreated back inside.

Tchaikovsky greeted her with a meow, then ran to his bowl, glancing over his shoulder to make sure she was following. Blair smiled and filled it up, the cat food made a pleasant clinking noise against the bowl, reminding her of bells. If she was really going to enjoy her break she needed to get into the spirit of things.

For the rest of the evening she watched silly, romantic Christmas movies that she found insanely corny but oddly enjoyable. While they played in the background, she ravaged

Gretchen's kitchen for some junk food. She even tossed some Oreos down into Cole's porch as a thank you. No more worrying, no plans, just self-love.

BLAIR WOKE up fully expecting the euphoria of her decision of not making any decisions to be gone, but instead she felt relaxed and worry free. She practically skipped to work, and enjoyed every carol that came over the intercom.

Rita groaned. "You're too chipper this morning. Stop it."

"You're a mean one, Missus Rita . . ." Blair sang.

"Oh, the noise, noise, noise!" Rita moaned dramatically, putting on her best Jim Carrey impersonation.

"So, what *do* you do for the holidays?" Blair asked, checking that her drawer was ready for the store to open.

"Nothing, holidays are stupid. I'll be here working late on Christmas Eve while people buy things, then I'll have to be here first thing on December 26 so that people can return all the gifts they received. I had to work on Thanksgiving, man, I don't *get* holidays. I don't get to go home to my family, or have a romantic date. I get this trashhole." Rita pointed at Blair seriously. "Don't you ever drop out of school. Take the loans, muscle through it, don't give up like I did, you don't want to be working in retail hell when you're thirty-one."

"I won't."

"Good." Rita straightened the shirt on a mannequin.

"Why don't you go back, Rita?"

"I'm going to." Rita grinned triumphantly and tapped the side of her nose. "This Grinch has been saving the green. Once I get my tax return next year I'll have enough to go to trade school. I'm going to take a HVAC course and get a real job."

Blair brightened. "That sounds great. Maybe I should do trade school."

"Nah. Get to the finish line. Don't bail out just because something else sounds easier, you've got what it takes to get there."

Blair knew she had promised herself not to make any decisions, but she made one then and there. At the end of break she would go back to school, no matter what.

BLAIR PULLED a double shift that day. The steady stream of people at the checkout counter gave her no time to acknowledge her sore feet and aching back.

Finally, Rita's voice came over the intercom announcing the store's closure. Blair pulled her drawer, counted the money, and gratefully left.

Back home, Blair shed her coat and collapsed onto the couch, exhausted from the long day. She heard the patter of Tchaikovsky's paws as he ran up to her. He meowed inquisitively, and Blair forced herself up to put fresh food in his bowl.

She heard something thump outside and realized it was her neighbor's door. Blair eagerly stepped outside.

"Thanks for the cookies," the voice greeted her.

"Handmade," she joked, sitting down and hugging herself against the cold.

"Damn, with an actual wrapper and everything. You'll get yourself a husband in no time."

"I just need to learn how to clean a house, bear children, and make a martini."

"The skills of a proper woman," Cole said.

Blair snorted. "But I'm *really* focused on my career right

now."

"Psh. Women today. And we let you *vote*."

"I kind of cheated on our deal today," Blair confessed to the patio floorboards.

"How?"

"I decided I'm not going to drop out of school," she said, pulling her hair under her nose to make a mustache.

"That's great, you should finish school. How is that breaking our deal?"

"We said no decision making." She let her hair fall back.

"Well, but that's different. I said no worrying, and it sounds like you're just staying on track with your original plan, so you're off the hook."

"Do the cookies help?"

"Oh yeah, cookies will bribe anything out of me."

Blair laughed.

"You get inside now, it's cold."

"Any updates on that snow?"

"It's coming, but not here yet."

"I'm interested to see if you'll actually get it right."

"You have to *believe* . . ." his voice trailed off through the opening of the door. Blair returned inside as well, grinning.

THE PHONE RANG. Blair groaned as she woke, tempted to just ignore it, but she saw Rita's name on the caller I.D. and answered.

"Blair, the morning crew called in sick, can you come in for a while?"

"Man . . . I already work tonight."

"I know, I'm going to try and find someone to cover you, but I really need help this morning. It's Saturday."

"Okay, okay, I'll be there as soon as I can."

"Thank you, thank you!"

Blair groaned, irritated at the thought of two double shifts in a row. She forced herself out of bed, skipped the shower, and got dressed.

Saturday before Christmas? Long lines of people packed the mall, rushing to finish shopping.

Rita stood at the cash register, struggling to check people out. Blair raced to the second register, where a mob of people who had been waiting in line quickly swarmed her. Blair checked them out at full speed, practically throwing shopping bags, urging people to get a move on.

When the line finally cooled, Rita gave Blair a hug. "Thank you. None of the other jerks who work here would come in, we're constantly understaffed, and do I get a 'thank you' when I pick up all the slack? Hell no." She sniffed. Blair sent her to the back room to rest.

After fourteen hours running the store, they finally got to close the doors. They stayed open an hour later for the holidays, and exhaustion weighed them down.

"Go home, you look like hell," Rita sighed.

"So do you."

Blair made the long trek across the parking lot to her car. She felt horrible, every part of her seemed to hurt. When she got home, she collapsed onto the floor in exhaustion. She felt herself begin to doze off and promised herself she would get up in a minute. She just needed to rest her eyes for a second, then she would go to bed . . .

Blair woke in the still-dark hours of dawn, coughing and slobbering. Mucus clogged her nose, her throat ached, and she was shaking violently.

Whimpering, Blair crawled down the hallway, pulling the clothes off her body. She hadn't even taken her shoes off when she got home. She went to bed, but even with three blankets and Tchaikovsky keeping her warm, Blair couldn't stop shivering.

A knock at the door woke her.

Startled, she quickly got up, blanket still wrapped around her trembling body. Blair looked through the peephole, but saw no one.

She opened the door. On the floor sat a Tupperware and a bottle of cold medicine. A post-it note stuck to the lid with a message that said:

I could hear you coughing. This should help.
    Cole

Blair felt herself tearing up. She picked up the plastic container filled with warm beef stew. Steam collected in the empty space below the lid. Homemade; she could tell that immediately by the thick cuts of beef and vegetables. Had Cole made this himself? For her?

Blair took her treasure to the table, and sipped at the flavorful broth. It tasted great. The warmth soothed her throat and ceased her trembling. Blair gulped down a mouthful of medicine and went back to bed. This time she fell asleep properly.

TCHAIKOVSKY WOKE her the next morning, running a sandpaper tongue over her nose. Blair giggled and rubbed his ears. She still felt stuffy, but her throat didn't hurt anymore.

She took some more cold medicine and shuffled to the kitchen, still wrapped in blankets. She had enough strength to make it to the couch.

Comfortable on the couch, it occurred to Blair to check her phone. She had one missed text from Rita from the day before.

I know you're on the schedule but don't come in today. You've worked two doubles in a row. I'll find someone else to do it. Get some rest!

Blair checked her schedule and saw that she didn't work today either.

Thank god. Blair sighed with relief, tossed the phone, and went back to watching a little boy and his dog try to save Christmas. At lunch time, Cole's soup was her saving grace.

Blair looked out the patio doors fondly, thinking of her mysterious neighbor living underneath.

"THANK YOU FOR THE SOUP."

Blair sat on the floor of the patio wearing Gretchen's bathrobe. She felt much better after her nap. She had waited all day for Cole to come home so she could thank him.

"Pfft, I didn't make you soup, got the cheapest can I could find. Pretty sure it expired six months ago."

"I *know* you made it yourself. Old family recipe?"

"Maybe. Not mine, I found it online."

"It really helped."

"I'm glad." The sincerity in his voice made her cheeks warm.

"Any premonition on when the real snow is going to hit? Those clouds look really heavy."

"It's close," Cole agreed, "I can feel it tingling in my skin. But it'll be a couple more days."

"You can feel it, huh?"

"I really can. You'll see."

Blair smiled and watched his cigarette smoke drift away. "I can't wait. I love the snow. It makes everything shut down, it's like nature telling the world to just *stop* and breath . . . then everything is quiet, everything is soft and white. Life isn't like that enough. Only when it snows."

"For the listener, who listens in the snow, and, nothing himself, beholds nothing that is not there and the nothing that is," Cole said quietly.

"What's that?"

"Wallace Stevens."

"You know a lot of poetry." She played with the belt of the robe.

"I studied it for a while in college. I memorized all my favorites. It makes me super douche-y and pretentious at parties."

"Hey, that's the goal. Do you write any?"

"Sometimes, but it doesn't pay any bills. It's a gentle hobby."

"I never have time for hobbies," Blair said ruefully.

"You will. School won't last forever. I thought it would, but graduation will surprise you and you'll have all the free time you need."

"That would be nice."

She heard him exhale, and watched grey smoke drift by. Then there was the crunch of his heel on concrete. "I gotta get inside, it's freezing. Any plans tomorrow night?"

"Oh yeah, big plans at work."

"Sounds like a party."

"Just a paycheck."

"Hey, gotta make a living. Good night, Blair."

Blair realized a grin had spread across her face. She didn't even notice the cold. "Good night, Cole."

She heard his door shut, then went inside as well.

Blair dreaded returning to work. When she woke up she checked the window, hoping for snow, but the world remained stubbornly green. She sighed and let her head hit the pillow.

"Tchaikovsky, you're lucky you're a cat."

Tchaikovsky flicked his tail in agreement. He settled in the bed with his paws tucked under his chest in contentment. She took some more medicine, went to the couch, and turned on the TV.

She stepped out on the patio to check for Cole, but his porch sat empty. Her dread for work deepened, and she considered calling in sick. It wouldn't be a complete fib, she *was* sick. She really wanted another evening chatting with Cole. His company brought solace from her loneliness.

She ate the last of Cole's soup for lunch. The meal sent her into a cloud of comfort.

She checked the patio again. No Cole.

The hour of decision drew closer. Blair would have to shower and start getting ready. If she wanted to ask off work she would have to do it now.

You need to go to work, she told herself with a defeated sigh. She pulled her cell phone out and pulled up some social media, wasting as much time as she could spare.

Caleb's face suddenly caught her eye, making her heart jump. Blair winced. She had forgotten to block him online. Well, she could fix that. Her finger hovered over his name, then she realized what the post actually referenced.

'Caleb is in a relationship with Megan!' The headline cried triumphantly. Blair jolted up so fast she accidentally sent Tchaikovsky to the floor. He ran off and scrambled up his cat tree, twitching his tail at her irritably.

Hot tears were building in Blair's eyes. A week? Five years and it had only taken him a week to find someone new?

Her cheeks burned as tears fell. Her hands started to tremble. She threw her phone across the room and pressed her face into a blanket, sucking in deep breaths to stop the sobbing that built up in her. She tossed the blanket away and went to the patio door. She needed air. She wanted Cole.

The fresh air helped, but it lacked the scent of tobacco. Blair took deep breaths, focusing on calming down. She called out Cole's name, knowing he would be able to hear her, but she didn't hear the door open. The night remained silent. She went back inside, wiping her face on her sleeves as snot and tears continued to build. She needed to get it together, she had to go to work.

Blair stumbled into Gretchen's room, unable to stop crying. She fumbled through her suitcase, looking for her work shoes, but tears kept blurring her vision. Something red and sparkling caught her eye instead, and Blair gazed up at the party dress hanging on the bathroom door. The dress that made her feel so sexy and confident. She reached out and touched the glittering fabric, and a decision suddenly clicked in her mind.

Blair tossed her shoes away and stood up, returning to the living room to find her phone. It was resting in the corner, thankfully unharmed. She scrolled through contacts until she found the store's phone number.

"Hello?"

It wasn't Rita that answered. It was Darrel, the other assistant manager. They rarely worked together, but when they did Blair always found his company less than pleasant.

"It's Blair. I'm not going to make it into work tonight."

Darrel paused. "I can't let you call in sick unless you have a doctor's note. It's extremely busy, and we're short staffed. I'm requiring everyone to have a doctor's note . . ."

"I can't afford to go to a d-doctor," Blair's voice cracked, fresh tears appeared. She thought of all the double shifts, of not having a place to live, of Caleb and his new girlfriend, and her red dress offering her a night away from it all.

"O-oh . . ." Darrel's 'I'm in charge' voice faltered.

"I can't come in tonight," Blair wheezed, "I'll see you tomorrow. If you want a doctor's note . . . that's your problem."

Then she hung up.

When she finished crying she just felt angry.

The anger surprised her. Blair expected remorse, fear, anxiety, expected to call Darrel back and apologize, but she didn't do any of those things. Instead, she gulped down a bottle of water and went to the bedroom where she threw off her cardigan and pulled on the red dress instead.

It hugged her dips and curves perfectly, complimenting her shape. The heels pumped up her calves and made her three inches taller. Blair stared at herself in the full-length mirror, thinking as herself, for once, as *hot*. Not just pretty or cute, but head-turning gorgeous.

Now what? Blair found her phone and did a google search of things to do in town. She found a club that hosted some sort of dance event. It didn't matter. It was open and Blair needed to have the college experience that her years of dating Caleb denied her. She wanted to forget all her fears, and lose herself to the night. No more anxiety, she was going to have *fun,* damn it.

She took a long swig of cold medicine, grabbed a coat, and ran out the door.

The night air hit her bare legs, but Blair didn't care. She stood up straight and tried not to shiver as she went to her car and blasted the heater. She turned on the radio and found a station that played pop music.

She drove through the empty streets toward downtown.

Blair had never been inside a bar. She and Caleb tended to stay at home instead. She used to roll her eyes at the girls who walked along the sidewalks in too-high heels and the sorority girls who partied during homecoming weekend, but now she wanted to be that girl.

Blair parked her car and decided to leave her coat. She didn't want anything blocking her dress, she didn't want to hide. Leaving her coat meant that she would have to leave her cell phone as well. She allowed herself enough cash to have a couple of drinks.

She stepped outside and ignored the blistering chill that wracked her body. She hugged her arms but otherwise stood up straight and headed for the only club that seemed to be open that night. Colorful lights poured out of the windows and pop music vibrated through the walls. People filled the club, all dancing. Blair gratefully stepped into the warm room and went straight to the bar, trying to ignore the nagging fear in the back of her mind.

I can't believe you left your phone. What are you even doing? You look ridiculous. What happens if someone tries to talk to you?

Blair focused on breathing. Focused on not *thinking*. She went to the bar and handed over her money. They didn't have a menu so she just asked for a cosmopolitan – a drink name she had heard on television plenty of times. It appeared to be the favorite of light-weight girls, and that described her perfectly. The bartender handed over two pink cocktails. Blair downed the first one quickly, then sipped the second. It tasted fruity and, despite not being a drinker, Blair really enjoyed it. She smiled and leaned against the bar, watching the dance floor.

A variety of people crowded the floor, some older, some younger. Some kept it simple by dancing in the corner, other couples did something more advanced in the middle, focusing on footwork, dipping each other, and performing practiced moves.

"You just missed the lesson," the bartender said.

"Oh?"

"Yeah, they just did this salsa class, I guess they're just free dancing now."

"Hey, you don't need a lesson to free dance." Blair drank the rest of her cosmopolitan, set the glass down, and propelled herself off the stool and onto the floor. She didn't look at anybody, just forced herself into the throng and started to dance. Her heels clipped rhythmically against the floor, and she tried not to overthink it, letting her body move to the beat. She waved her hands in the air, swayed her hips, bent her knees, whatever felt appropriate.

It felt amazing.

Terrifying at first, yes, but the lights kept her hidden, the bass of the music pounded in the air, the drinks kicked in, and she felt *good.*

Why was I always so scared before? Blair wondered briefly. *It's so much easier to just not care.*

She felt body heat against her arm and glanced over to see a younger man dancing next to her. He took her hand, and before Blair could even think about protesting he had pulled her into his arms and guided her through a dance.

Blair giggled nervously as he twirled her under his arm. They moved to the fast-paced music. He wrapped his elbow around her waist and dipped her back so that her hair cascaded to the floor. Blair lifted her leg to wrap around his, and her cheeks started to burn with surprise at her own forwardness.

Am I really doing this? I never *do stuff like this.*

The man smiled and lifted her up again, twirling her out,

then pulling her back in. He appeared to have red hair, but the lights made it difficult to be sure. Blair smelled smoke and sweat on his shirt. He smelled good.

The song suddenly switched into something slower. Blair stumbled to a halt, flustered. She felt like her whole body was blushing. "Th-thanks . . ."

He pulled her in, taking one hand in his, and placing her other against his chest, while his arm went to the middle of her back. Blair realized her hand trembled, and she grabbed his shirt to steady it.

He started leading her through another dance, but Blair didn't know the footwork. Her toes kept nudging his, but he only smiled, and focused instead on turning them along the floor. Blair smiled back.

"How about a drink?" he said.

"Uh huh."

He took her hand and pulled her off the dance floor toward the bar, and Blair gratefully went to a stool. Her feet hurt, and the dancing and loud music made her dizzy.

"That's a beautiful dress," he said waving to the bartender.

"Th-thank you. I found it at a thrift store."

The bartender handed them a fresh cosmopolitan and a soda.

"I don't think I've seen you at the practice before."

"N-no." Blair shook her head and took a long drink. "I just came out tonight. Just looking for some fun."

"Well, if you want to stick around I'd love to teach you."

"Yeah, that's . . ." Blair cleared her throat, reminding herself to sit up straight and calm down. "Yeah? What did you have in mind?"

"Whatever you like."

Blair took another drink. *What am I doing? Am I going to*

go home with this guy? Does he like me? Why does my stomach hurt?

"Here, I'll show you something easy." He set his soda down and hopped off his stool. Blair followed, stumbling a little. She shook her head and straightened up, staying composed as they returned to the dance floor.

Her feet ached in the heels, but she did the dance moves that the gentleman taught her. Right foot back, then to the side, then left foot forward, sway the hips.

"This is the rumba," he said over the music.

Blair got into the dance. She swung her hips to the music, enjoying the simple footwork and letting him guide her through more intricate moves. She forgot about her foot pain and grinned wide as they spun and swayed together. More dips followed, and her head started to rush, the world blurring in a rush of lights. She tried to regain her footing and stumbled. The dancer's arms caught her.

"Whoa, are you okay?" He studied her with concern.

"Yeah, yeah, just, really dizzy all of a sudden . . ."

"How much did you drink? Have you eaten anything?"

Did I? Blair tried to remember if she had eaten dinner, but didn't think she had. *Did I give Tchaikovsky his dinner?*

Dimly, she realized that he guided her back to the bar. She took a seat on the bar stool, and he asked for a cup of water. She drank it and sighed, resting her head on the bar. She felt very hot.

"Do you have someone who can take you home?" He tilted his head, trying to look at her face.

Blair shook her head. She couldn't drive like this.

"How about I call you a cab?"

Blair groaned. "I don't have any money for a cab."

I'm never drinking again. Look at this mess. I should have just stayed home . . .

"I can give you a ride if you want but . . ." He rubbed the back of his head awkwardly.

"But what?"

"I mean, you don't have a friend you can call?"

"They're all out of town for the holidays." *Plus, I can't call Rita. I'm supposed to be sick.*

He shrugged. "I can take you home if you want."

Sure, what's one more bad decision?

"Where's your phone?" He asked.

Blair frowned, then remembered. "It's in my car."

"Really?" His eyebrow rose in concern, and perhaps with a little judgement. Blair groaned and rubbed her temples.

"Let's go get your stuff out of your car, okay?" He motioned with his head, and they headed to the door, Blair stared at the floor, shuffling her feet as they walked. Her benefactor took his jacket from a hook on the wall – *they have coat hangers?! I could have brought my damn coat* – and put it around her shoulders. The heavy, warm fabric comforted her. She took his arm and let him lead her out the door, huddling down into his jacket as the cold air hit. The air felt good against her skin after the sweltering heat of the bar. She led the dancer down the sidewalk toward her car, where she retrieved her phone and coat from inside.

"Am I drunk?" she asked

"I think you're just feeling poorly. You're really pale," he said sympathetically.

Blair suddenly remembered the cold medicine she had taken, that on top of not eating . . . "God, I'm so stupid."

"You seemed like you were having fun."

"I was, but I'm also being stupid. I'm going to be even more stupid and get in a strange man's car."

"Here." He reached into his pocket and pulled out a little pocket knife with an ebony handle. It looked tiny in his hands, the kind that would get through an airport. "If I try anything, you can stab me with that. I give you permission."

"I don't want to take your knife . . ."

"Call it a Christmas present. Let's go, it's cold as balls out here."

Blair clutched the little blade and shuffled after him, wincing as they stepped off the curb to cross the street. each step shot agonizing pain through her. She hissed through her teeth, trying to keep up. He looked over his shoulder at her.

"Do you need me to carry you?" He asked, a little exasperated.

Blair nodded. She wanted that very much.

He wrapped an arm around her shoulders, and slipped the other under her knees, lifting her off her feet. Blair melted, feeling warm and pain free.

They arrived at his car and the man set her down. He opened the passenger door and helped her inside. Blair wrinkled her nose at the strong cigarette smell and trash at her feet, but felt too grateful for a chance to sit down to complain. The man quickly joined her in the front and turned the car on, blasting the defrost to get rid of the icy build up on the windshield.

"Well, you got me in your car, do you at least have candy?" Blair tried to joke.

"Actually . . ." The man reached into his cup holder and produced a little plastic bag covered in snowmen, filled with festive candy. He pulled out a chocolate Christmas tree and handed it to her. Blair stared at the candy, something finally clicking in her brain. The smell of cigarette smoke, his voice, the chocolate tree...

She stared at him, saying nothing.

She told him where she lived, and he grinned like the Cheshire cat.

Once the car started moving and the air began to circulate, Blair drifted off, eyelids suddenly heavy. She glanced at the digital clock on the dashboard and felt shocked to see how much time had passed. She still held the knife in her hand, but she put it in her pocket next to the chocolatey treat, and dozed off.

A gentle hand on her shoulder shook her awake. Blair fumbled in the dark for her purse, muttering a soft sorry. The door opened and her chauffeur helped her out. He immediately took her back into his arms as she stumbled out of the car, almost falling to her knees. He carried her into the building and up the stairs. Blair found the keys and opened the door.

Tchaikovsky trilled at them as the lights came on, yawning and stretching himself awake. He jumped down from the couch and ran up to rub against their ankles, meowing loudly.

"Oh, Tchaikovsky, I didn't feed you. I'm sorry." Blair went to the kitchen and the cat bowl, but her guest stopped her.

"I'll get it, you go change and lie down. You're about to pass out."

Blair didn't argue. She went to the bedroom, peeling off the dress in exchange for sweatpants, long socks, and her cardigan. Getting out of her heels was the most rewarding feeling she had ever experienced.

She could hear things happening in the kitchen – the clink of dishes and opening of cabinets. Blair fell into bed and slithered under the blankets. Before she could fall asleep again the smell of food hit her nostrils and her stomach lurched eagerly. As she forced herself to rise again, the door opened and her new friend came in with a plate of toast and a mug of tea.

"Eat this, you'll feel a lot better. Bread is good for alcohol."

Blair wolfed down the first, buttered slice, then washed it down with a long drink of tea. The man placed the orange tabby on the bed. Tchaikovsky purred and settled himself into the circle of Blair's legs.

"Nothing like a cat to make you feel better."

Blair stared up at him, feeling like this was the strangest, most amazing night she ever had. She realized that her guest would probably leave, and she reached out and took the cuff of his sleeve between her fingers. He tilted his head, watching her with a gentle expression.

"Stay with me."

He chuckled a little and sat down on the bedside. "You don't even know me," he reminded her.

"I know you." *You're the voice on the other side of the wall, the poet, the giver of candy.*

He smiled and touched her head, catching a strand of hair in his fingertips. He pulled the blankets up to her chin, forcing her to lie down. Blair's head touched the pillow and her brain began to swirl, draining into the vortex of sleep.

"Don't go." She wanted to raise her arms and grab him, but he had tucked her in tightly.

"I'm only downstairs," he assured her.

"But there's always something in the way . . . work . . . money . . . a floor . . ." Her heavy eyelids fell shut.

"They don't have to be in the way," he told her. His voice was close, so close she could feel his warm breath.

Blair blinked her eyes back open, staring at his gentle expression. He was close enough for a kiss. Instead he pressed his forehead to hers, and her eyes fluttered shut again.

"Sleep well, Blair. There will be snow tomorrow."

✳

WHEN BLAIR OPENED HER EYES, she didn't feel as bad as she thought she would. She felt magnificently cozy. Tchaikovsky lay in a perfect circle on her stomach, the blankets felt warm and heavy, and filtered half-light came through the window.

Snow.

Blair craned her head to look out the window. The sky looked overcast, and on the ground . . .

Green grass.

Blair sighed and set her head back down, disappointed, but too content to let it bother her. She freed an arm from under the blankets and found her phone on the bedside table, plugged in and fully charged. She didn't do that, it must have been . . .

Cole.

Blair heaved a deep sigh and turned her phone on. She saw several texts from Rita and her heart skipped a beat.

Shit, I'm fired. I'm so totally fired.

She winced, hitting the message and preparing for the bad news. The text read: '*Darrel told me what happened, don't worry, I got it sorted out. Take all the time you need.*'

The breath she had been holding came out in a long, shaky sigh. Tchaikovsky murred and raised his head, yawning widely. Blair smiled and pressed the phone to her chest.

'*Bless you, Rita.*' She texted back.

Her phone vibrated with a response.

'*Do you need tonight off?*'

Blair laughed and answered: '*We're all getting the night off. It's going to snow.*'

Blair didn't leave bed until late afternoon when she started to get hungry. Her mind kept wandering back to the night before. She felt like she should be embarrassed. She kept remembering the way he taught her to dance, the way his arms felt as he carried her to the car. He helped her, complimented her dress.

He promised her snow.

Blair found his little knife in her coat pocket and fiddled with it as she ate her cereal, laughing quietly through her nose remembering all the jokes he made. For some reason, she just couldn't bring herself to feel ashamed. Cole had made it all seem so . . . unimportant, so adventurous.

That had been her goal, to have an adventure and forget about everything else. She dressed up, danced, drank too much, made a fool of herself, and no one cared.

More importantly, *she* didn't care.

She busied herself looking for more snacks and didn't notice the first snowflakes as they began to fall. When she entered the living room fresh powder covered the ground.

The last bit of daylight began to fade from the short winter day. Filtered grey light slipped through the clouds to reveal the beautiful snowfall coming down. Blair stared at it through the window, entranced. Tchaikovsky jumped up on his cat tree to watch, his pupils shrank to narrow slits.

Blair put on her coat and shoes and stepped out onto the patio, grinning at the falling snow. It fell fast and heavy. The snowflakes were the size of half dollars, and the powder quickly became a heavy blanket. The streets sat empty and still, the only movement came from the twinkle of Christmas lights from the houses across the way.

She took a deep breath of the icy, snow-scented air, and released a long stream of white. As her breath drifted away, a grey puff of smoke joined it.

Blair felt her heartbeat quicken with excitement.

"You called it," she said to the floor, "snow."

"I told you, I always know when it will snow," Cole said.

"It's beautiful...everything's so quiet."

"'And now I am listening hard, in the grandiose silence of the snow.'" Cole said quietly.

Blair tilted herself forward, peering over the side to try and see him. He stood out of sight under the patio, and another cloud of smoke drifted by.

There's always something in the way.

They don't have to be in the way...

Blair looked down at the building pile of snow, already so thick it made all the grass disappear. Blair swung her leg over the patio railing, rested her boots on the edge, took a deep breath, and jumped.

She crumpled into the snow as she landed, making the white powder burst all around her. It didn't hurt, and Blair stood up triumphantly. She turned to see Cole staring at her, mouth dropping so that his cigarette fell away and hit the ground in a shower of sparks.

"Wh- You just . . . we have stairs you know."

Blair grinned and dusted the snow from her pants. "I was tired of talking to you through a wall."

Cole stepped forward, studying her face. "Are you okay?"

"The best I've felt in a long time."

Out in the open, the snow quickly accumulated on their clothes and hair. Cole's light brown hair filled with snowflakes. His warm brown eyes sparkled.

"Thank you for last night. For teaching me to dance. For helping me."

The corner of his mouth rose in a bemused smirk. "You're welcome."

"Did you know it was me?" She asked.

"Not at first. But once we got outside and you started talking and making jokes, I recognized your voice."

"Me too. It was the candy. You gave me a chocolate tree when we first met."

The other corner of Cole's mouth joined his smile, and he rubbed his hair bashfully, casting off the snow that had built up there.

"I was going to invite you, you know, to go dancing. I'm part of this dance club. But you had to work."

Blair nodded. "I called in sick. I found out my ex-boyfriend is dating someone new and . . . I just wanted to get out. I was tired of hiding away every time something bad happened. I wanted to just feel free, to stop worrying . . ."

"I don't know why you worry at all. You looked . . . I mean, you were kind of amazing last night."

"It was a pretty sexy dress."

"I don't just mean the dress. You were all by yourself but you went out and danced. You were really cool."

Blair laughed loudly. "Me? Cool?"

"You're the coolest person I know."

Her cheeks warmed in the night. The street lamps and strands of Christmas bulbs shining on the horizon provided the only light. Blair stared at Cole, feeling safe, feeling confident.

"I like you, a lot."

Cole looked down at his feet, but his smile was big. "I like you too."

Blair stepped forward and rose up on her toes. Cole leaned forward and met her halfway. Their lips met. His kiss warmed her, setting butterflies loose in her stomach. It felt wonderful. Blair slipped her arms into his jacket, wrapping around his waist in a hug, huddling into him as the snow swirled around them. The warmth of their bodies clashed against the white world around them. His arms went around her back; Blair felt completely encased in him, breathing in his scent, relishing the soft touch of his mouth.

They parted softly, like a melting snowflake, but kept hold of each other, eyes soft and shining, cheeks burning red, snowflakes lingering in their hair and eyelashes.

"Stay with me. . ." Blair whispered, reaching up for another kiss.

This time, he did.

BLAIR FELT bittersweet about that Christmas Eve. She missed her family terribly, even after taking a video call with them. It didn't feel the same without a tree and her mom's tres leches cake, but Cole kept her company. They spent the night together, talking, drinking hot chocolate, and watching the snow fall all night long. They sat on the floor in Gretchen's apartment, wrapped in blankets with all the lights turned off so that they could see the holiday lights of the surrounding neighborhood. Tchaikovsky lay curled up in Cole's lap, happy and purring.

"Are you off tomorrow? For Christmas?" Cole asked.

"Yeah, the one day off we get," Blair said.

"Good. We should get dinner. And you should definitely wear that red dress when we do."

Blair giggled. "You're not visiting family?"

"Not until later. We all have a hard time lining up our schedules. My sister is visiting her husband's family, and then we'll get together on the twenty-sixth."

That made Blair feel better about her own situation. She would see her family soon. It didn't have to be Christmas. With Cole at her side, she finally felt that everything would be okay.

She snuggled closer to Cole, feeling sleepy as the night continued. At the stroke of midnight, Cole gave her a soft kiss and whispered, "Merry Christmas, Blair."

"Merry Christmas," she whispered.

BLAIR PATTED her new mattress fondly. She didn't have much to unpack, unlike her new roommate, who would be busy for the rest of the day.

"Do you need any help?" Blair asked absently, putting on a coat and filling her mug with coffee.

"Nah, Tchaikovsky's giving me a hand," Gretchen said. The cat jumped from box to box, hiding and attacking bubble wrap while Gretchen worked.

"Thanks again for taking me in, Gretch."

"Hey, I'm just glad they had a two-bedroom for us to move into. You should have told me sooner that you needed a place to live, this is going to save me a ton of dough."

"It was mostly Tchaikovsky. We connected and I just couldn't part ways." Blair zipped her coat up and stepped outside through the sliding glass doors. They lived on the first floor and had a concrete slab that acted as their porch. Snow from last week's fall still covered the ground, and heavy, white clouds crept across the winter sky.

A little puff of cigarette smoke drifted past her. Blair turned her head and smiled at Cole, who sat on his own patio next door, watching her. He patted the chair next to him, and Blair strolled over to join him. No walls separated them.

"Think it's going to snow?"

Cole looked up and smiled. "Oh yeah, there will be snow."

FATES' BUTTERFLY CHRISTMAS

SADIE MAY

FATED EVENTS

*T*his isn't just some typical, cliché, Christmas Hallmark movie love story, okay? It's different. Well, alright, no, it's not actually all that different. Honestly, the plot is pretty similar to every other Hallmark holiday special where you've got the Midwest girl falling in love with some handsome young man and a "should-we-shouldn't-we" vibe, but I'll tell you why this story is different. For one thing, I'm not blonde. Secondly, I'm not skinny. And thirdly, he's not white—or American. As you can see, this Hallmark movie love story is clearly very different because I've already turned the top three clichés on their head! Does this mean my story is going to inspire feelings other than an eye roll, a scoff, and a "can you believe this sappy crap?" No, not necessarily; however, if you're ready to hear how a fat, white Kansas woman fell for a skinny, brown, Sri Lankan man in time for Christmas, then I've got just the story for you. As with all Hallmark love stories, ours starts with a coffee shop.

Fate has a funny way of arranging moments in our life

months, sometimes years, before we even recognize the importance of those events. A simple conversation, a slip on the ice, or having to rush home one morning before work because you forgot your phone, all seem innocuous in the moment, but could ultimately change the course of your life. Some call this "the butterfly effect." The term originally came from a man named Edward Lorenz who applied his metaphorical and mathematical model to weather as a way of explaining how small causes can have large effects. Others, inspired by this observation, took it and ran with it as a philosophy in life. Johann Gottlieb Fichte in his *The Vocation of Man* declared that "you could not remove a single grain of sand from its place without thereby...changing something throughout all parts of the immeasurable whole". A single placement of sand in a desert can make all the difference. A single moment in time can do the same.

Some call these seemingly connected events in life "the butterfly effect," some call it coincidence, while others declare it to be "God's plan." I suppose I wrap all of these notions into one idea, one word: fate. A dictionary definition of the word fate will tell you that fate is a noun and represents the "development of events beyond a person's control, regarded as determined by a supernatural power." What that supernatural power might be to you is up to your own determination. I don't have an answer for what my life's laid out plan looks like, the events that will take place, or even the wherewithal to always recognize when something momentous and life changing is happening. I simply live my life the way everyone else does: oblivious and moving forward as much as possible, flexible to the changing tides of fate. Without notice, the thread is spun, its length predetermined, and cut free to the wind.

CLOTHO - THE THREAD IS SPUN

"Somewhere, something incredible is waiting to be known"
– Sharon Begley

SOCIAL ANXIETY IS A CRUEL BITCH. She makes everyday tasks, simple social interactions such as ordering a coffee from a cute boy, a tremendously difficult task. *What if I get up to the front and I forget what I'm going to order because I get lost in his eyes? What if I drop my change? What if our hands touch when he hands me my cup and we fall in love, get married, have three and a half kids, and then one day he gets hit by a bus on his way home and dies, and I'm stuck with three and a half kids I never wanted and*—see where I'm going with this? It starts innocently enough, logically enough, and before you know it you've created a made-up world that ends in death and despair all because you decided to buy coffee at the college student center's Starbucks. Christmas lights draped and glittered around the edges of the counter, twinkling on and off in alternating blinks. The usual holiday and seasonal versions of the drinks were out and those that resembled ice cream more than coffee tempted me most.

"It could happen, right?" I ask, turning my chin slightly to the left, so that my friend can catch the words that I'm not so quietly whispering, eyes still locked on the cute guy working the Starbucks' counter. She rolls her eyes, exasperated because we've been standing in the same place for the last three minutes as I try to make up my mind on what I want to order, rehearsing the order in my mind multiple times to make sure I've got it without flaw, and switching weight from leg to leg, trying to time my waltz up to the counter, so that the cute barista would be busy and I could just order from the "not as cute" one.

"Yeah," Amelia scoffs, quickly jabbing her elbow into my side. "It could totally happen all because you get up to the counter and buy a damn coffee, not because you've been standing here staring at the poor kid for the last, what, five minutes now? You think messing up your order would be weird, but not this?"

I mean—fair. She's not wrong. At this point, standing off to the side and looking like someone who can't figure out how to order from a Starbucks is definitely weirder than if I'd just ordered the damn Starbucks. Okay. Time to do this. I could do this. It's just a simple coffee order. How could I mess that up? Wiggling my shoulders to release the tension, I stepped up to the counter, eyes locked on the *not* as cute barista, only to be greeted by a deep voice in front and slightly to my left.

"Hi, what can I get for you?"

Internally, I groaned. Outwardly, my gaze shifted up toward the voice that did not come from the barista I had waltzed up to, who had by now wandered off after hearing his co-worker step in, but to meet the very brown, shining, and focused eyes of the *cute* one. I don't know if my jaw had actually gone slack, but it certainly felt like it. He offered a small smile and tilted his head a little to the left, and I realized that he wanted my order. Caught off guard, I quickly looked past his head and stumbled out a quick, "Venti iced coffee, please." I could feel my heart beating in my chest as I fumbled with the clasp on my wallet, grabbing my card out and shifting my gaze to stare intently at the card reader.

"Venti iced coffee, got it. That'll be $3.75"

I nodded, and pushed my card chip into the reader, only to be met with an angry beep.

"Sorry," he apologized, "I don't think it was ready".

Oh god. I had tried to pay too soon and now I looked like an idiot. Laughing slightly, I took the card out and shrugged, holding it close to the machine as I waited for it to reset.

"No, sorry, I guess I wasn't paying attention," I offered as an excuse, eyes still very much locked onto the card reader, so I could see when it was *actually* ready to take my payment.

"Alright, should be ready now."

I could hear the smile in his voice and a slight vibrato that seemed to lace each word because of the timbre of his voice. Without vocalization, I once again inserted the chip into the card reader and waited for it to say that the payment had been processed before withdrawing it and sticking it back in my wallet.

"Receipt?"

"No, that's alright, I don't need it", I replied, eager to step away from him and begin my descent into embarrassment. I had already started walking toward the end of the counter where Amelia stood with a bemused smile on her lips. "Oh, shut up," I said while sweeping past her and leaning my elbow on the counter.

"I didn't say anything"

"You didn't have to. I could see it in your face that you saw my embarrassment from afar."

"Hey, it wasn't that bad. It's not like you spilled something all over him or dropped your cash all over the floor," she offered.

"It was still embarrassing! I wasn't expecting him to be the one to take my order. I specifically walked up to the other guy, so that I wouldn't have to talk to the cute one! Then he just took over and I got all flustered. I mean, did you see his eyes? And his *ass*," I emphasized, finally turning to look at her. She laughed and raised an eyebrow, "How could you even see it when he's behind the counter and wearing an apron?"

I waited to answer as the other barista walked over and slid my coffee across the counter to me, hoping I hadn't been speaking too loudly. "Thanks", I said as I grabbed my coffee and turned to walk away from the Starbucks, Amelia in tow. When we made it out of the general coffee area, I finally answered her.

"It's a talent I have, I suppose. Being able to spot a nice ass. I mean, it's not like I was looking for it, but when he turned around, you could just kind of see the shape, y'know? How can I not get flustered by a cute boy with nice eyes, a cute smile, and a great ass?" I questioned her.

She laughed again, "Whatever you say. You're ridiculous".

And that was that. We headed to class and I ruminated over the embarrassing event for another two hours before eventually forgetting that it had ever happened. Something that had seemed mortifying and built up in the moment quickly passed into the recesses of my memory as a non-event. It would be three years before I would return to this memory again, and when I did, Christmas would look a little different.

WALKING INTO REVERE, the popular downtown coffee shop, I felt the uncomfortable and temporarily forgotten mixture of nausea and nerves that comes along with a first date coil inside my stomach. It had been nearly three years since I had gone on a first date and only two months since I had broken up with my boyfriend. Was it too soon? Was I even over my ex enough to go on a first date? I had just gotten off work and it wasn't a hair wash day, so my hair was looking a little limp and probably more than a little bit greasy. I felt self-conscious and I wondered if that radiated from me as I walked to the back of the shop to a secluded area where I could keep my eyes on either entrance to the coffee shop, hoping to catch a glimpse of my date before he saw me. I didn't do well with first dates in general, but because my last relationship had deteriorated into nothing over time, the concept of dates existed only as a faint memory—no use to me now. Did I remember how to act on a date? What were the expectations? I checked my phone and saw that I had arrived a good ten minutes early. That gave me enough time to order my own drink, so I didn't have to deal with the awkwardness of someone else paying and I could focus on taking a few deep breaths to calm my nerves.

Picking up my drink from the barista, I turned toward the table I wanted by the window and paused when I saw someone who looked as lost as I felt. He had come in from the front door and lingered a few feet away from the counter, near the wall where I'd stood upon entering. He was taller than I had expected, with black hair that drifted over his eyebrows as he stared down at the phone in his hand. I could see a worried crease take over his forehead and a wrinkle to his eyebrows while his slender fingers went to tap the screen. His body posture and overall demeanor radiated nervousness, and somehow, that eased my own. He looked enough like his pictures, and his uncertain energy convinced me that this was my date. Instead of sending him a quick message like an "I see you," or an "I'm over here," I walked up right behind him.

"Hey. It's pretty busy in here, isn't it?"

He jolted slightly and his eyes flashed up quickly from his

phone to me, surprise and mild confusion running across his face before a look of recognition came over it.

"You're here already. I was looking for you...about to text you. It's really busy. I wasn't expecting that," he admitted.

I hadn't been expecting it either. I'd never been to this coffee shop before and I wouldn't have thought that a Friday after work in February would be so crowded. Luckily, the spot I had chosen for us to sit remained relatively free of people; only half the shop seemed to be packed with people, most of the patrons preferring the cushy chairs and booths to the window stools.

"Yeah, I was surprised when I came in. I've never been here before, but it seems nice. I actually just got here not too long ago and ordered my drink. I found us a free spot over by the window," I gestured toward the back of the shop behind us. It was then he noticed the coffee I held in my hand.

"You already got your drink? Oh, I—why? I'm supposed to buy your drink." Confusion flashed over his face. It was sweet. Smiling, I shrugged my shoulders and *meant* to say something like, *I just wanted to figure out what to drink so you didn't have to wait on me.* What *actually* came out of my mouth was, "Well, you're a student and I make more money than you, so I didn't want you to have to pay for me." As soon as the words left my lips, I wished I could retrieve them, feeling very much an asshole as well as embarrassed. I couldn't even think of a way to recover from that kind of statement, and didn't have the time to as he shifted his weight to his left leg, obviously a little taken aback.

"Oh. Okay," he said. "Uh, I'll order mine now then. Where do I...?" I saw my chance to recover! I stepped forward a little bit and nodded to the counter in front of us where a young woman stood, waiting with a smile. "She can take your order right there and they have their menu right above," I offered, trying to be helpful. He simply nodded and stepped up to the counter, seeming as if he already knew what he wanted. It was something simple: a small black coffee with two sugars. I stood nearby, so that we could walk to our seats together, and I heard the barista behind the counter ask for his name.

"Theodore," he told her.

"No, like, what's your real name?" I overheard.

Did I overhear that correctly? I lingered behind them both, but I stared at the girl with wide eyes, amazed at the audacity to ask someone that. I don't think she meant her question offensively—I could tell that she was genuinely curious why this tan skinned, somewhat accented young man in Kansas was using a very *English* name (and an uncommon one at that). Still, it reminded me of the movie *Mean Girls*: "*Oh my god, Karen. You can't just ask people why they're white.*" I could tell that he was also surprised, perhaps slightly embarrassed, as he responded with, "Tharindu." Not having noticed the awkward air that she had created, the barista smiled brightly and nodded her head, enthused and spurred on by the response.

"That's a nice name! Where are you from? You don't look like you're from here..."

Every word that came out of this woman's mouth appalled me further, and my eyes shifted between them as though they played a tense tennis match. Should I step in? Steer the conversation away? Was this weird or was I just reading too much into it? Why couldn't she just take the order and not continue to make conversation? I moved to step forward and stand by his side right as another barista handed his drink over to the inquisitive one. To his credit, my date gave an awkward chuckle and held his hand out to receive his order, still answering her question. "I'm from Sri Lanka. Thank you for the coffee." She handed it to him without further comment and I led us over to the spot I had found, still discombobulated by the whole encounter I saw take place.

"I can't believe she just asked you what your *real* name is," I told him, settling onto the stool to his left as he joined me.

"Who even asks that?" I questioned.

He shrugged and took a sip of his coffee before answering sagely, "I guess she was just curious because I don't look like a Theodore."

I couldn't help it; I laughed. "Yeah, well, to be fair, there's not that many white people that are named, or look like, a Theodore. Out of all the names you could have chosen, that was probably one of the more uncommon ones." He laughed with me and agreed, "I only used it because some of my friends used to call me Theodore—because they said I look like that Chipmunk from the movies." He did, a little. He had a pleasantly round face, large eyes, and when he smiled, his upper front teeth showed in a way that made them appear slightly rounded and, well, chipmunk like. I could see the resemblance.

In some ways, I had to internally thank that socially confused barista who took his order because the whole situation helped relieve some of my own anxiety and nervousness. It gave us a funny situation to talk about and I didn't have to be the one to ask him about the name from his Tinder account, because let's be honest, how many foreign brown men have *you* met named Theodore? It wasn't impossible—I had met one named Marlin, after all—but it remained rather improbable. We slid comfortably into conversation now that someone else had broken the ice for us, and we spent two hours slipping in and out of conversation about topics like work, school, his home country, his friends, and our own dating expectations. I learned that he had previously worked for the Starbucks in the student center and felt an itch in my brain that caused me to look at him a little closer.

"You used to work in the student center's Starbucks?" I asked for verification.

He stared at me a bit puzzled, "Yes. I worked there about three years ago and mostly worked in the mornings." His face looked slightly familiar and the itch in my brain kept touching on some recess of my memory before it dawned on me and I leaned in a little closer.

"I think I remember you! I'm pretty sure I saw you working one day and thought you were super cute!" He laughed and the memory of three years prior burst forth from my memory. I could almost see the image of his back turned toward one of the machines, a green apron tied around his waist and a cute butt clothed in khaki pants.

"No, seriously" I said, "I remember because I was so nervous to go up and order from you because I thought you had such a nice smile. I tried going to the other barista, but you took over the order and he walked off! I was so flustered because I can't make eye contact with cute people!"

He laughed again and took a sip of his coffee before responding, "Sorry, I don't remember you."

I waved my hand as if to wave off his concern, "Don't worry about it. I'm sure you met a lot of people while working there." We continued to talk about all the people he had met, the commonalities of white girl names and their various spellings that came through Starbucks (Emily, Caitlyn, Rebecca), and eventually, we transitioned into talking about where we saw this date going. He looked down bashfully at his hands, spinning the cup around with his fingers, "This is actually my first time using a dating app. My friend set up my account for me, but I wasn't sure what to put on it," he admitted and I laughed, thinking back on his profile. It had three pictures with friends, making it difficult to tell which one he was, and a profile that only showed three emojis.

I grinned mischievously and rested my chin on my hand, "Yeah, to be honest, I almost didn't swipe right on you because it was pretty empty, but I thought 'Eh, he's cute enough." His eyes lit up with amusement at first before his entire expression fell into one of seriousness.

"Listen, I had a really great time tonight and I'd like to see you again," he offered. "I'm not sure how dating works or what I'm supposed to say or do, but I'd like to take you out for dinner."

He only needed one date to know that we were something worth pursuing, and I found out later that he had deleted the dating app after our first date, but I needed a little more time. I agreed to a second date, and a third, until it seemed unimaginable to want to be with anyone else.

LACHESIS - MOMENTS MEASURED

"The trouble is you think you have time"
– Gautama Buddha

TIME IS something we all take for granted, especially when we're young. Einstein's theory of special relativity essentially explains that time slows down or speeds up depending on the speed you move relative to something else. Tharindu used to tell me that Einstein won a prize for explaining time's relativity by saying "When you stand next to a hot oven, time seems so slow, but when you stand next to a hot woman, time passes by quickly." I still don't believe that Einstein explained time using hot women analogies, but Tharindu always seemed to believe it himself, and I preferred to nod along with his explanation rather than check his factuality. Whether Einstein described time based on a hot woman wasn't the point—only our perception of time mattered. It passes whether we acknowledge it or not. Whether we feel that it passes us quickly or slowly, it passes all the same. One day we wake up and realize that we're further than when we started—our life continued moving and events, significant or otherwise, have taken place without us appreciating each moment. We take for granted that we will wake up each day, that our loved ones will continue to exist, and that we will be able to maintain our happiness. After all, an object in motion stays in motion unless acted upon by another force, right? Happiness in motion stays in motion…unless acted upon by another force. Time, however, is acted upon and influenced by nothing. It continues forward regardless.

WE HAD two months to decide. Two months for a "make-or-break" decision that would impact the rest of our lives. We all have those pivotal moments in life where single choices change the course of our futures. Remember when I mentioned the butterfly effect? One choice could change all outcomes from there on out. Sometimes we're not capable of seeing those moments as they come—like a trip to a coffee shop—but sometimes we're attuned enough to know when such a situation is placed before us. This is almost worse because you are acutely aware that the choice you make cannot be undone and you will have to live knowing that you brought each event on yourself. The stress of a momentous decision can lead to fear, indecision, and regret. Moving forward becomes difficult and you become ever more aware of time as it passes you, seemingly speeding up with each day that you hesitate to decide. Each day, you wake up and consider the pros and the cons, track the possible futures laid out before you, and count the ways that you could be making a mistake. One choice, numerous futures, all waiting. On you.

We started talking about marriage in August. The idea had been floated here and there, touched upon lightly with a smile and a tentative plan of "someday." What hurry was there, after all? We were only six months in; we still had our whole lives ahead of us. What was the rush? We had time…didn't we?

All of a sudden, it seemed like we didn't.

It started with tweets from our President. It started with his policies—many damaging ones in place before we even realized the significance—and increased over time. In December of 2016, President Trump's administration shut down the Military Accessions Vital to the National Interest (MAVNI) recruitment program, leaving more than 4,000 immigrant recruits in limbo. The MAVNI program, facilitated by the U.S. Department of Defense, provided a path toward citizenship for legal non-immigrants who wanted to serve the United States and had been around for eight years, starting under the George W. Bush administration, with great success.The Trump Administration's explanation for the program's suspension and termination came as an unenthusiastic and entirely baseless claim about national security.

In 2019, the U.S. Immigration and Customs Enforcement agencies doubled down on their initiatives to corral and deport immigrants deemed illegal. Families were rounded up and separated—placed in detention facilities. The horrific conditions of overcrowded fenced in areas holding families at Border Patrol processing centers exploded into the public's attention. We learned about the pain, disease, and abuse happening within our own facilities while immigrant children went missing and died while in U.S. custody.

The Trump Administration voiced their distaste for the Diversity Immigrant Visa a.k.a the "green card lottery," created in 1986 which aimed to diversify the immigrant population in the United States, by selecting applicants from countries that historically had a low number of immigrants in the previous five years and successfully halted the immigration of millions who had been awarded the Diversity Immigrant Visa in 2020 on the basis of the 2020 global pandemic. The pandemic became the perfect opportunity for the administration to lock down the nation and lead the U.S. toward isolationism. Policies that had previously allowed foreign workers and students into the U.S. on various visa types eroded slowly over time. Each year, fewer were granted, fewer approved. With the pandemic, it became near impossible for those not born in the United States to ever see a possibility of not only immigrating to the U.S., but to even dream of citizenship. Even those who had become citizens in recent years did not feel safe.

We did not feel safe.

IT WAS a Tuesday night in early August when we began to talk seriously of marriage. He came over after work, like he did every Tuesday, weighed down by melancholy. I had learned by this time the ways that his body crippled under stress. I could see it in the way his shoulders sloped downward and his brow furrowed. We sat on the couch together and I waited for the thoughts hidden behind contemplative eyes to make their way past his lips. When he spoke, he held both of my hands in his and kept his gaze down.

He began his sentence the way he did every time something was burdening him, "Listen. I think we should get married." I stared at him dubiously, but I knew he had more to say, so I waited for him to continue.

"We've been dating for some time and I'm ready to settle down. I'm twenty-seven and I'm not interested in being with someone if there isn't a point. I deleted Tinder after our first date, and I think, if we wait until after the election, that we might lose our chance." I shifted uncomfortably and squeezed his hands with mine. I had always told myself that I wouldn't marry anyone unless we had dated for a minimum of five years because I thought that's how long it took to really know someone... right? Although, even five years of dating didn't guarantee that your partner wouldn't cheat on you or that your marriage would last. Furthermore, foreign and immigration policies had changed so rapidly and without notice in the last four years under the Trump Administration and had only escalated significantly since the start of the pandemic that his fear for the "after"—because there would most certainly be a "before" and an "after" once the elections were over, had merit.

If we waited to marry, we ran the very real threat of finding our path to marriage and his ability to remain in the U.S. closed before our eyes. I felt the burden of his suggestion land on my shoulders as I realized that where we went with our relationship now rested in my hands. It seemed, in some ways, a difficult choice to make. We had only been dating since February. We hadn't even lived together yet! I thought to myself, "how could we even imagine marrying so quickly?"

Yet, how could we not? I knew, deep down, that he was my person: only time stood in our way.

I sat there with his hands in mine, thinking to myself, "had we known one another longer, had he been here longer, had this happened, had that happened, wouldn't the decision be made so easy?" Realistically, is the decision to marry ever easy? I had to look at both worst case scenarios and decide whether I could imagine a life where we were stuck in relationship limbo, or one where we took a leap of faith.

We made our final decision in September.

We would get married.

ATROPOS - CUT FREE

"There is no real ending. It's just the place where you stop the story" – Frank Herbert

I WATCHED his face pinch in consternation as he focused intently on making sure the tree was fluffed to perfection. He took his task seriously as he helped decorate a Christmas tree with me for the first time, wanting to make sure that each fake branch splayed out just right to hide the gaps. I couldn't help but smile as his forehead furrowed in concentration. It didn't matter what he did, he always took time and care in every activity, a trait I appreciated and loved. I felt happiness settle into my chest while I watched him, finding it hard to believe that I was here in this moment. The holidays had never been a time of happiness for me because they acted as a reminder for the lack of family that I had always felt. My mother tried her best, but I wanted what I saw in other families. More family, more gifts, just... more. I had longed for years to have a family of my own—traditions of my own—so that maybe I wouldn't feel so lonely. Sitting on my living room floor and watching as my husband leaned back, satisfied with his handiwork, I finally felt: a sense of belonging.

"Done!" he exclaimed, looking to me with satisfaction on his face. "What's next?"

"Next, we can hang our lights and ornaments. It's probably easier to hang the lights first, that way we don't knock things down when trying to wrap them," I explained. He nodded, already reaching past me to grab the white lights.

"I'll do it. I know you get frustrated with this type of thing" he stated, already beginning to wrap the bottom of the tree. He was right; I got frustrated with simple tasks like wrapping Christmas lights on a tree because they never aligned themselves the way I wanted. I appreciated that he noticed those kinds of quirks and took the initiative to be helpful and take over the tasks that I found tedious. He had always been great at noticing changes in my voice and what it meant, seeing the tasks that I struggled with, or the odd little habits I had. It might seem like something small, but it showed that he paid attention and that he cared. He often noticed things that I didn't even know about myself. Although he remained attentive and detail-oriented in all areas of his life, his attentiveness meant more when he focused it on me. Maybe that made me a narcissist. I didn't care.

I watched patiently as he finished wrapping the lights around the tree before grabbing his hand in mind and interlacing our fingers.

"I remember the first time I saw you, it was around Christmas time, and you were working at the Starbucks. I know you don't remember that moment, but I do—and I'm glad that I do. It feels like that moment was some kind of foreshadowing that I didn't realize until later," I admitted. His hand squeezed mine before he unlocked our fingers and used his arm to pull me against his side, his right hand coming up to gently cradle the side of my head and tilt it toward him so he could place a gentle kiss to the top of it.

"I wish I could remember that moment too, but I know I'll always remember this one," he stated, resting his cheek on the top of my head.

"Oh, look at you being cheesy,"I teased, leaning into him fully as my eyes looked over the ornaments sprawled out on the floor before us. I reached out to pick up one in particular: a tiny house shaped ornament with 'our first home' engraved on it. My mom had bought it for us, despite the fact that I had purchased the house three years ago and he had only lived with me since October. She explained "they didn't have any that said 'my first husband.'" I'm still not sure if she meant the comment tongue-in-cheek as a subtle jab at our fast union, or if she had simply phrased it poorly, but I appreciated the gift all the same.

"Let's hang this one first," I said, holding it up in my palm for him to see.

"Yeah, okay," he agreed, unwrapping his arm from around my shoulders and taking the ornament from my hand, so that he could place it delicately—front and center—on our tiny tree. He placed the first ornament and we quickly arranged the rest—most of them random baubles I had collected over the years, but some we had picked out together specifically to remind us of memories we shared. A Kansas City ornament represented our first trip out of town together, a pumpkin for our first pumpkin patch visit and Halloween, two cat ornaments symbolizing our "kids"—as he called them—Sugar and Jim. Each made me smile as we placed them on the tree, so that by the time we were finished decorating, it looked like a visual representation of the year we'd had and all the years we hoped to have going forward.

"You know," I began, placing my hands behind me and leaned back, "When we first started dating and you broached the tentative idea of marriage during the second month, I wondered if it was a red flag. I was like, 'is this guy just wanting a Green Card from me?'" He gave a flustered and indignant exclamation as I laughed. Before he could defend himself, I sat back up and wrapped my arms around his waist, leaning into him and picking up my sentence.

"But I also wondered if I was crazy because I seriously considered it! Growing up I had always told myself that I wouldn't marry anyone unless I had been with them for a minimum of five years first. I never understood the people that got married in such a short timeframe. How could they be so sure that this person was the right one? Then again, I guess we can never be sure, right? Even couples that are together for five or ten years before marriage sometimes get divorced." He nodded in agreement, a small frown tugging at the edges of his lips, as he wrapped his right arm around my shoulders and squeezed me close to him.

"I promise I did not marry you for a Green Card. I told you, right? Divorce is not an option in my mind. We can work through anything and someday we'll be *so* old together. We could have waited longer if you wanted...do you regret it?"

I looked up at him in surprise and unwrapped one of my arms from around his waist, reaching it up to cup his cheek. "I don't regret it. Somehow, we moved both fast and slow at the same time. It's all relative, yeah? Like your Einstein analogy?" I suggested as he laughed. "Life is unpredictable. We never know what's going to happen. Plenty of people wait longer and still end up divorced, but I choose to trust in us.

We've proven we can work through things together and love is about choice. We might not always like one another, but as long as we choose one another every day, we can do it. I chose you and I will continue to choose you every day."

Tharindu nestled his cheek into my hand and closed his eyes, soaking in the words before he looked at me.

"I choose you every day too. I promise to always choose you. I'm glad to spend this first Christmas with you—I don't need Santa because I have everything I could want." His cheesiness made me smile and I used my fingers to gently pinch his cheek that I was still holding.

"Ugh, okay, we're getting too cheesy, it's squirming me out," I said. We both laughed at our vulnerable sentimentality.

"Now that we've finished our tree, let's go have breakfast," I said, pulling away from him and standing up with a stretch.

"I can't wait until Christmas day, so you can see what I got you!"

THE LETTER

ALEXA ROSE

*M*aya poured herself a cabernet sauvignon, filling the glass halfway and wiping a garnet drip from the bottle's lip. She shooed Korra, the blue point Siamese mischief maker, from between her feet and rounded the island, lowering the living room's lighting as she went. White and pink holiday lights glowed along the wall, and the Christmas tree twinkled in the living room's far corner.

"Sure you don't want any?" Maya asked her wife.

"I'm good, hon," Haydee said, her eyes electric as she gripped her controller and glanced from the screen to flash an exaggerated smile.

Walking past the couch, her nails trailing along its back, Maya passed her wife and dragged her fingers through that tangle of black hair. Korra raced ahead, smoky gray tail raised, and looked over her back when she reached the sliding door.

"I'm coming, Miss Korra," Maya said. She sipped her wine and slid the door open. Korra darted onto the balcony and began to purr in the cold December air.

"Close the door," Haydee called. "It's freezing out there!"

Maya slid the glass closed and bent to pick up Korra. The year-old Siamese purred and nuzzled her chin. Holding Korra close to her chest, Maya took in the night. She could see all the way onto the Nellis Air Force Base's runway where red and blue lights flashed in the night. A jet moved across the runways and turned, facing in her direction.

Tapping the sliding door with her wine-held hand, Maya waited for Haydee to look, then made their sign for takeoff. Her wife gave a thumbs up and kept playing. On the runway, the jet started to move forward. A second later, the incredible thunder of its engine grew closer and closer. Korra's claws came out and dug into Maya's skin, but she ignored the pain and stared, transfixed by the approaching rumble and roar.

The single light on the jet's front landing gear tilted upward, and a cone of flame chased it. Maya recognized the single cone as an F-16 Fighting Falcon. Of all the jets that took off and landed at the base, she most liked the Falcon. B-52 Stratofortresses and B-1B Lancers shook the condo too much, and Raptors disappeared too fast.

The condo rumbled as the fighter jet passed overhead. Maya watched it as long as she could, then she sipped her drink and opened the door. Heat washed over her, and Korra leapt to the hardwood floor and zoomed toward the master bedroom, no doubt going in search of whichever warm spot her sister, Buffy, had found.

Haydee's phone dinged on the coffee table beside paper containers of Chinese food and a styrofoam cup dripping with condensation. Grabbing the iPhone, Haydee held it up, let the screen unlock, and tapped her text. A second later, she pressed the power button and dropped the phone into her lap. Maya said nothing as she dropped onto the couch and pulled her legs beneath her. She leaned against the armrest, wine glass raised as Overwatch characters leapt and ran across the screen, and thought of Christmas dinner and when she would start cooking. She went as far as the kale bruschetta when the Play of the Game erupted onto the screen.

Maya set her glass down and turned to Haydee.

"Was that your friend?"

Haydee tossed her controller onto the cushion between them and stood up, taking her phone as she headed into the kitchen.

"Yes," she said. "Becca wanted to play a match. She texted me when I missed a super."

"She's still awake?"

Ice cubes clattered into a glass. Soda fizzed. Something extra splashed in. A moment later, Haydee returned, drink in hand, and resumed her seat.

"She is. And we are not going to discuss this."

Maya sipped her wine and focused on the pink lights.

"They are boarding a plane in-." Raising her wrist until her watch face lit, she continued, "five hours. That means she won't get any sleep. The flight from Madison to here is like two hours or something, which means she and her fiance are going to get here and be tired. And then what? I'm feeding two sleepy people?"

Haydee tipped her glass and drank a third of it.

"We're eating Christmas Day. It's a new plan."

Staring at her wife, her pulse loud in her ears and her fingers tight on the glass's stem, Maya asked, "When were you gonna tell me?"

"Oh, calm down, Maya," Haydee said. "You're as excited for them to visit as I am."

"Am I? I've never talked with either of them," Maya said. "I don't know anything about them. Do they know anything about me?"

Haydee drank another third, took a deep breath, and

drained her glass. She set her glass aside and slid across the cushions to wrap her arms around Maya and set a brief kiss against Maya's cheek.

"They are my friends, and they'll love you."

"Are they staying here?"

Haydee squeezed Maya's shoulders and said, "Stop it. They're lovely women."

"If you say so."

"Give them a chance, babe. That's all I'm asking."

Maya sipped her wine and set the glass on the floor. She lifted Haydee's arm from around her, and she clasped her wife's hand in hers. Looking into Haydee's bottle-green eyes, she smiled and said, "I trust you. And I will give your friends a chance. But you have to promise me they won't be transphobic."

Haydee leaned in with another kiss and said, "I promise. They are wonderful, and they would never even think such a thing."

"Okay," Maya said. She stood and pulled Haydee after her. "It's getting late, and we have to be up early. Are you coming to bed, or do you want to game some more?"

Haydee laughed and turned off the Xbox.

"As if any game could compare."

Laughing, Maya set her wine glass on the mantle and led the way to their bedroom where Korra and Buffy had curled near the pillows.

Feigning resignation, Maya said, "Looks like we'll just have to cuddle between them."

Haydee turned out the light and said, "I think we can make do."

Twin purrs rumbled across the bed, competing with the rustle of clothes and the distant jet's roar.

※

MAYA WOKE to a cat kneading her belly and the rattle of the day's first jet. Her watch showed 6:03, and the gray of pre-dawn pressed against the window. A small part of her hummed with giddiness. Christmas Eve had always been special in her family. Maya slid out of bed, upsetting the cat, and padded into the living room.

Flipping the lights on, she ignited the fireplace and opened the blinds. The holiday lights came next, glittering diamond and rose along the walls. Korra and Buffy came as twin shadows from the bedroom, tails up as they raced one another to their dishes. Seeing them, Maya filled each dish and set down fresh water.

Through the sliding door, the city and air base stood in muted colors. *The sun will come soon, and color will come with it.* Smiling at the thought of an artistic sun, Maya popped in a k-cup and set her favorite mug in the machine. She turned the mug so the stack of five kittens in the colors of the trans flag faced her.

The bathroom came next. On her way through the bedroom, she leaned over the bed and kissed Haydee's forehead, earning a smile and a sleep-mumbled "Hi" as her reward. She pulled the sheets around Haydee's shoulders and brushed strands of dark hair from her wife's face. Temptation almost slid her under the covers to cuddle and coil around Haydee's warmth, but she pushed off the bed and returned to the morning ritual.

Gathering her clothes, Maya closed the door and started the shower. Setting her clothes on the counter, she arranged them in the order they would go on, jeans on the bottom, undergarments on top, socks in the middle with her top laid out so it wouldn't wrinkle. She set out the makeup brushes and tubes she'd need. A quick brushing of her teeth, a flurry of pajamas scattering across the warm tiles, and she stepped into the spray of hot water. Her shower started and ended in just moments, and she dressed and applied her makeup to the whisper of the bathroom's fan and the low-volume rhythm of AJR's 'Bang!' coming from a silver radio tuned to Mix 94.1. She finished with a spritz of Bombshell, a touchup of her wings with a Revlon eyeliner pencil, and a misting of Rimmel setting spray. Turning out the lights, Maya passed the empty bed as she returned to the kitchen dressed in blue jeans and pink socks, a lavender long-sleeve top and a hair clip holding her unwashed, blonde hair out of the way as the setting spray dried.

Haydee huddled on the couch beneath a blanket with both cats clamoring for her attention. The TV lit with the main screen of Halo: Reach. Seeing the stack of blue, pink, and white kittens in her wife's hand, Maya harrumphed and didn't say a word as she stomped through to the kitchen and glowered at Haydee.

"Morning, babes," Haydee said, her voice small.

Maya almost said something, but she refused to begin Christmas Eve with a fight. So, she took her second favorite mug off the mug tree and set it in the machine. Another k-cup. More waiting. The faerie dragon painted in splashes of blue and pink against the mug's white background froze in mid-flight. Staring at that image, Maya let go of her frustration.

"Good morning."

"I thought it was for me. I'm sorry."

"No, it's okay. You'll need it. We're leaving in like 20 minutes to get your friends, right?"

"What? No. I texted them. Their flight got in like an hour

ago, and they're having breakfast at McCarran. So there's no rush. I told them we'd be there by like 8."

Taking her dragon cup, Maya went to the couch and sat on her side, legs curled under her. She sipped her hot chocolate and peered at Haydee from over the rim.

"You're going to leave them at the airport for three hours?"

Shrugging, Haydee said, "They brought Switches, and there's a ton to do there. Plus, come on. It's Christmas Eve. Traffic is going to be stupid. If we leave at 7, we might get there on time."

"I just think it'd be better if we left now. No one wants to sit in an airport."

Haydee rolled her eyes and sipped from the stolen mug.

"But Becca said she was cool with it."

Her mind made up, Maya stood and plucked the mug from Haydee's hands. She pointed toward their bedroom. "Shower. Now. Because I'm not cool with it. And don't dawdle. I'm not giving your friends a bad first impression of our hospitality."

"Fine," Haydee pouted, standing and letting her blanket fall. "But you're driving."

"Deal. Just hurry, okay? I'll put together a breakfast for you to eat on the way."

The pout flipped into a smile, and Haydee came close to kiss Maya's lips.

"Okies. Imma go be nakey."

Maya laughed, her hot chocolate nearly spilling. If she ever started to wonder why she married Haydee, she only needed to hear her wife's playful side. She went to the kitchen and set the mugs aside, laughter still bubbling from deep within.

Using her mom's hand-me-down cherry wood cutting block, Maya prepared a bowl of kiwi, mango, papaya, and grapefruit wedges. She added a splash of lemon juice, a torn-apart mint leaf, and a dusting of lime rind. Popping on the Tupperware bowl's lid, she set out a fork, washed up, and went in search of her wife.

She found Haydee leaning over the bathroom sink in matching magenta undergarments, tweezers plucking her brows at lightning speed.

"Are we stopping anywhere else?" Haydee asked.

Maya stepped behind her wife and wrapped her arms around that full waist. She set her chin against Haydee's shoulder and said, "Only if you want to, babe."

"Then I'm just wearing leggings and a big sweater."

Looking around, Maya didn't see leggings or an oversized sweater. She did see loose caps and tipped bottles, puddled water and toothpaste in the sink.

"You're so messy," she said. "Good thing you married me."

Haydee smiled and asked, "Could you get my beige sweater and black leggings? They should be on top of the basket."

Maya parted with a squeeze and a kiss. The cats had resumed their places on the queen-sized bed, and she patted each as she crossed to Haydee's side and rummaged through two baskets of washed clothes. Once upon a time, she would have folded these clothes and put them away. Now, she kept her opinion to herself, fought her urge to organize, and pulled out the black leggings. To her surprise, the beige sweater hung on a hanger, which Maya snatched off the dresser and carried into the bathroom.

"Hey, as a thing, did you take the car in for servicing?" Haydee asked as she rubbed blush into her cheeks.

"I did last week," Maya said, setting the clothes down and

tidying the countertop. "We just hit three thousand miles, too. Only took a year."

"I keep saying we should go for a ride to, like, San Diego or take a week and go up to Seattle."

Wiping up the puddles with a hand towel, Maya said, "I like it here. And what about Korra and Buffy? They don't travel well, and I'm not gonna crate them."

"Right, but Lara said she'd stop by to check on them."

"And what? Pour food in their dishes? Set out water? They need love."

"So we're never going to travel because of the cats?"

"Don't be mean, Haydee. We will travel once we know they'll be okay."

Haydee finished her routine with a daub of cherry lip paint. Setting the NYX tube aside, she turned and pulled Maya into a hug.

"I don't want to fight. I love Korra and Buffy just as much as you do."

Maya returned the squeeze and handed Haydee the leggings. She helped her wife into the sweater, pulled it to one shoulder so a bra strap showed, and kissed where her neck and shoulder met.

"If you're ready, I'll grab my coat and breakfast," Maya said.

"I'm ready," Haydee said, reaching around to give Maya a light pinch on her bottom. "See you at the car!"

Giggling at the moment, Maya grabbed her charcoal peacoat. She took two bottles of sparkling water from the fridge and slung her purse over her shoulder. Sliding the fork into a pocket, she carried the container of fruit into the garage.

"Goodbye, kitties," she called from the doorway. "Mom and momma will be home in a while. Be good."

The garage door opened, and the heather-gray Aston Martin Vantage growled to life. Haydee opened the car door from inside, and Maya passed along the food and water. She set her purse behind her seat and tossed her peacoat onto the back seat. Dua Lipa sang from the speakers. Haydee already had her Switch out, and Maya saw the signal bar for the car's 5G hotspot.

She settled into the driver's seat and closed the door with a whispered *thwump*. Fastening her seatbelt, Maya adjusted the mirrors and tapped the touchscreen until the radio menu appeared.

"Playing with Becca?"

"Yep. They're having cinnamon rolls, and I guess Fiona's bored, so it's good we're going now."

"What're you playing?" Maya asked, waiting for the car's temperature gauge to move just a little.

"Smash Bros. It's something we can all play, but Fiona's being a punk and spamming Pikachu."

"Be nice to her. If she's bored, help her smile. And who cares if she's spamming. Not everything is about winning."

Haydee set her Switch down and picked up her iPhone. Her thumbs danced across the screen, and she closed the game. A moment later, Animal Crossing's logo appeared.

"Fiona's been trying to organize her island, so we'll help her with that."

Beaming, Maya let out the emergency brake, shifted the car into first, and pulled out of the garage. A tap of a button, and the garage door came down. A tap on the inset display screen, and the volume rose as their driving playlist started. Maya turned onto the street just as Britney Spears's "Toxic" came on.

Haydee's prediction for traffic proved wrong. No one else shared Lake Mead Boulevard with them. Maya accelerated toward I-15 while her wife dug up trees and laughed in her bucket seat.

Feeling overcome with joy, Maya stopped the playlist. She put on Christmas music and sang along.

THE RIDE DOWNTOWN went faster than expected. Maya had planned to arrive at the airport by 7:15, but she pulled off the interstate at 7:04 and followed the signs to Arrivals.

"You're going to the curb?" Haydee asked, setting down her Switch and picking up her phone. The fork rattled in the empty fruit bowl between Haydee's feet.

"Yeah. I don't want to park and go in search of them. And I'm sure they're ready to be out of there."

Haydee tapped her screen, laughed at a response, and said, "They'll meet us. Becca's been here before. She said she forgot what it's like to see people bundled up when it's sixty degrees."

Maya rolled her eyes and said, "She's one of them? Like, this *is* cold for us. That'd be like us going to Madison in the summer and being like, what, it's 90 degrees? Come talk to me when it's actually hot."

"Calm down, hon. She's just joking. I told her to take it easy with jokes around you."

"You what!? Why? She's going to think I don't know how to laugh."

Haydee pointed up and down from Maya's head to her hips and said, "Right now, all this is anxiety talking. Stop being so anxious. They're really nice. Fiona is a lot like you. I bet you'll even like her if you give her a chance."

"Is Becca like you?"

Haydee laughed and nodded.

"Yeah, kinda like a long-lost sister. But she's really nice."

Maya wanted to ask why Haydee kept calling her friends nice, but the airport loomed. Traffic had piled up at Arrivals and Departures. She saw an opening at the curb and nosed in, leaving the car's rear in the road. Shifting into neutral and setting the brake, she asked, "Do they know where w-"

Her words died on her tongue as two early-20s women in matching pride-flag masks came running to the car. They looked tall in the crowd, and the blonde arrived first, leaving the brunette to slow to a walk and come the rest of the way out of breath.

Haydee stepped out of the car and folded her seat down. The blonde stepped in and held up Maya's peacoat.

"Want this anywhere?" she asked in a thick midwest accent. She pulled down her mask and took a deep breath.

"Haydee can put it in the trunk," Maya said. She turned as far as she could to see the woman behind her. "Hi. I'm Maya."

The woman waved and said, "Hi! I'm Becca."

Fiona moved to step into the back seat, but Haydee stepped in first, sitting beside Becca and pulling the seat upright. She set Maya's peacoat on her lap.

"Front seat is all yours," Haydee said. "Just buckle up because this one takes corners pretty fast."

A murmur of an "Okay" came from the brunette as she sat down. As soon as her door closed and she buckled in, she pulled down her mask, folded her arms around the backpack in her lap, and glanced at Maya.

"Hi," Fiona said.

"Hi," Maya said. "Don't mind Haydee. Words just fall out of her big mouth."

Becca laughed and elbowed Haydee, saying, "You married a real firebrand, girl."

Maya's knuckles turned white on the steering wheel.

"Everyone set?"

The car moved before anyone responded. Maya backed into the road, drawing angry horns. She shifted into first, eased off the clutch, and tapped the accelerator, throwing everyone backward.

"Sorry," she said, her voice slipping into a flippant Valley-girl tone. "I totally forget what I'm driving sometimes."

Haydee glared at her. Becca looked angry. Fiona smiled and leaned over the console.

"This is a really nice car."

"Thanks, hon," Maya said. "Do you want to see the Strip, or do you want to go back to our place?"

"I've never seen it."

"We're going the long way home," Maya said loud enough for the backseat, but Haydee and Becca had fallen into a deep conversation about League of Legends.

Following Maya's gaze in the rearview, Fiona looked over her shoulder and relaxed. She slid her backpack to the footwell, kicked off her boots, and curled her feet under her.

"Do you play any games?" the brunette asked in a less nasal midwest accent.

Following the signs to Las Vegas Boulevard, Maya said, "I do. MMOs, mostly. I played Warcraft and Star Wars back in the day. Now, it's mostly Final Fantasy."

"That's cool," Fiona said. "I don't play much. Really not at all. I watch Becca play, and I write and work on my podcast."

"You have a podcast? That's so cool!"

Fiona turned toward Maya, and her voice rose as she said, "Yeah. It's a lifestyle podcast about eating right and exercise and being really gay."

"Sounds great."

From the back seat came, "Oh, it is. She's so good on air."

Fiona blushed and faced forward.

Maya guided the Vantage through intersections and onto the south end of the Strip. As soon as she saw the press of traffic, she moved into the left lane.

"We'll kinda cruise through to Tropicana so you can see most of the Strip. There isn't much to see during the day anyway. I'll bring us down here tonight to see the lights."

"Okay," Fiona said. She took out her phone and started typing in Notes. Without looking up, she asked, "What's your favorite hotel here?"

"Mine? I don't know. I never stayed at any of them." Glancing over her shoulder, she asked, "Hey, babe, which casino do you like to stay at?"

Both her and Becca responded with "Bellagio."

"Have you gambled here?" Fiona asked.

Maya shook her head and said, "Nope. It's a waste of money." She peered at Fiona's screen and asked, "Is this for your podcast?"

"Yeah. Can I put the window down and take photos?"

"Sure, just don't leave it down. It's cold outside."

As Maya said that, she looked in the rearview and watched Becca's face. The blonde hadn't heard her. Instead, she and Haydee stared at an iPad.

The window went down, and Fiona's phone clicked dozens of times in all directions. She swiped it into video and panned it around until Maya slowed at Tropicana and waited for the green arrow to turn.

"There's so much to do here," Fiona said, rolling up her window.

"It's fun to come down here every once in a while. Get

dressed up and go out for drinks. But it's expensive, and there are always so many people. Now, with the pandemic, it's better to stay home."

"But we're coming back tonight, right?"

Maya nodded.

"We will. The city is really pretty at night, and there will be Christmas lights and stuff. Did you bring anything nice?"

Fiona opened her photos and scrolled to a white-and-lavender strapless cocktail dress that looked fittingly scandalous for this ritzy city.

"That's the one you brought?"

"Yep. Becs and I bought new dresses before flying out."

The arrow turned green, and Maya pulled through the intersection. She swept into the right lane, sped to third gear, and guided the beast of a car onto the on-ramp. As soon as she merged onto I-15, she said, "Hang on."

Pressing the accelerator all the way down, she skipped a gear and tapped the gear shift into fifth, backing off when the car hit 70. Grinning, she studied the rearview where all attention remained on the iPad while lanes and jungles remained the topic of the hour.

"Will we get pulled over if we go faster?" Fiona asked.

Maya laughed and said, "Doubt it. But we'll see."

She stomped on the gas, shifted into sixth, and sped back to North Las Vegas.

MAYA HELD the door for everyone to come inside the condo. Haydee and Becca passed in conversation, and Fiona came last, backpack in her hands and sleep heavy on her shoulders.

"Once we're upstairs, I'll set up my office so you can lay down if you want a nap."

"No, I'm okay," Fiona said. "It's just been a long morning. A little coffee will wake me up."

Maya followed Fiona up the tiled stairs and said, "I can run for coffee, but we don't keep any in the house. Just hot chocolate. Or tea."

"Can we run for a coffee? I'll need it."

"Sure."

Upstairs, Maya set her stuff down. Becca followed Haydee into the guest room, and Maya pointed for Fiona to follow.

"You'll be staying in there, so get set up and stuff, then we'll go for coffee."

Leaving the other three to unpack and talk, Maya checked the cupboards and fridge, making sure she had everything for tonight's meal. Christmas Eve dinner should stand out, and she hoped it stood out for its flavors rather than it being entirely vegan. Maya took out the dry, room-temperature ingredients one-by-one and arranged them on the counter. She set the pots on the stove, put the pans in the oven, and laid out all the utensils she would need. Measuring cups went by the sink, empty bowls went on the island.

Maya set out and lit Christmas candles, filling the condo with pine and cranberry. She passed the guest room where all three chatted away, and she eased into the master bedroom where both cats sat on the edge of the mattress and stared at the hallway.

"They're friends," Maya said. "So be nice."

Korra licked her paw. Buffy licked Korra's ear. Neither cat cared about Maya's opinion.

Maya retrieved a large cardboard box from the closet and dragged it into the living room. Only Haydee saw her, and she flashed her with a grin. Pushing the box beside the Christmas tree, Maya opened its top flaps and set out the dozen gifts contained within. Some shapes gave away the gift, like the twin Xbox Series X consoles labeled for Becs and Fi. Others remained mysteries behind pink paper with yellow bows and metallic-silver paper with sky-blue ribbons. She artfully arranged each gift beneath the tree, turning the Pride-scarf-wearing snowman tags outward so recipients could see her neat handwriting.

Returning the box to her closet, Maya came back to the living room with one cat in her arms and the other following, smokey ears pert as laughter spilled from the guest room.

Becca saw Korra in Maya's arms and melted into a loud "Awwwwww!" Everyone came into the living room to pet the cats, and to Maya's relief, both cats purred and soaked up the attention. Siamese cats displayed possessiveness, so she hoped they wouldn't turn mean later.

Patting Korra's side, Maya said, "This one is named Korra, and the prissy one is Buffy. And they're being really nice right now."

Haydee added, "Yeah, they usually bite by now, so get your pets in before they get bitey."

Fiona carefully ran her hand down Korra's back and made happy faces where the cat could see. Becca dropped to all fours and scratched beneath Buffy's chin, calling the cat beautiful and pretty.

Looking at Fiona, Maya asked, "Ready for that coffee?"

Fiona nodded and pulled on a pink hoodie that read *cutie*. Becca stood and brushed cat hair off her black yoga pants.

"Coffee? Can you get me one, Fi?"

"Yeah. Black or something else?"

"Something tasty, like a holiday flavor."

Fiona kissed her fiancée's cheek and slid her clutch into the hoodie's large pocket.

Calling across the living room, Maya asked, "Want anything, hon?"

"Nope," Haydee said. "We're going to play some games and stuff. Need help starting the meal?"

Maya shook her head as she put on her peacoat and knit hat.

"Nope. I'll start it when we get back. Won't take long."

"Stay warm."

"Yep. Ready, Fiona?"

Fiona yawned and nodded, covering her mouth with a sleeve.

"Sure you want to go? We're walking."

"Can we drive? I'm too tired to walk."

Pausing for a moment, Fiona dropped her coat onto the couch and said, "Yeah. We'll drive. There's a nice coffee place on Craig."

"If you're going that far, can you grab donuts? A half dozen of whatever," Haydee called out. On the screen, Becca flipped through PUBG's menus.

Maya hoped her wife would do more than play games with two friends who flew across the country, but she didn't say anything. However, if she came home to League of Legends being played, she knew she'd lose her cool. *Haydee knows the rule*, Maya thought. *No tournament stuff in the house.* She thought of how that game had nearly cost their marriage two years ago. It remained Haydee's main source of income, and though she had incredible skill, Maya did not want to hear all the shouting and rage because some kid didn't stick to their lane or an enemy ganked a beast.

Grabbing her purse, Maya led Fiona to the stair, into the garage, and around the car. She held open the passenger door, closed it when the sleepy woman had all her limbs inside, and thumped her chunky heels around the front bumper to drop into the driver's seat.

"Sometimes, I just can't," Maya breathed.

"I know," Fiona said.

Without another word, Maya pulled out of the garage.

KEEPING the car to a sedate speed near the military base, Maya turned onto Craig and followed the anemic morning traffic. She saw the sign for the mom-and-pop bakery, but slowing down did not appeal to her just then. Speeding up, she changed lanes, flung the Vantage around a cluster of three cars, and slowed down to the speed limit.

"We're getting Krispy Kreme," Maya said.

"I haven't had those in a long time," Fiona said. She had leaned against the door, her eyes mostly closed, as she twisted her engagement ring around her finger.

"I don't like their filled donuts, but I just want to drive. So, a little farther sounds better."

Fiona nodded, her attention focused on the passing storefronts.

"Farther sounds good to me," she said. "I don't want to watch Becca play more games. I just want to visit and talk."

Maya knew what Fiona meant. She dreaded going home to twelve hours of video games and video game talk. With two gamers, the topic would never change. She raised her watch and said, "Hey Siri, give me directions to Krispy Kreme on Spring Mountain Road."

The city map popped up on the car's display. Turn-by-turn instructions had been off since she'd first driven with Siri, so she saw the turn onto I-15 and moved into the right lane.

"This will be a longer drive," Maya said. She turned the radio volume down to a whisper, kept the car in third gear for the on-ramp. "You can put your seat back and have a nap, or we can chat or just listen to music."

Fiona moved her seat back and reclined a little. She turned sideways as much as she could and slid a hand between her head and the cushion, but she kept her eyes open.

Maya merged onto the interstate and headed southward, shifting to sixth and riding the engine at a low growl near 75 mph.

"Can I ask you a question?" Fiona asked.

Maya put both hands on the wheel, kept her eyes on the busy highway, and swallowed. Her stomach fluttered. Her voice guarded, she said, "Yeah, sure."

As silence filled the seconds, Maya glanced at her passenger. She saw Fiona's fingers pulling at her sleeves. Saying nothing, she returned her attention to the road.

Then, a whisper.

"When you married Haydee, was your mom upset that you chose a girl?"

Maya looked across the console to that half-awake face and its resignation. She saw fear.

Memories of her mom came to mind. She remembered transitioning in middle school and her mom defending her choice to be given puberty blockers. She remembered her parents taking her out of school when the bullying started. She saw her tutor sitting across from her and her mom when she started homeschooling. She heard her mom's calm voice describe how puberty would turn her into a woman when she stopped taking puberty blockers at age 16. She felt her mom's hand squeezing her fingers as nurses rolled her toward the operating room on her 18th birthday.

"Not at all," Maya said. "She had told me she loved me and was happy I'd found someone special."

"Oh." Fiona paused, then asked, "What did Haydee's mom say?"

"She didn't say much. As I recall, she took the news of our engagement like she'd taken everything else in life: laying down with a drink in hand." When Fiona didn't laugh, Maya asked, "Is everything okay?"

"I guess," Fiona said. "I mean, yeah, it's really good. Becca is amazing."

"But your mom won't go to your wedding?"

"She said she will, but I don't want her to. She'll make a scene. I know she will."

Maya focused on the road, steering around cars as she waited for Fiona to continue.

"Did anyone make a scene at your wedding?"

"No. We were married at the courthouse, and we invited friends and a few close family members for a huge party afterward."

"Did that work?"

Maya kept to the far-left lane and said, "Yeah. But we had to be so careful because some people on both sides really didn't want us to marry."

Fiona's eyes opened all the way as she asked, "Why's that?"

Glancing at the wide-eyed brunette, Maya said, "Did Becca say anything about me to you?"

"No?"

Maya had been beside Haydee when Becca found out over chat. *If Becca didn't trust Fiona with that information . . .* Maya let the thought fade, deciding she wouldn't out herself. She smiled and said, "There are bigots on both sides of our families, so we thought it'd be easier to plan and host it ourselves."

"Oh. Does it have to do with you having money?"

Maya laughed before covering her mouth and waving away Fiona's stare.

"No, it doesn't."

"I'm really prying, and I'm sorry," Fiona said. She leaned back in her chair and nestled her cheek against her hand. "We don't meet many married women, so I just wanted to know."

"No, it's okay," Maya said. "It's kinda odd your fiancée didn't say anything, though. This money isn't given to us. Haydee gets hers through tournaments and stuff, and I'm an artist. I create for Wizards of the Coast and freelance for indie games. I've shown at a few galleries in town and at Comic-Con. My Patreon does well, too."

Maya's watch vibrated against her wrist. She changed lanes to the far right, slowed to 70, and watched for her exit.

"I want to marry Becca in January," Fiona said. "In a snowy park. But then my family will show up, and they'll ruin everything."

Without thinking, Maya said, "Marriage is tough."

Fiona blinked. She opened her mouth. Hesitated. Closed it.

"You and Haydee seem happy."

"We are. And I'm not saying don't do it. Just, marriage is tough."

"How so?"

Maya put on her blinker and pulled off the interstate, following Siri's directions into the tangle of surface streets. Traffic had picked up. Jingle Bells came on the radio and played in the background against the car's throaty growl.

"Haydee and I met at 17," Maya said, her attention fixed on her mirrors and the road ahead. "We were friends right away. She came with me to the hospital where I had my surgeries. As soon as I could stand, I proposed. We married at 18. Her parents bought us the condo and helped us pay bills and stuff. We went to UNLV, studied hard, got our degrees, and when we had no milestones left, we started to argue about what came next.

"She wanted to travel. I wanted to settle down and draw, start my career. When we chose to stay, she focused on gaming, which meant we saw each other less. I traveled often for jobs, conventions, and galleries. We almost divorced two years out of college, so we each sacrificed something. She gave up games during the night, and I stopped traveling so much. I worked with local galleries, and I renegotiated my contract with Wizards to only work from home."

They rode in silence for several blocks. When Maya pulled up to the Krispy Kreme, Fiona didn't move. Rather, she stared straight ahead. Maya turned off the engine and set her purse in her lap. She checked her lipstick in the mirror, smiled to make sure none had transferred, and brushed her hair back with her fingers.

"Want to come in?" Maya asked.

Fiona nodded and followed. She stayed silent the whole time.

Coffee and donuts in hand, Maya returned to the car as Fiona hurried to hold the door, then dropped into the passenger seat. Handing everything over, Maya settled behind the wheel. She'd barely closed the door and started the car when Fiona spoke.

"Do you think everything will work between Becca and me?"

Maya thumbed the ignition. She met Fiona's gaze as she shifted into reverse and aimed the Vantage toward the tangle.

"Yeah," she said, shifting into first and checking for traffic. Seeing her opportunity, she sped onto the street, skipped to third gear, and settled the car for its return trip. "It'll work out. Just don't keep things bottled up. If you're afraid to tell Becca something, make a point of saying it. That's my advice."

Fiona took out her phone. Maya recognized the Medium app's layout. Fingernails tapped against the screen as a torrent of words spilled from those delicate hands.

Raising her watch, Maya said, "Siri, take me home."

COMING THROUGH THE DOOR, Maya held it for Fiona and their breakfast. The sounds of electronic battle echoed down the stairs, and twin shouts of faux anger chased the battle. Hearing the clamor set Maya on edge, but she kept her smile in place as her passenger and guest shuffled her feet through the garage.

Fiona passed with donuts and coffee and stumbled to a stop, ponytail bouncing, as the wall of sound buffeted her.

"I'll take those," Maya said, lifting the Krispy Kreme from Fiona's hands. She led the way upstairs and set everything on the kitchen island. Thumping her purse against the counter, she rummaged in the cupboards for paper plates, letting each door thud shut.

On the third door, Haydee stood, controller in hand, and raised her shoulders into a shrug.

"What are you looking for?"

Maya held up a stack of paper plates and said, "We're home with breakfast."

Haydee cocked her head. Her shoulders settled. Setting her controller aside, she tapped Becca's shoulder and came into the kitchen.

Maya handed Becca a plate and said, "Take whatever you want." Turning to Haydee, she added, "Can we talk for a sec?"

Haydee nodded as she plucked a blueberry cake donut from the box and followed Maya, who stepped around her wife and led the way into the bedroom. She let Haydee pass and closed the door with a last peek down the hall where Fiona and Becca embraced and sought a stolen kiss.

"What's going on, Maya?" Haydee asked. She sat on the corner of the bed and patted the plush comforter at her side. "Did something happen?"

Maya sat and leaned her head against Haydee's shoulder.

"That girl needs something good in her life," Maya said.

"Which girl?"

"Fiona. She's lonely. Becca came out here to see you, and I think Fiona followed because Becca is her whole world. Did you know her family doesn't accept her?"

Haydee leaned away, taking Maya's face in her warm hands.

"What are you proposing, Maya?"

"Fiona wants to marry Becca, but she doesn't want her mom to ruin the wedding," Maya said. She met her wife's patient gaze and set her hand against Haydee's cheek, running her fingers from apple to jaw, over the ear, and into that thick, black hair. "I want to pay for them to be married someplace snowy and perfect. Like Aspen. Lake Tahoe. The Swiss Alps. Someplace Fiona's mom won't ruin their memory."

Haydee leaned close and pressed her lips against Maya's. They lingered for a moment, all warmth and softness and happiness, until Haydee withdrew. She beamed and set a kiss on Maya's nose.

"I think that's a wonderful idea," Haydee said.

"Yeah? Should we wait to offer to pay?"

"No, babe. Absolutely not. It's Christmas Eve. Write something in your calligraphy, and leave the letter in here. I'll come get it when we open gifts tonight."

"Okay, babe. Maybe you should go visit with them. Tell them I'm changing, and that I'll start our meal as soon as I'm out there."

Haydee planted a parting kiss on Maya's cheek and departed.

Alone, Maya pulled a sheet of cream paper from her desk and twisted her fountain pen. Without searching for the best words, she wrote, *"The perfect wedding should never remain a dream. You choose the destination and the details, and we will see to the rest. Best wishes and all our love, Haydee and Maya."*

Setting the paper and pen aside, Maya stood, undressed, and slid into loose jeans, a flowing peach top, and black slip-on shoes she only wore around the apartment. The cats had curled inside the closet, and she left them to their slumber.

MAYA SET out the last of the appetizers, arranging the baked apple chips and the kale bruschetta beside the savory meatless meatballs in their cranberry glaze. She stirred the vegan pozole on the stove and opened the oven to peer at the main dish and the sides, which bubbled and steamed in their pans. Leaving the heavy dishes to finish, she wiped her hands on her apron and set out plates.

Beyond the kitchen, Becca leaned against Fiona on the couch's far end, and Haydee snuggled beneath a blanket on the near end. The L Word: Generation Q played in 4K, filling the living room with drama and lovely voices. Maya watched long enough to see Tess cross the screen, then she set forks and knives on each plate.

"Apps are ready," Maya said. "And the pozole will finish soon. Come get your plates."

Haydee paused the show and set aside her blanket, rising first and stretching her arms toward the ceiling. At the far end, Fiona slumbered beneath Becca, who took Haydee's blanket and drew it over her and her fiancée.

"Looks like we're eating alone," Haydee said as she came to the counter and transferred a stack of apple chips onto a plate.

"Don't be mean, hon," Maya said. She returned to the pozole, wooden spoon in hand. "Make a plate for them. Just a little of everything. I'll bring the soup and main course to the table."

Haydee set a small stack of apple chips, three bruschetta, and two meatballs on another plate. With a wink and a smile, she returned to the couch and set the plate within Becca's reach.

A hand came from beneath the blanket and found a bruschetta.

Fiona's tiny voice squeaked from beneath Becca.

"I want a bite."

The show started again to a chorus of crunching. Maya listened to the dialogue, but she kept her eyes on the soup and the baking pasta. The rolls had browned well, and she smelled the garlic radiating from them.

With everything needing another minute or two, Maya fetched her phone from her back pocket and searched for hotels in Lake Tahoe and Aspen. Having heard of the Grand Residences by Marriott, she clicked on it and put in dates for late January. The quoted penthouse rate of $285 landed well within her estimated budget. Hotel Aspen came back at $400 with less space and fewer amenities. Maya closed the Hotel Aspen tab, clicked off the screen, and slid her phone into her back pocket.

Oven mitts on, Maya opened the oven and removed the ratatouille baked penne and rosemary garlic biscuits. One by one, she carried the dishes and the pozole to the dining room table where clean, white plates with inlaid butterflies waited near each chair.

Maya removed her mitts and untied her apron. She set everything aside, took a pitcher of cranberry juice from the fridge, and brought it and a bottle of chilled moscato to the table. She popped the cork, poured cranberry juice for everyone, and took a deep breath. As the final detail, she lit four candles around the table and turned down the condo's lights.

"TV off, babe. Time to eat."

The screen went dark a moment later. Haydee stood, and Becca and Fiona followed. Everyone nibbled on something, and when Haydee walked by, Maya kissed her cheek and took an apple chip.

As everyone found their seat, Maya finished her chip and sat last.

"There's moscato here, if you want any. The ratatouille is hot, so careful with the pan. It's filling, so if you haven't had it, small servings are a great starting place." Maya paused for a moment, looking from face to face. "Does anyone want to say anything before we begin?"

Becca poured wine into her glass, filled Fiona's, and passed the bottle to Haydee. She sipped, set her glass down, and said, "I want to thank you both for inviting us out here. Haydee, seeing you has been a treat. Maya, your hospitality is amazing. Thank you for this meal."

Fiona met Maya's eye and smiled, but she said nothing.

Haydee filled her glass, splashed some wine into Maya's glass, and said, "You're so welcome, Becca."

Maya filled her plate first, and as everyone took their share, she ate in silence, enjoying the flickering candlelight and the sound of so many utensils poking and scraping along plate and bowl. It had been too long, she decided. And she meant to do this more often.

HAYDEE HELPED Maya clear the table as Becca and Fiona returned to the couch. Before they could settle in, Maya detoured from the dining room to turn on the lamp near the Christmas tree.

"We'll have the table cleared in a moment, and then we have gifts to share."

Becca spoke first.

"Gifts? You didn't have to."

Haydee spoke from the dining room.

"Of course we didn't *have* to, but we wanted to. So we did."

Fiona moved to the tree and stretched out like the teenager she had been a year or two earlier. Maya smiled as the woman sorted the gifts into piles and grew louder and louder as hers and Becca's piles became substantial.

Haydee gripped Maya's elbow and whispered, "Get the letter. I'll put the last glasses in the sink."

Maya padded into the bedroom and took the letter from atop her dresser. The cats woke and yawned near the pillows, watching her with judgmental blue eyes.

"You'll have your condo back in a few days," she said. Neither cat seemed impressed. Still, she filled their dishes and gave each a pat before returning to the living room.

The piles had grown, and Fiona grinned from behind hers. Both she and Becca had pulled the largest boxes onto their laps, and like excited children, they waited for Maya's approval to tear into the paper.

Settling onto the plush carpet, letter in hand, Maya said, "They're your gifts. Open as many as you'd like."

Haydee clapped, and both women tore at the wrapping paper. In a frenzy of ripping paper, each revealed an Xbox Series X, and each squealed with delight. Next came the custom-colored controllers; Fiona's with the lesbian flag and Becca's themed pink and blue after Jinx from League of Legends.

Games followed. Gift cards. Flannel bathrobes. Cute tops, flowy skirts, matching bracelets.

When they had nothing more to open, Maya slid the letter to Fiona and smiled.

"Our car ride gave me an idea," Maya said. Haydee reached out and took her hand.

Fiona unfolded the sheet of paper. Her eyes danced across the page as she gasped. Her hand covered her mouth. Tears followed.

Becca shot a curious look at Maya, glanced at Haydee, and took the letter from her fiancée's hand. She read it aloud.

"The perfect wedding should never remain a dream," she said, eyeing Maya over the letter. "You choose the destination and the details, and we will see to the rest." She looked up again, this time with tears in her eyes and her lower lip heavy with emotion. "Are you serious?" she asked.

"We are," Haydee said.

"We really are," Maya said. She took out her phone, unlocked the screen, and slid it to Becca. "That hotel is at Lake Tahoe, and it looks lovely. If you want to go elsewhere, just tell us."

Becca showed the hotel to Fiona, who nodded and said, "Yes! I want to get married there."

Haydee kissed Maya's cheek and stood. She helped Maya to her feet and said, "Now might be a good time to go for that ride. I think we could all use some quiet and a few sights."

Letter and phones in hand, their other gifts forgotten, the couple from Wisconsin got to their feet and followed Haydee and Maya to the car.

Only Maya brought shoes and a coat. Everyone else wore their lounging clothes and drifted as though in a dream. When everyone clambered inside the Vantage, Maya opened the garage door. Outside, fireworks echoed from far away, and the sounds of Christmas music drifted from open windows.

Maya smiled. Pulled her coat tight. Satisfied with the moment, she slid behind the wheel and patted Haydee's thigh.

"Ready, babe?"

Haydee smiled, her face lit by the instrument panel's blue glow. "With you? Always."

SHORTBREADS

L.T. WARD

*S*ugar and flour dust floated in the air of the Bakery, a filter of sweetness and promise throughout the kitchen. The seasonal shifts began with Winter sprinkling powdered sugar onto the world. They dipped their fingers through the sugar glass globe encasing the ball known as Earth, shaking the white flurries over the land, the people inside delighting with shouts of *Snow!*

The Bakery's aromas from Autumn's pumpkins and apples preferred recipes faded to Winter's molasses and ginger. Cinnamon, allspice, and clove lingered. Autumn stood at their long, wooden kitchen block, tucking the people cookie cutters and baking sheets onto the shelves below. Spring and Summer stood kitty-corner at their own workstations, the four seasons working tirelessly in their cycle around the sugar glass globe in the center. With a deadline of nine months to prepare their cookie people and no longer on vacation, Summer got back to work. They pulled out their ingredients—berries, citrus fruits, whipped creams—the lightest tastes and flavors belonging to the summer-born children.

Winter slaved over their workstation. Now was their

season and it was their responsibility to deliver the winter newborns. This year, Winter had adapted their usual recipes adding cayenne, cranberries, and coriander to some of the doughs.

Of course, the staples of flour, brown and white sugars, eggs, and yeast were in the starter. Winter whisked the starter from scratch as soon as Spring finished their turn at the sugar glass globe. For most of the year, Winter, like their seasonal siblings, prepped, rolled, and cut the dough, then decorated each cookie child to their individual perfection.

Most cookie children took nine months to develop, but some were a little more rushed. Those were the ones the Bakers always felt pangs of guilt over, but they were loved just as much as the others despite the urgency in their deliveries.

All cookie children were loved by their creator.

Autumn plucked a dish towel off their designated counter and began wiping down the walnut surface. "This is always such a hard time of the year. When I've released my children and have nothing to do. I never know what to do with myself."

Kneading a ball of whey colored dough, Spring said, "Relax, dearie."

"Baking is my relaxation and I can't begin new batches for three more months. I've tried reading and have consumed everything our little cookies have ever written. Beyond that, nothing feels right. I'm not one for lounging around. I'm not designed for unproductivity."

"Our little cookies never have that problem," said Summer. They lined up a silver cutter above terra-cotta shaded dough, then swept their arm like a calibrated piston across it. With one hundred human etchings created in a breath's time, they paused to admire their work, a proud smile on their lips.

"That's not true," argued Winter as they rushed towards the glass sugar globe. Carefully, with fingers coddling the delicate and detailed cookies in their hands, they rested the backs of their hands on the sugar glass. Dipping their hands slowly through and into the world, Winter spread their fingers wide. The cookie children disappeared from sight, destined to reappear in a few moments at their births to their human parents.

"Plenty of the little cookies get bored from time to time," they continued as they hurried back to their workstation to collect the next batch of tiny humans.

"Okay," conceded Summer. "They do, but then they concoct plans, projects, even events to fill their time. They give themselves a purpose. Don't you ever watch them? It's what I do when I'm on hiatus."

"I used to," said Autumn. "It has been a while."

"You know, Autumn, with your time off, you could go visit some of our little cookies," offered Spring. With circular movements of a pestle, they mashed raspberries in a stone bowl held in the crook of their arm.

"Ooh! Yes! You should do that!" cheered on Summer.

Autumn hitched one shoulder. "I guess."

"Don't you ever wonder what happens to our little cookies once they've finished baking?" asked Winter.

"I mean, it's been nearly a millennia since I last went through the sugar glass." They paused in their cleanup and glanced at Winter and the sugar glass globe. The world was beautiful. "Where would I go?"

"Oh, I know!" Winter dipped their hands again through the sugar glass, stretched their neck to peer down, ensuring their cookie babies were safe inside, then freed their hands from the globe. "In a little more than a week, two of my favorite cookies will be having birthdays. Same day actually. They were delivered three years apart. You could go check on them. Come back and tell me how they celebrated the anniversary of leaving the Bakery."

Autumn cocked their head. "That might be fun. Which ones?"

Winter sighed fondly as they piped last-minute details of eyebrow hair and dimples on the next batch of cookie children. "Eva and Hugh. They were each made from a curry ginger cookie recipe. Of all my sweet babies, curry ginger cookies tend to have a fiery kick with a bold sweetness. I really should whip up a few more of those batches this year."

"Go dearie," said Spring, dusting their countertop with sifted flour. "Do something nice for Winter. Take the vacation."

Autumn grinned a toothy smile. "This might be fun."

ONLY AN HOUR after Autumn's entry into the sugar glass globe, they already regretted their decision to take a vacation. Dressed in a flannel shirt, jeans, Timberland boots, and a wool-lined black denim jacket, Autumn shivered with Winter's latest snowfall blustering about. The sidewalk was shoveled clear, but every breeze sent a shockwave of sharp, frigid air along Autumn's spine.

"What are they thinking?" they mumbled, their hands cupped together as they huffed a heated breath to warm them. "Winter, this cold is overrated."

Cold is wonderful, Winter responded, their voice clear inside Autumn's head.

Pulling their jacket collar higher, Autumn trudged through

the Peoria city streets. As much as they wanted to get to the fun of the trip—finding Eva and Hugh—they felt cold in ways they never experienced in the Bakery. They needed to find a hotel.

After another twenty minutes of schlepping along the urban sidewalks, Autumn found one along the riverfront. They entered the foyer, thrilling at the forced heat at the entrance.

"Good afternoon. Welcome to the Sleep Suitely Inn. How can I help you?" asked the concierge with a name tag reading *Betty* on her chest. A wisp of peaches and almonds. Betty was a summer-born cookie.

"Good afternoon, Betty. I'm in need of a room."

"Would that be a double or a single?" she asked through a beaming, scarlet painted smile, tapping away at her computer as her grey eyes remained on her guest.

Autumn had no idea what Betty meant. Did they somehow look like two people? They had designed their corporeal body in the image of one of their own cookies. A butter pecan inspiration with maple flavorings.

Or did a double mean two rooms? That would be much too much space. They only needed the room as a place to get out of the cold. Bakers never slept.

"Um, single?"

"Very good," Betty's red lips widened. Her fingernails clacked away at the keyboard. "And how long will your stay with us be?"

Autumn quirked an eyebrow. "Eight days?" Eva and Hugh's birthday—December 8th—was in 8 days.

"Very good. All I need now is a name and a credit card for payment."

Autumn pulled a wallet from their back pocket and slipped the card to Betty. Summer had whipped up the necessary human accessories with their fondant before Autumn had left the Bakery.

"Autumn Baker," she said, reading the name off the plastic. She offered a slip of paper for Autumn to sign, then returned the credit card as well as handing them a black key card.

"Room 223. Second floor. Just take the elevator to your left and your room will be at the end of the hall. Riverfront view."

"Thank you," they said, pocketing both cards.

"Thank you for choosing the Sleep Suitely Inn. I hope you enjoy your stay with us."

Autumn nodded and headed towards the elevator, leaving Betty with her peach and almond perfume to her duties.

AFTER A HOT SHOWER, Autumn felt thawed, refreshed, and ready to set out to find Eva then Hugh. Winter had known where they'd dispersed Eva and Hugh, and given as many details as they could to Autumn. Both had been delivered in the Peoria area, thirty-eight and thirty-five years ago respectively. Autumn had checked the Bakery's cookie logs and discovered both still resided in the area.

Before Autumn had descended into the sugar glass globe, they had repeatedly inhaled a batch of Winter's curry ginger dough. The aroma was savory with an earthy sweetness. Quite distinct. Autumn needed only to allow their divine nose to lead them to the little cookies. Finding them now came down to sniffing them out.

Literally.

They stepped out of the temperate hotel onto the brisk, empty streets of the downtown area. Autumn walked hunched over their folded arms, shivering. The pale grey skies offered no warmth. The brick buildings provided excellent protection from the winds; the gusts only reached them when they passed by the alleyways. But the buildings also blocked out any of the faint sunlight that snuck past the grizzled clouds, casting chilling shadows across the sidewalks.

Autumn shook themself and stood upright. They weren't inside the sugar glass globe to experience the misery of winter; they were here to find Winter's joys.

They stretched their neck, closed their eyes, and took a deep inhale through their nostrils. A flood of scents. Autumn's keen mind sorted through the delicate odors until they honed in on curry ginger cookies. There were forty-eight within a fifty mile radius.

Autumn exhaled to clear their nose, then slowly, ever so slowly, inhaled again, filling their head with the air. Nineteen of the curry ginger cookies smelled fresh. Young. Still in the care of older cookies.

Sixteen were going stale. Autumn felt a wave of sadness as they had forgotten about the ending of a human's life. Winter's older cookies were not long for this world and would soon be turning to crumbs.

On the last thirteen curry ginger cookies, Autumn honed their olfactory senses. One more chasmic inhale and they narrowed their search down to four cookies.

Autumn locked onto the strongest, nearest scent. Nose tipped to the sky, they navigated the sidewalks. At the passing of a raspberry-scented human and her swaddled apple cinnamon child, Autumn temporarily lost the curry ginger trail. The baby wafted a scent so potent, so rich that Autumn knew the littler cookie was one of their most recent batches. Autumn's face split with a wide grin.

The sun continued its game of hide and peek throughout

the late afternoon until night's early darkness arrived. Autumn closed in on the first of Winter's curry ginger children; they picked up their pace and rushed at a fast clip before finding themself before a glass door. The smells of coffee beans, flour, and sugars from inside permeated through the walls of the storefront. The painted sign above read *Shortbreads*.

They walked inside and immediately felt nostalgia for the Bakery. Autumn made their way to the back of a short line and took in the ambiance of the shop. People hovered over mugs of whipped cream topped hot chocolates as they sat at wooden tables and chairs. In the booths lining the walls, more humans sat together with plated biscotti or muffins on the side of cups of espressos and cappuccinos. Some patrons livened the air with conversations while others wore earbuds and stared intently at laptops.

Everyone seemed relaxed.

"Next person in line," came a chipper voice.

Autumn turned towards the woman behind the counter. An apricot basil perfume. One of Summer's cookies.

"Good evening. I'd like to order a fun drink, but I have no idea what."

"Well, what sorts of flavors do you like? And are you interested in a coffee or tea or something sweeter? Like a hot chocolate?"

Autumn's lips puckered into the corner of their mouth. "Um."

The barista pointed to a brightly painted chalkboard bolted to the wall behind her. There were names like Snickers, Mud pie, and Wintergreen in curvaceous prints with their ingredients listed below. With more than two dozen options, Autumn wasn't sure which would be the best.

"So, we have a lot of choices and can custom make anything you want."

"I usually like apples and pumpkins and heavy buttered flavors," they said. At least, they knew they loved the smells.

The barista sucked air between her teeth. "Ooh. Sorry. All of our fall flavors and syrups are done. Once they're gone, they're gone. How about a peppermint latte? It's fresh, but very seasonal."

"That would be fine. I'll have a peppermint latte, please."

"For here or to go?"

"Here, please." Autumn pulled out their credit card, swiped the purchase, then stepped towards the Pick Up window to wait.

To their left, beside the open door to the backroom kitchen, hung another painted chalkboard.

Your barista today: Maritza

Your barback today: Jonathan

Thought of the Day: Words cannot espresso how much we love our customers!

Any questions, concerns, or gushes of love for Short-breads, please reach out to the owner, Hugh Shellstrap.

Hugh! Autumn took a deep inhale. Sure enough, a strong waft of curry ginger drifted from the kitchen.

"Peppermint latte?" announced the barback—Jonathan—as he slid a glass stein filled with milky brown liquid, and topped with chocolate shavings on a swirl mountain of whipped cream across the counter.

"Mine," said Autumn, slipping their hand under the handle to grab the heated glass mug. "Thank you."

Jonathan smiled and nodded. Autumn reciprocated, then walked over to a nearby table with a view of the backroom kitchen.

Their first sip ebbed a wave of soft, cool dairy over their

tongue, but was immediately chased by the burning sweet liquid.

"Ouch!" Autumn spewed the word and a spray of latte as they popped up from their chair, the legs screeching against the floor as it was pushed away. They set the offending stein onto the table. The room's attention focused solely on Autumn, the other customers hiding sniggers or sharing knowing grins.

"I'm so sorry about that," said a man with a black mustache and beard. The man offered Autumn several paper napkins. He took a hand towel hung over the waistband tie of his apron and wiped away the latte dribbles on the table. "Sometimes the milk steams need a minute to cool."

Dabbing their shirt front, Autumn said, "It's alright. It was my error."

The man whipped the towel at the dry table and stood with a toothy smile gleaming through his sable whiskers. The snap caused a brief breeze and Autumn caught a whiff of curry ginger cookie.

"Hugh, correct?"

Hugh's brows furrowed. "Yeah. How did you know?"

Autumn pointed over his shoulder. "The sign. I'm assuming Maritza and Jonathan are the ones behind the coffee bar."

Hugh shook his head with a chuckle. "Of course." He tucked his hand towel back over his apron tie and said, "Well, welcome to Shortbreads. If you need anything else, just let us know." He then returned to the coffee bar.

After allowing the peppermint latte to cool, Autumn leaned back in their chair to eavesdrop on Hugh.

"I'm not sure how I'm going to manage," Maritza said.

"You'll get through," Hugh replied. A hiss of steam put a pause in their conversation.

"I don't know. My Bio class plus lab work are taking up so much time. I'm either in class, here, or studying. I barely sleep enough as it is, let alone finding time for my other classes. These finals are going to kill me."

"What about taking some time off?"

"You wouldn't fire me if I took two weeks off during the busy season?"

"Listen, you're one of my best employees. If we need to rework your hours, we can do that. If you need the time off, we can do that too. Your job is safe and your education matters."

"Really, Hugh?"

"Of course."

A few more customers came in from the cold, ordered their treats, then moved along to find seats. An elderly man towing a small child by the hand approached the coffee bar, and instead of placing an order, said, "This here is Lilly. She's my granddaughter. She and I have been spending the week together, having adventures. Today's been our best one yet. Right, Melanie?"

Autumn side-eyed the pair. The little girl clung to her grandfather's hand with both of hers and buried her face into his thigh.

She did not speak, so her grandfather continued, "We went to the Riverfront Museum and saw the planetarium. We took a riverboat ride. We even went ice skating at the Owens Center. Didn't we, Melanie?"

The child peeked from behind her grandfather. She gave a slight nod with her cheek pressed against his leg.

Hugh walked around the counter and squatted before her. In an enthusiastic whisper, he said, "Wow! That is an adventurous day!" He looked up to the grandfather. "If it's alright with your grandpa," turning back to Melanie, "would you like extra chocolate shavings on your hot chocolate? Today was winter's first snow *and* it sounds like you had a day that deserves extra chocolate."

"Can I, Grandpa?" she breathed excitedly.

The man's shoulders bounced from laughter. "Of course, Melanie."

Autumn liked Hugh. The thirty-two year old man wore an easy smile and handed out compliments quicker than his coffees. Sincerity laced his kind words and his untroubled movements garnered a comforting calm. Each person who spoke with Hugh was treated with the same easygoing dignity, humor, and gentility.

Once their mug had been drained, Autumn went up to the front counter to request a second drink. This time, they ordered a caramel latte and waited until the glass had cooled before taking a swig. They sat, a rapt audience to the live action entertainment of watching the Bakery's cookies.

While Autumn sugared and caffeinated themself inside Shortbreads, listening to acoustic indie rock songs and cookie watching, the shadow sky of evening had changed to a night's indigo. Autumn didn't want to go back to the hotel. Instead, they had an urge to stroll the Peoria streets. Of Winter's three remaining nearby cookies, Autumn hoped that one of them was Eva.

Autumn returned to the nippy outdoors and vibrated with each twitchy step.

They stopped short when a gust of wind smacked them hard in the face. Pulling their jacket collar high around their neck, they smiled. Curry ginger hung in the air.

Over the course of two blocks, the parabolic potency of the scent faded, then thickened until they reached the stoop of Frigg Renovations. Autumn stared at the elegant wooden doors and brick entryway. Without the undercurrent odors of foods, drinks, and other cookies at Shortbreads, this curry ginger smell was even stronger. The hours placard above the brass handle noted the business would be closing in fifteen minutes. They quickly went inside.

The overhead bell's tinkling was answered by a voice coming from the back of the store. "Be out in a minute!"

Autumn meandered between showroom displays. Kiosks with staged home and business, interior and exterior, samplings. Each showcased a well-coordinated example of the work Frigg Renovations offered—reminding Autumn of the variances and beauty of the workstations back in the Bakery.

Autumn plucked a pamphlet from a bolted plastic folder. The cover displayed a house with a russet roof, white shutters, and goldenrod siding.

Making your dream home come true is our dream.

Let Frigg Renovations help make the impossible possible. Contact Eva Frigg, Proprietor, for more details.

They smiled. Cute.

And lucky.

"Sorry about that," said a man, walking from the backroom. "My name's Ben. What can I do you for?"

Coconut and German chocolate. One of their little cookies.

"I hope I'm not interrupting anything. I got caught in the cold and saw you were still open so I came inside to warm up."

"Ah," he said. "Well, you're lucky we're open late on Thursdays. We're closing soon, but you're welcome to stay here until then. If you change your mind about needing help, I'm going to be just over there," he pointed towards a desk tucked away in the corner with stacks of paper spread all over.

"Thank you," Autumn said. Ben walked over to the desk and sat down. As they stood in front of one of the displays, another human came out from the backroom. Curry ginger. Eva.

She smiled in Autumn's direction and asked, "Have you been helped?"

"Of course," piped in Ben. "They're a soul coming out of the cold for a bit. I told them they could stick around until closing time."

"Absolutely," she said. "We'll be here a little longer than our closing time and you're welcome to stay until then."

Autumn slowly moved between the kiosks with eyes glazed over as they eavesdropped on Ben and Eva. The minutes passed and they lost track of time while the pair worked on opposite sides of the desk—Eva on a tablet and Ben on a laptop.

Ben tossed his hands in the air. "What do we do about the Feldmans' basement? They want an Irish pub, but what they have now is the usual room layout."

Eva rose and walked to behind her employee. She bent over to peruse his laptop.

"Here," she said, tapping the screen. "We can remove this wall. It's not load bearing. If we open that space." She pinched her fingers against the screen, then stretched them wide. "We can then move them to create the open bar area. And over here, we can tear the drywall down to studs and put up brick.

" I think dry burnt bricks would look best, but that's going to cost, depending on class and their timetable."

"Which class do we need to use?"

She stood straight, crossed her arms over her chest, and smiled.

"What's the purpose of the brick?"

Ben swiveled his chair around and looked up at Eva. His face shifted from frustration to that of an eager student. "It's supposed to be reminiscent of a pub, *but* we the Feldmans also like clean lines. At least they do in the rest of their house."

"Right. And that means first or second class brick. So give me the pros and cons for the classes in regards to the Feldmans' needs."

Ben rattled off the lists as Eva nudged him along with hints of aspects he might not have thought about, displaying her vast knowledge base. Autumn found the conversation fascinating. Eva listened to her employee, then skillfully followed up with questions to draw the answers from Ben as opposed to her simply telling him what needed to be done.

She was more interested in teaching Ben than getting the project wrapped up immediately.

In-between the serious discussions, Eva cracked jokes. Autumn found her delightfully comical and had to duck behind the displays as they muffled their laughter, lest their eavesdropping be discovered.

Just like Hugh, Eva was easygoing, quick to laugh, and truly likable.

Winter's talent at baking shone brightly through these little cookies.

The tinkling of the doorbell drew Autumn away from their snooping. They startled, dropped their jaw, then clamped it shut quickly, hoping no one else would notice. The someone else coming in after hours into Frigg Renovations was Jonathan from Shortbreads with a cardboard tray and three paper to-go cups in hand.

Gawking more than they meant to, they watched as he crossed the showroom floor purposefully to Eva and Ben.

Ben rose from his seat, leaned over the desk, and planted a kiss on Jonathan's lips.

"Finally," Eva gushed, reaching for one of the cups. She took a sip, shoulders dropping and eyes closed as she lived in the zen moment. A blush bloomed over her cheeks. "Nothing like hot ginger tea."

Autumn tucked their chin to their shoulder, shuddering from their restrained laughter. A curry ginger cookie loving ginger tea was too cute.

"Sorry, but we're going to need to close," she said.

Autumn straightened themself up and with sincerity said, "Well, thank you for letting me stay as long as you have. I wasn't dressed for the weather, but I'm much better now. You have a wonderful business, by the way."

They opened the front door and took an imperceptible deep breath to enjoy one last whiff of the perfumes from the three little cookies inside Frigg Renovations.

STILL TOO PUMPED up from a successful day to return to the hotel, Autumn wandered through the downtown area until they found a fast food joint. Curious by the long drive-thru line wrapping the building and the nearly filled parking lot, they went inside and ordered a strawberry milkshake. They carried the drink back to the Sleep Suitely Inn to enjoy.

Instead, they were treated to a lackluster concoction that had no touch of real strawberries. It was nothing like the drinks from Shortbreads and the experience left Autumn missing the Bakery.

After discarding the still-full cup into the wastebasket, the little cookies returned to the forefront of Autumn's mind. Eva and Hugh were as endearing as Winter had remembered and they couldn't help but wonder what would happen if the two should meet.

"Winter," Autumn said aloud.

Yes, Autumn? I'm fairly busy at the moment. Did you find Eva and Hugh? Winter replied.

"I did. Surprisingly fast, too. It's no wonder they're two of your favorite cookies."

Good, good, Winter mumbled in a distracted tone. *How are they doing?*

"Very well. Eva runs a construction company. A builder by nature. And Hugh has, get this, a coffee and treat company!"

Winter gave a prideful chuckle. *My special little cookies.*

"They're fantastic. Somehow, though, they live near one another, have people in common, and seem like they should know one another, but they don't. At least I don't believe they do." Autumn tossed themself backwards onto the bed. The poofy comforter smooshed around their human form and they wriggled in whimsical joy. "I was wondering if I could introduce them."

You know we're not supposed to affect the cookies. Once they're in the sugar glass globe, they're free to do as they wish.

"True, but they'd really like one another!"

Well, if you figure out a way to not break the rules, I'll help. I need to get back to work.

"Blessed baking, Winter."

As Autumn didn't need sleep, they turned on the television and browsed the channels to pass the time. A few minutes into each show or the start of commercial breaks, they flipped the station until they landed on Hallmark Movie Channel. A holiday marathon. The beautiful crimsons, forest greens, and shimmery white snowfalls danced on the screen.

The visuals were comforting in a portrayal that wintertime is a fantasy time with optimism, hope, and seeking warmth with loved ones. As much as Autumn found the greyness and chills of sugar glass globe winter to be miserable, Winter the Baker was like the movies—gorgeous inside and out.

As the morning sky's pale light crept into the hotel room, Autumn pulled at the thread of an idea within their mind. What Hugh and Eva needed was a meet cute. If they bumped into one another under the right circumstances, surely they would become fast friends.

A meet cute. The movie tutorials all evidenced that the most successful were ones orchestrated for the couple to meet under ordinary circumstances that were touched by the extraordinary. However, bound to not directly interfere with the little cookies, Autumn couldn't walk up and introduce one to the other.

They got off the bed and walked to the window. A steamboat sat roped to a pier on the slate currents of the Illinois River. Winter's powdered sugar floated lazily onto the riverfront and the street below. It was a picturesque scene filled with natural magic.

Autumn snapped their fingers.

"Winter!"

Yes, Autumn. Still busy here. What do you need?

"I need you to send down more sugar. Maybe even some heavier granulated bits. But I need you to do it right over one place in particular."

I don't know…, their voice dropping off.

"I promise it won't break any rules! You can drop sugar all over, but I need you to drop a huge amount on Shortbreads, Hugh's shop."

Autumn swayed in place and stared at the eggshell ceiling. Patience came more easily when there was something to do.

After a few minutes, Winter sighed, *Okay. I'll send some sugar after I drop in the next peppermint chocolate cookies. Will that work?*

"Perfect!" Autumn squealed.

They took another hot shower then bundled to head out to Shortbreads. The temperatures began dropping before Autumn reached the coffeehouse. Once they were seated at Shortbreads near the electric fireplace with its dancing flames and a cup of hot wintergreen tea, the sugar outside began to fall. Well, it didn't fall. It dropped. Thick flakes *tink*ed against the store windows, leaving behind streaks of melted water.

Autumn lost themself in the beautiful chaos of whiteness on the other side of the glass. Their season preferred rains, breezes, and humid heats followed by dropping temperatures. Winds Autumn kissed with a heated breath into the globe, whisking the air with promises of celebrations catered by recent harvests. A transitional season that sometimes included Summer's color smears frosted across the sky at the sun's rise or set, or a soft sprinkling of Winter's sugar snow.

But the full-blown snow was different.ballet

The cold bits danced through the air in a ballet so elegant and refined that even the frigidity couldn't detract from its beauty.

"Looks like it's coming down hard," Hugh said strolling up to the glass. He pulled a phone from his pocket and tapped the screen. "The forecast changed. Now they're saying a massive storm is coming in."

"Does that mean we'll be closing early?" shouted an eager Maritza from behind the counter.

Hugh smirked. "We'll see."

After Autumn finished their tea then a caramel marshmallow latte, the storm kicked up. Winds blew howling whistles above the piped-in acoustic music. Glistening snow mounded into the corners of the outside window panes. Passersby scurried away, bundled in puffy or wool coats, their heads wrapped in scarves and hats and with eyes shielded from the elements.

"Sorry folks! Storm isn't going to let up so we're going to have to close early. Last call to the bar!" Hugh announced to the room, an apologetic smile on his lips. "Don't want any of our customers or employees to have to be out in these conditions."

Autumn quirked a smirk, ordered themself a to-go white chocolate latte, then left Shortbreads, the delight from their working plan keeping them warm.

THE NEXT DAY, Winter's storm continued unabated. Autumn remained in their hotel room. They took several hot showers, watched more Hallmark movies, and dreamed of scenarios about what it would be like for Eva and Hugh to meet. Once the sugar snow stopped the following morning and the streets had been plowed, Autumn felt ready to risk the cold. They headed straight for Shortbreads.

A *Closed* sign hung in the window. The shop should have opened three hours earlier.

Peering through the window, the reason became clear. Snow and broken ceiling and roof laid across the coffee bar and floors. The roof had collapsed beneath the weight of the snow.

"Sorry," said Hugh from behind Autumn. "Looks like we'll be closed for a while."

Autumn spun around.

Fatigue wore heavy in Hugh's smile. "You were just becoming one of my best customers, too. Hope when we reopen, you'll be coming around."

"I'm sorry about the damage. Have you already figured out how you're fixing it?"

Hugh bobbed his head. "Yeah. Insurance is moving through quickly and I've already lined up Frigg Renovations to do the work. Helps that one of my employees knows one of theirs. I'm not sure if any other businesses were affected by the storm, but if there were, the connections should help move us up on their list to get the job started soon."

Autumn buried their joy behind sympathetic straight lips. "That's at least something, right? You'll be back up and running before you know it. And I'll definitely be back around once you are."

"That's awesome to hear," said Hugh. "Truly appreciate it."

Autumn gave a nod, then turned to walk back to the Sleep Suitely Inn.

THE WEEK PASSED with the same routine. Each day, Autumn strolled from the hotel to various eateries, Shortbreads and Frigg Renovations always on their route.

While they sampled the many concoctions of seasonal brews Peoria had to offer, none tasted as delicious nor satisfying as the ones at Shortbreads. Despite their good intentions to connect Eva and Hugh, they felt guilt at having asked Winter to bombard the business with sugar snow.

Depriving the city of such a wonderful establishment was collateral damage they hadn't thought about.

The flutter of hope that Eva would arrive at Shortbreads

on day one to oversee the project quickly disappeared. Instead, Ben was the project manager. Autumn could smell his coconut and German chocolate from across the street, but not the duplicate potency of two curry ginger cookies.

Autumn asked Winter to not add any more sugar to the sugar glass globe, at least not in Peoria, so that the construction could progress. With the snow held in the clouds, the white tufts drifted languorously across the early December cerulean skies. The temperatures below warmed to moderate, pleasing conditions.

On day five, Autumn, with the bitter Sleep Suitely Inn continental coffee in hand, parked themself on a bench across the street from Frigg Renovations. They faced the riverfront and sat under the pretense that they were another person having a leisurely morning taking in the glorious view of bobbing geese on the grey waters.

In truth, they were using their divine hearing to listen to the workers across the street.

"Another week and Shortbreads should be able to reopen," Ben said.

"You're a miracle worker," replied Hugh. "The longer we're closed, the harder it'll be to get back our clients."

"It's why we're putting in the extra hours. Eva knows this is a big deal. That storm coming out of nowhere was crazy, right?"

"Yeah. Gotta love the Illinois weather. Or hate it." They both laughed at Hugh's joke while a wave of relief washed over Autumn. At least Hugh was forgiving about the snow damage.

"Speaking of Eva," Hugh said, "when do I get to meet her? I've got to thank her for putting such a rush on this project. I gotta imagine Frigg was swamped with projects."

"Actually, it's the darndest thing. Only Shortbreads had a

roof cave in. Sorry," Ben said with sincere condolence. "But at least that meant we could put a rush on the supplies and had the labor available to get you back up and running."

"I truly appreciate that."

"Oh, and tomorrow. Still on for our party, right?"

"Of course. I wouldn't miss a party invite from one of my favorite employees. Speak of the devil!"

"Why are my ears burning?" asked Jonathan.

"Hugh confirmed that he'll be in attendance to our little soirée tomorrow night," Ben said.

"Ah. Yeah. You'll have a great time. Promise."

"I'm sure I will. I could definitely use a fun distraction from this past week."

Hugh's voice changed to suspicion. "This wouldn't happen to be a surprise birthday party, would it? If I remember correctly, you did know that tomorrow is my birthday."

"Your birthday? Really?" asked Jonathan.

Autumn caught an underlying tone they could not place, almost like buried laughter beneath the words.

Hugh didn't notice. "You promise?"

"Actually, I'd totally forgotten yours was tomorrow. Nope. This is just a fun between the holidays party."

"Okay, then. Well, I need to run over to the insurance office to drop off some of the receipts for the claims. I'll be back in a few hours. Keep up the good work, Ben. And Jonathan, see you both tomorrow."

Ben and Jonathan bade Hugh goodbye and after the ginger curry had left the area, Ben asked, "Do you think they know?"

"I doubt it," said Jonathan.

"I've already verified. Eva's confirmed she's coming too."

Autumn's ears perked. Apparently, they weren't the only one thinking Eva and Hugh were meant to meet.

THE NEXT MORNING, after yet another marathon of Hallmark movies—an addiction they realized they were forming—Autumn took their last hot shower. They reveled in the simple joy of water pounding then trickling over their temporary human skin.

They dressed and headed downstairs to the lobby to check out. Betty with her peach and almond perfume greeted them.

"Have you had a good stay?"

"I have." They slid the key card across the desk

Betty took the card and said, "Wonderful. Thank you for visiting us at the Sleep Suitely Inn." She flashed a beatific, scarlet smile that warmed Autumn even more than the shower had.

They took a quick sniff of her peach and almond perfume, turned on their heels, and headed out to Shortbreads. Summer would need to hear how wonderful a batch peach and almond cookies were.

The weather along the river felt particularly warm. Hugh had been right about the erratic Illinois weather as the air hung a humid breath akin to fall. Autumn overheated in their jacket, having to strip it off before they found their place on their usual bench.

Hugh was already on site when Autumn arrived. He hovered near the front entrance with a coffee urn, handing out to-go cups to the Frigg Renovations workers. It was nearing lunchtime for the crew when Autumn first smelled an additional waft of curry ginger before hearing, "How're my people doing?"

"Hi. You must be Eva," Hugh said.

Autumn squirmed with excitement in their seat, fighting the urge to turn around.

"And you must be Hugh," Eva said. "Nice to meet you. So? How're they doing?"

"You've got an impressive crew. I can't believe how much they've gotten done in just a few days. I should be able to reopen in another week."

"Wonderful. That's what I like to hear."

The two continued to talk. Small chat banter.

Autumn twisted to peek over their shoulder. Hugh offered Eva a cup of coffee. When she reached for it, his hand lingered on the cup. The pair stood, still talking with flushed faces and wide smiles, each with a hand wrapped around the cardboard.

After a few heartbeats, Hugh let go and hooked both of his thumbs on his pants front pockets. Eva held the cup in both hands and took a step closer to him.

Neither paused their amiable conversation.

Autumn turned back towards the river. They were unsure if this was a real human connection or politeness, but an instinct in them swelled like yeast that Eva and Hugh were becoming something more than professional acquaintances.

After the construction workers returned from their break, Eva left her conversation with Hugh to check on her employees. The afternoon breeze was pleasant and Autumn lost themself in staring at the sparkling waters of the river. The glittering current flowed like caramel.

"Here you go," interrupted a voice.

Autumn startled and turned. Hugh extended one hand holding a to-go cup.

"Don't think I haven't noticed that you've been around. Thought you might like a cup of coffee on the house. Definitely don't want to lose someone who was becoming one of my best customers."

Autumn's jaw dropped. What could they say?

Hugh registered their surprise and interjected, "Don't worry. I added extra sugars and creams. You ordered so many of the sweeter drinks, I'm sure you'll like this."

Autumn's cheeks warmed. "It's not that. I've been here on vacation and today's my last day."

Hugh cocked his head with a bob. "Ah. No worries. The joe is still on the house, if you want it."

Autumn accepted the offer. They took a sip. Hugh was right. The coffee was sweetened and creamed to perfection.

"And look, if you're ever back in the area, hope you'll look us up or recommend us to your friends."

"I certainly will. Thank you," Autumn said.

Hugh smiled. "Appreciate it. And safe travels." He crossed the street and returned to Shortbreads.

With the best coffee they'd tasted, Autumn strolled the streets, cookie watching. They planned to stay through the evening and spend the last of their vacation on a casual walk. They felt homesick and missed the other Bakers, ready to go home.

The day waned until the blue-grey sky turned into sherbet oranges and pinks. The sun dropped quickly, pulling the beautiful colors with it until there was only a navy sky and a smattering of stars.

Autumn found themself walking down a broken sidewalk. Somehow, they lost track of their path and wound up in a residential section. Streetlamps appeared and Autumn could see their breath in wispy puffs. They played with it. Puckered blows made barely a ghost of air while a hearty huff produced a thick hanging cloud.

They laughed and when they inhaled, the aroma of curry ginger filled their nostrils.

The street beside them was filled with parked cars. Two walkways ahead, Autumn saw them.

Standing under a porchlight were Hugh and Eva. Each blushing. Each swaying with nervous energy, their hands in their coat pockets.

Autumn knew they shouldn't be watching. This was an intimate moment, but as with the movies they'd binge watched, a feeling that something was about to happen hung thick in the crisp night's air. They didn't want to miss it, if only to be sure they were right.

Hugh's swaying stopped and Eva paused in her own pendulum movements. They locked eyes with one another. Their lips whispered words Autumn couldn't hear.

Eva shuffled a step closer to Hugh, and he mirrored her.

Giddy excitement flooded through Autumn.

As icy powdered sugar fell around them, Autumn turned to leave for the Bakery and give the couple their privacy, but not without one last glance as Eva and Hugh shared a kiss beneath a porchlight and a bit of hung mistletoe.

ONCE IN A LIFETIME

TIFFANY PUTENIS

*D*elicate snowflakes danced on the light wind that blew just beyond the large bay window. Gemma stood beside it, watching the flakes dip and turn to the music of the breeze. Mark walked through the back door and shed his jacket and hat, dusting off the snow and hanging them on the hook before walking into the living room. He stared at her silhouette, smiling at the sight of her rounded belly. Their due date approached rapidly, and the excitement became more palpable by the day. Gemma, sensing Mark's presence, turned to look at him, a wide smile on her face.

"Hi babe," she said, rubbing a hand over her rounded belly.

"Hi love." He walked over and wrapped his arms around her, dropping a kiss on her forehead. "How are you feeling?"

"Like the Titanic, except I only have one passenger," she said with a laugh. "I'm glad you're home from work, because I'm ready to decorate for Christmas."

"I'll go get the boxes out of the basement and bring them up. Do you want to eat dinner first?"

"I have a pot roast in the oven, but we have another hour before it'll be ready. Let's start decorating."

Mark nodded and headed toward the basement stairs to get the decorations and haul them upstairs. While he grabbed everything, Gemma admired the large Balsam fir they had picked out at the Morris Family Tree Farm a few days before. The branches had settled nicely, and the scent of fresh pine filled the room, adding to her festive mood. She walked over to the chaise lounge and sat down, leaning back into the soft velvet cushions and running her fingers along the fabric. She felt a twinge of pain and a cramp in her lower abdomen and flinched.

Another Braxton-Hicks contraction, Gemma thought. *They've been happening so much more frequently the last week.* She absentmindedly rubbed the area where the muscles tensed and squeezed, watching the logs crackle with flames in the old stone fireplace.

Mark's footsteps thudded heavily up the stairs. He emerged through the door, arms laden with clear plastic storage boxes. Reds, greens and golds shone from one large box, while the other glittered in shades of ice blue, white, and silver. He strode across the room and set them beside the chaise, then sat beside her.

"You ok?"

"Yeah, I'm fine. A little tired, another Braxton-Hicks contraction, but I'm fine," Gemma said. She stretched her legs and wiggled her toes in the cozy cabin socks Mark surprised her with the week before.

"I'm glad. Ready to decorate?" Mark smiled and placed his hand on her thigh, gently stroking it with his thumb.

"You'll have to help me up!" Gemma smiled at him, giggling as he stood to help her from the chaise. She'd been having increasing difficulty standing after reclining or sitting for more than a few minutes at a time. He grabbed her hand and pulled her from the chaise.

"Have you decided what ornaments you want to use?" Mark asked, the glow of the fire warming his eyes.

"I keep thinking about the ornaments we found last year. Remember the pale blue, silver, and teal ones that made me think of Jack Frost?"

"Yeah, I remember those. The ones you insisted we absolutely had to have, even though they don't go with any of the decor we already own?" Mark chuckled and shuffled the bins around, peeking under the lids to look for the strands of warm white lights that they put on the tree every year. He found the strands and opened the box, removing the coiled strands and plugging them in.

Gemma sighed, a thrilled smile on her face, as the lights flickered to life. Their warm glow made Christmas seem much closer, and her excitement felt nearly overwhelming. She bent carefully and picked up the glowing coils, handing one end to Mark and keeping the other. He began to wrap them around the tree from the top down, walking behind the tree to pass the lights back to her. A few more passes back and forth and the tree sparkled with a warm glow.

"It's perfect," Gemma said, her breath catching in her throat as she stared at the tree. "I love the way the lights peek through." She picked up a few different ornaments and took a step back, holding them up and looking at them with the tree in the background. She spun a delicate red and gold filigree orb between her fingertips, admiring the way it glittered in the lights from the tree. She repeated the action with a small icy blue and white star, studying it in the lights. A small crease formed between her eyebrows. Finally, she held up a gold and silver tree, decked in small green crystals, and studied it against the lights.

"Is it wrong that I hate the way the pale blues and whites look against the lights we have? The ornaments are a different shade of white than the lights, and it looks terrible." Frustration leaked into her voice as she looked at Mark. He laid the red and black buffalo check plaid runner across the fireplace mantle and set the candles back in place before turning to look at her.

"Show me," he said, gesturing to the tree. "Let's see how it looks on the tree before you make a final decision."

Gemma walked over to the tree and carefully placed the three ornaments on branches at eye level, then backed up a bit and studied the tree closely.

"What do you think?" she said after a few moments passed. "I still don't love the pale blue and white one."

"I see what you mean about the lights," Mark said, turning away from the tree to look at her. "The different shades of white make it feel a little weird. The reds and golds and greens look beautiful."

"They feel right with the warmth of the lights. We need different lights if we want to use the other ornaments."

"Do you want me to go get different lights?" Mark wrapped his arm around her shoulders. "I can run to the store."

"No, it's ok. The warm lights make me so happy, and I don't want to change them when they look so pretty with the other ornaments." She leaned into Mark, enjoying the warmth of his arm around her. She looked at the tree, stroking her hands over the swollen mound of her belly. The baby's wiggles slowed down whenever she moved around, but she could feel stretching and gentle bumps now that they were still. "He's wiggling again," she said, giggling.

Mark reached over to stroke her belly and she turned toward him slightly, giving him easier access. Their little one greeted him with a hearty kick, and Gemma giggled again. Her enjoyment at the baby's movements hadn't dimmed as their pregnancy dragged on.

"He sure does love to kick you whenever you're touching my belly," she said, laughter filling her voice.

"He's excited to meet his daddy in a couple weeks," Mark said. His wide smile brought out his dimples and made his gray eyes twinkle in the lights. "Ready to put the rest of these ornaments up?"

Gemma nodded, happy-hearted, then walked across the room to turn on the radio. Her favorite station started playing Christmas music the day after Thanksgiving, and she loved the cheerful, upbeat pop versions of the popular carols. The last verses of a soulful rendition of "Silent Night" came over the speaker system, the husky alto of the singer's voice providing the perfect backdrop to finish trimming the tree. Mark handed Gemma one of her favorite ornaments, a small golden snowflake covered in rhinestones that glimmered when the lights hit them. She studied the tree closely before placing the snowflake a little more than halfway up on its front, where it caught the light from the fireplace and the Christmas lights. It glowed, shimmering, and brought a broad smile to her face.

"I love when you smile like that," Mark said, hanging another ornament on the tree. "It reminds me of the day we met."

"What a beautiful rendition of 'Silent Night,'" the announcer's voice came over the speakers as the final bars of music played in the background, "and what a silent night we have ahead of us. The snow is just starting to fall here, folks, but these flurries are going to turn into something serious over the next few hours. The local meteorologists have been calling this a 'once in a lifetime' storm. We're expecting 24-

28 inches of snow over the next 8 hours. Not looking good for anyone with travel plans over the next few days. So stay inside by the fire, spend some time with your families, and enjoy this rousing rendition of 'Rockin' Around the Christmas Tree.'"

"A once in a lifetime storm?" Gemma repeated, her voice quiet. "That's a little terrifying. It didn't look that bad on the radar earlier when I watched the news." She looked out the bay window near the sofa, watching the delicate flakes fall. "It doesn't look that bad now."

Mark pulled out his phone and checked the weather app, pulling up the radar.

"Babe, it's bad. Look at this." He showed her the radar screen, where light blue enveloped their town, with the deep sapphire color of a severe snowstorm heading in their direction. He glanced at her, seeing her eyes widen as she realized the severity of the storm that approached.

"Ok, so it's about to get really bad." She walked closer to the window and stared outside, watching the flakes falling.

"Yeah, that's what it looks like," Mark said. "I'm glad we did the groceries early. We should be fine to make it through until they're able to get the roads plowed."

Gemma nodded, still watching the snow fall outside of their windows. Mark, sensing her anxiety about the storm, rubbed her shoulders. She leaned into his hands and sighed.

"We should finish decorating," Gemma said. "I'd love to just relax tonight and enjoy the fire."

"Let's finish up, then, and we can eat dinner by the fire tonight." Mark kissed her cheek quickly, then they went back to trimming their Christmas tree.

❄

FINALLY FINISHED with decorating and full from dinner, Gemma settled onto the couch near the fire. She put her feet up on the large upholstered ottoman and snuggled into the cushions and pillows to watch the flames dance among the logs and kindling. The firelight reflected off of the delicate stained glass of the star that topped the tree, sending prisms of color around the room. Mark walked back into the living room carrying two steaming mugs and handed her one, setting the other down on the side table.

"Cocoa! Oh thank you, Mark," she said, taking a sip. "It's perfect."

"It seemed like the perfect night to have cocoa," he said, picking up his mug before wrapping his arm around her shoulders and pulling her closer. He watched the firelight flicker and smiled, feeling Gemma relax against him.

"Oh," she says, jumping slightly. "That was different."

"What was different?"

"He just shifted down a bit, and it felt strange." She rubbed her belly, then leaned over to set the mug down. "Definitely strange. I feel like he's not as high up in my lungs anymore."

"Well, that's a plus, at least." Mark smiled at her and leaned to kiss her belly. "Hi buddy, be nice to Mommy for a little bit and let her rest."

Gemma threw her arms around him, giggling. They held one another and Mark felt the baby move and chuckled. She settled in to snuggle against him again as he rested his large hand on her belly. Sighing with contentment, she placed her hand on top of his and leaned her head against his shoulder. The baby wiggled for a few more minutes before settling down. Mark continued to stroke her belly as they sat together.

"We really need to get the mattress pad and sheet on the crib mattress," Gemma said, nuzzling her cheek against

Mark's shoulder, "and we need to get the last load of baby laundry folded and put away."

"We can fold the laundry and get the crib bedding together tomorrow. I washed the bottles and parts for your pump last night."

"I saw that, I put everything away this morning. Thank..." Gemma trailed off, gasping.

"Babe? What happened?

Gemma gasped again, grasping her belly and curling into herself in pain. She struggled to remember the breathing exercises she learned in birthing class but couldn't bring them to mind.

"Gemma, what's wrong?" Mark rubbed his hand up and down her back, feeling the tension in her body.

The seconds ticked by at a snail's pace while she panted and struggled to catch her breath. Mark kept stroking her back, unsure of what else he should do to help her. He felt her body begin to relax and she slumped backward. Catching her gently, he leaned her back into the cushions of the couch.

"Gemma?"

"That contraction was different," she said, her voice wavering. "It hurt a lot more than the others have. I'm sure I'm fine now."

"Maybe it was another big gas bubble? That happened the other day," Mark said, turning his body and pulling her closer to him.

Gemma relaxed into him and he stroked his hand up and down her arm. She rested her head against his chest and sighed, enjoying the feel of his hand on her arm. With his free hand, Mark brushed the hair back from her face, inhaling the scent of honeysuckle flowers and vanilla that surrounded her. He pressed his lips to her forehead and another small sigh escaped her throat. She nuzzled her cheek against his chest. A smile turned up the corners of his full lips as she snuggled closer to him. He gazed out the window, watching the large snowflakes fall outside.

"Mmm, that feels nice," she said as he continued to stroke her arm.

"Good, I'm glad. Looks like the snow has really picked up," he said. He felt her stiffen beside him. "Gemma?"

She didn't respond, but pain painted her face as her eyebrows drew together. She squeezed her eyes shut, her breath coming in harsh pants. Mark looked at his watch and began to time the pain. Her hand reached out to grasp his leg, squeezing with all the strength that she could muster. Her long nails dug into his thigh and he gritted his teeth, determined not to let her see his pain as she suffered through her own. When he felt the grip of her hand slacken, he stopped timing the contraction.

"62 seconds," he said, rubbing her back. "That's a long one. The other one was that long, too."

Gemma nodded at him. She slumped back into the couch, resting her head against the cushions.

"Ok, I'm pretty sure you're in labor. I'm going to start timing the way Dr. Johnson taught us during the labor and delivery class." Mark made a note in his cell phone of what time the second contraction happened and how long it lasted.

"Ok, babe. That one was really bad." Gemma looked pale. "Could you get me some water?"

"Coming right up." Mark ran to the kitchen to grab one of the stainless steel water bottles from the fridge. He handed it to her and watched as she drank deeply.

"Thank you," she said, closing the bottle and setting it beside her on the couch. "How long has it been?"

"Almost five minutes. How are you holding up?"

"I'm ok. Very nervous, but ok."

"Let's see how far apart they are and then we can call the doctor." Mark glanced out the window again. A thick blanket of snow covered the street. The bushes outside the windows were almost indistinguishable from the rest of their front lawn.

"The snow is so pretty," Gemma said, noticing Mark studying the scene. "This little guy picked an interesting night to come into the world."

"I hope they come by to plow soon. Everything is completely covered right now."

"They will. The town is always good about getting that done early on so that people can get home safe." She stretched her arms above her head, then tilted her head from side to side, stretching her neck. As she rolled her shoulders back, she tensed again, a low moan ripping from her throat.

"Another one? Six and a half minutes apart, then." Mark took note, then sat back down beside Gemma on the couch and pulled her back against him. He rested his hands on her belly and felt the muscles in her abdomen clenching. He breathed with her, trying to lead her through the breathing techniques that they learned in the birthing class. "I wish I had paid closer attention to the breathing techniques. I'm trying, babe."

Gemma panted in response, gripping the couch cushions as the pain from the contraction coursed through her body. Mark glanced at his watch, checking the seconds that had passed, and rubbed her belly.

"57 seconds," he said as he felt her begin to relax again. "We need to call the doctor now."

Gemma nodded at him, catching her breath. A light sheen of sweat covered her forehead.

"Ok," she said when she could speak again. "I'll call him now." She grabbed her phone from the ottoman and dialed the number for her obstetrician. Putting the phone to her ear, she listened for the first ring signalling a successful connection. Silence greeted her. "Nothing at all. It's not even ringing."

"It's not ringing?" Mark looked perplexed as he stared at her. "How is it not ringing?"

"I don't know, Mark. I don't know. What are we going to do?" Her voice rose in panic.

"I'm going to go clean off the car. We'll go to the hospital." Mark walked to the front door and threw on his boots and heavy jacket, grabbing the ice scraper. When he opened the door, a gust of wind blew a flurry of snow into the foyer. "I'll grab the shovel, too."

Gemma stayed on the couch. She went through the relaxation exercises she learned from her meditation app, focusing on her breathing and attempting to relax her body one part at a time. She startled when the door flew open again.

"We aren't going anywhere," Mark said, frustration filling his voice. "There's at least a foot of snow out there, and the car is stuck. It drifted against the back end of the car, and I can't dig it out."

"What are we going to..." Gemma trailed off as another contraction hit.

"Less than 6 minutes apart now. 5 minutes and 44 seconds." Mark shrugged off his coat and shook off the snow that accumulated during the few short minutes he struggled with the snowbanks outside their home. He checked the second hand of his watch as he walked over to where Gemma leaned against the arm of the couch.

Her breathing began to level out again as he sat down. She tried to smile at him as she relaxed.

"61 seconds that time," Mark said. He brushed the hair back from her face and gazed into her eyes. "You're doing great."

"What are we going to do, Mark? If we can't leave, nobody can get here."

"We'll figure it out. You haven't been in labor very long, so we have some time. Isn't one of our neighbors a doctor?"

"I don't know, Mark. Other than Alex and Alicia across the street, I don't spend a lot of time with our neighbors."

"I'm pretty sure the old man a few doors down is a retired doctor. I'm going to walk over there. He's only three houses away."

"You might be right. I think I remember him. They have the old Victorian with the pretty trim, right?"

"Yup, that's his house. I'm going over there to get him. He'll be able to help us."

"Ok. Bring your phone, just in case? If service comes back, I can call you and tell you what the doctor says when I get in touch with him."

"I'll bring it. I'll be back as fast as I can." Mark wrapped his arms around her, pulling her into him and kissing her softly. "I love you so much."

"I love you, too," Gemma said, cupping his face in her hands and pulling him in for another kiss. "Be careful."

"I will." He walked back to the foyer and pulled on his still-damp jacket and boots. Putting the hood of his jacket over his head, he pulled on his gloves. He waved to Gemma and opened the door, heading out into the swirling white of the storm.

"Please keep him safe and bring him home to me," Gemma said, touching the small cross that lay just below her collarbones. The notepad and pen sat beside her on the couch, and she glanced at her phone as she felt the first pangs of pain begin.

"5 minutes and 38 seconds," she mumbled, struggling to

write it down on the pad of paper. She panted, focusing on breathing and getting through the contraction. The pain began to ebb and she struggled to stand up. She put the pad and pen into the pocket of her hooded sweatshirt and walked to the fireplace.

The fire had begun to burn down, but the temperature outside would tax the heater unless she kept it stoked. Shivering slightly, she grabbed a log off of the curved wood rack beside the fireplace and tossed it into the fire. She studied it again, deciding to grab a second log and added it, then used the bellows to fan the flames. As the fire roared back to life, she sat down on the chaise, angling her feet toward the flames to enjoy the warmth. Watching the flames distracted her from the anxiety building in the pit of her stomach as each minute ticked by.

GEMMA RODE out each contraction as it came, tracking the time between them and trying not to focus on how long Mark had been gone. Nearly two hours had passed, and her anxiety level increased with every passing moment. She picked up her phone and tried to call him again, but it still wouldn't connect.

"Why did the cell towers have to go down today, of all days?" Irritation filled her voice as she set her phone down on the chaise. "I shouldn't have to be alone right now."

She stood up and began to pace in front of the fireplace, stopping whenever a contraction hit. The fire crackled in the background but the soft sound failed to relax her. Visions of Mark stranded in the snow, freezing and alone, danced through her head as she walked. She looked across the room toward the window, where heavy blankets of snow continued to fall. She thought she saw a light in the distance but refused to give herself the chance to hope.

Turning, she faced back toward their Christmas tree, smiling slightly at the stained glass star at the top. She began to pace back toward the tree, then felt warmth run down her leg.

"No. No, no, no. This can't be happening," she said as she rushed to the bathroom. She checked, anxiety threatening to overrun her system, and confirmed that her water had broken. She sighed. "Well, I guess I need to find new pants."

She walked down the hallway, past the kitchen, to the cozy bedroom she shared with Mark, too tired and anxious to appreciate the sloped ceiling and warm colors that filled the room. She grabbed a pair of soft fleece pajama pants and clean underwear, changing into them and putting the wet clothes into her hamper. No longer damp, she headed back toward the living room and the fire. The creak of the front door startled her, and another contraction hit as she struggled to walk to the foyer.

"Gemma?" Mark's voice rang through the hallway.

She screamed in response, leaning against the wall, and heard the clatter of his boots as he ran toward her. He gathered her into his arms and carried her to the living room, heedless of the snow falling from him as he walked.

"I have Dr. Alexander with me," he said as he set her down on the chaise. She squeezed his hand, her face twisted in pain as she rode out the rest of the contraction. "How far apart are they now?"

Gemma pointed to her notebook, which lay on the table beside the chaise.

"5 minutes, got it." Mark looked toward the foyer, where Dr. Alexander struggled to free himself from his snow-encrusted winter coat. The stiff yarn of his gloves prevented him from gripping the zipper, and they stuck to his hands. Mark stood to help him, divesting himself of his gloves, coat, and boots as he arrived back in the foyer.

"How is our patient?" Dr. Alexander asked quietly as Mark assisted him in removing his winter gear.

"She's been in labor for about three and a half hours now," Mark said, glancing at his watch. "I know she's anxious, and that last contraction seemed worse than the ones she was having before I left."

"That will happen. Let's get in there and check on her." Dr. Alexander walked carefully around the wet spots on the floor from the discarded snow, trying to keep his socks dry. "How are you, my dear? I'm Dr. Alexander."

"My water broke just before you got here," she said, looking at the doctor and studying his age-lined face.

"Things are moving along, then," Dr. Alexander said, pressing gently on her belly, checking the baby's position. "He's head down, which is good. The contractions are five minutes apart?"

"Yes," she said, stretching her legs slightly. "Are they supposed to hurt this much?"

"Everyone says that, dear."

"Mark, can you please make sure the jackets and gloves and things are hung up on the coat rack near the fire? Also, you and Dr. Alexander need to change into dry clothes. You're both soaked." Gemma smiled at the doctor and looked over at Mark, who looked confused.

"You want me to worry about changing and hanging everything up?"

"Yes. And please grab some dry clothes for Dr. Alexander so that he can change, too. The fire is warm, but you've both been out in the storm for God knows how long. We have time."

"She's right. Gemma, I'll need you to change into a night-gown, as well," Dr. Alexander said. "We need to check to see how dilated you are so that we can gauge where you're at in your labor."

Mark walked into the bedroom and changed into dry clothes, bringing out a spare set of sweatpants and a t-shirt for Dr. Alexander and a nightgown for Gemma.

"Thanks, my love," Gemma said, accepting the gown he handed to her. "Dr. Alexander, the bathroom is down the hall, first door on the right, if you want to go change." She flinched, then gasped as another contraction started.

"I'll go change, and I'll be right back," he said, heading down the hall.

Mark sat on the floor beside Gemma, holding her hand as she focused on breathing through the contraction.

"You're doing great, baby. I'm so proud of you," Mark said, kissing Gemma's hand. She squeezed his fingers with all her strength. Relief flooded his system as he felt her hand relax and her breathing returned to its normal rate.

"Ok dear," Dr. Alexander said as he re-entered the room, "I need you to go change now."

Gemma nodded, and Mark stood, helping her up from the chaise. She walked into the bathroom to change into the short nightgown. The rush of the fabric over her skin didn't give her the same thrill she normally experienced. Anxiety threat-ened to overwhelm her, despite the calming presence of the doctor.

"Mark, do you have a spare shower curtain that we can put on the chaise and cover with a blanket? I want Gemma to be comfortable, but I don't want to ruin such a beautiful piece of furniture."

"Yeah, we have an extra in the linen closet that I can grab. Should I put more pillows to support her back?"

"That's a great idea."

Mark grabbed extra pillows and shower curtain, then grabbed a black knitted blanket from the back of the couch. Together, he and Dr. Alexander arranged the shower curtain and blanket, then stacked pillows to provide additional support for Gemma's back.

"Oh," Gemma exclaimed. "Thank you for the extra pillows and the blanket."

"You're welcome. Dr. Alexander recommended the blanket. We put the extra shower curtain liner beneath it to protect the chaise," Mark said, helping her settle herself back onto the chaise.

"Ok, Gemma, I'm going to check to see how dilated you are now," Dr. Alexander said as he pulled on a pair of gloves from his medical bag.

Gemma leaned back against the cushions and pillows as Mark sat beside her on the floor. Dr. Alexander checked her progress, then removed the gloves and put them into the trash.

"You're about nine centimeters right now. Almost there, Gemma. It won't be much longer now." Dr. Alexander stood and walked into the bathroom to wash his hands again.

"You're doing so great, Gemma," Mark said. He leaned forward and brushed her hair from her face. He gently pressed his lips to hers. "I love you.

"I love you, too," she said, smiling at him. "I was so scared when you hadn't come home yet."

"I made it, I'm here."

"So am I," said Dr. Alexander as he returned to the room, "and women all over the world have had home births for centuries. Everything will be just fine."

"Mark," Gemma said, looking at the embers burning

down in the fireplace, "could you put another log or two on the fire. I'm a little cold."

"Of course," Mark said. He stood and added a few logs to the fire, using the bellows and poker to ensure that they caught. The fire roared back to life and he smiled.

"There's so much pressure," Gemma said, looking at Dr. Alexander.

"Let me check you again. It might be time to push. Mark, I need you to grab towels." Dr. Alexander crouched at Gemma's feet, slipping on another pair of latex gloves and checking her again. "Ok, Gemma. You're fully dilated now, and the baby is crowning. When your next contraction starts, I need you to push."

Seconds ticked by as they waited for the next contraction to start. At the first twinges of pain, Gemma groaned.

"Ok, Gemma," Dr. Alexander said with his hand on her belly. "Push."

Mark blanched. Gemma's fingernails dug into his hand. Her scream echoed through the house.

"Good job, Gemma. Breathe now."

Gemma's breath came in sharp pants, and she laid back against the pile of pillows. Mark held her hand and leaned against the chaise. She ruffled his hair, then caressed his cheek. He smiled and turned his face into her hand, kissing her palm.

"I love you," she said quietly.

"I love you, too."

Another contraction rippled through her, and she pushed again. Mark flinched as her nails dug into his hand for the second time.

"Keep going, baby. Keep going," he said.

"Ok, Gemma, breathe," Dr. Alexander said, pushing his hair back with his forearm.

Gemma took several deep breaths and smiled at Mark. He grinned back at her, kissing her hand.

"One more push, Gemma, maybe two."

She nodded, focusing on breathing. Mark stood up and stretched his legs, then sat down behind Gemma on the chaise. She leaned back against him, resting her head against his chest. He kissed her cheek, stroking his hands up and down her arms. Gemma grunted as her abdomen began to clinch again.

"Push, Gemma. Big push."

She screamed, her body arching forward. Mark rubbed her back and shoulders as she pushed. She slumped backward, and the wail of a newborn baby echoed in the room.

"It's a boy," Dr. Alexander said, grinning at them as he wrapped the baby in a clean towel.

"He's here, Gemma," Mark said, pride filling his voice. "You did it."

Gemma smiled, exhausted. Dr. Alexander brought the baby to them and set him on her chest. Tears spilled from her eyes as she beheld her son for the first time.

"Hello, little boy," she said softly, awe filling her voice.

"Mark, can you take the baby for one moment? Gemma, one more push," Dr. Alexander said.

Mark took his son from Gemma's arms and held him against his chest, amazed at the tiny child they had created. His heart swelled as the little boy in his arms opened his eyes slightly and looked at him.

"Hi, little guy. I'm your daddy," he whispered.

Dr. Alexander stood and cleaned up the mess from the delivery, gathering the soiled towels and trash into a bag to be taken out. He set the bag by the front door, peeking out the window. The snow had stopped, and the sound of plows on the road reverberated in the distance.

"Ok, give me the baby and I'll get him cleaned up for you. Mark, do you want to grab him some clothes?"

"I'll do that now," Mark said, leaning down to kiss Gemma on the forehead. "Why don't we get you up so you can change and rest, Mommy?"

"Good idea," Gemma said as Mark helped her to her feet. She blew him a kiss as she walked toward their bedroom to change and get comfortable.

Mark collected the blanket and shower curtain and brought them into the kitchen to put in the trash can. He walked back down the hall to the nursery, grabbing a newborn sleeper and onesie from the dresser, and a diaper from the basket beside the changing table. He carried them into the kitchen, where Dr. Alexander washed the baby, gently cleaning him before wrapping him in another clean towel. Mark stared at the little boy, tiny in the doctor's large hands, and an overwhelming sense of pride filled him.

"Here you go, Doctor," Mark said, a wide grin on his face. "He's perfect."

Dr. Alexander diapered and dressed the infant, then handed him to Mark.

"He is," he said. "I'm so happy to have been able to help."

"Gemma was terrified when labor started and the phones didn't work. Thank goodness you were home."

"I couldn't have been anywhere else," the doctor said. "Mrs. Alexander doesn't like it when I drive in the snow."

"Gemma is the same way. She worries."

"Well, she has too much to be happy about to worry now. Let's take the little guy over to her."

The doctor and Mark walked in companionable silence into the living room, handing the newly dressed infant to his mother. She lounged in her favorite spot on the couch, dressed in clean pajamas with her hair up in a neat bun.

"Hi, little guy," Gemma said, smiling as she kissed his forehead. The baby's face wrinkled and he let out a huge wail, startling Gemma.

"Sounds like he's hungry," Dr. Alexander said, showing her how to nurse him.

The baby latched after a few tries, his tiny fist resting against her chest. Gemma sighed, happiness filling her as her son nursed. She gazed down at the little boy, a soft smile lighting her face.

"You're a natural," Dr. Alexander said.

Gemma smiled up at him, radiant and full of joy, from her spot on the couch.

"Thank you for walking here in a storm to help us," she said, her eyes misty with tears. "I don't know what we would have done without you." She beckoned the doctor over to sit beside them on the couch. "I am so grateful for you."

"Have you chosen a name?" The doctor asked.

"We had chosen his first name a few weeks ago. This is Jacob," Gemma said, stroking his head as he nursed.

"Jacob Alexander," Mark added. "After the doctor who delivered him in the middle of a blizzard."

Tears welled in Dr. Alexander's eyes, and he clapped Mark on the shoulder.

"That is the biggest honor of my life," he said, smiling at the new family before him.

WHERE THE WILD ROSES GROW

EMILY JONES

J visited the garden for the first time on Christmas Eve- a time long before I could remember and long before I could walk alone. Not my own experience as such, nor my own memories- but a story pieced together by my mother's stories and lingering nostalgia. Glimpses of staring at the sky from a metal framed stroller as she pushed until the path narrowed, then held me above the thorns and the ice in her arms.

We called it the garden but really the meadow of wild roses sprawled like an ocean before Whatever name it took over the years fell somewhere in between habit and the unknown- it became our secret and therefore better off nameless. One of those few and far between places known only to the small few that stumbled upon it, even having known the hills their entire lives.

It could be found nestled in the grounds of a crumbling manor house, allegedly destroyed during the war. The house, long since decayed and ruined by time and snow, stood before the meadow, giving way to a more inviolable architecture, evergreen trees and winter roses that persisted against the cold. The hills surrounding the manor had once separated it from the village, the rich from the poor. Now they provided enough protection for the garden to lie untouched- so much so that it was never discovered by travellers or those hungry for photographs- the classic small town English Christmas card. We kept it safely away from those who cared about it far less for it than we did.

To us, the meadow represented tradition- something passed down through generations. How my mother found it I never knew. I always guessed she discovered it through her mother, who had learned from her mother and so on. In the way that every child sees their back garden as the world, and their village as a universe- the rose garden and the stories that came with it were my reality, thus what I thought existed to everyone.

As a toddler, I learned how to walk down those dirt tracks, one fawning step after another, my mother or father bundled in sweaters clappin mitten clad hands when I reached them. Though at first the roses felt like canyon walls towering on either side of me and the trees felt like mountains in the distance, it always felt like a home away from home.

It became our routine every December, come rain or snow or shine to make our way to the garden to pick holly leaves and pine to weave wreaths from willow branches stolen from the boughs that hung over the river.

My father begrudgingly carried along a basket of left overs with us on Boxing day. We'd sit, huddled under one big blanket, savouring the last bites of turkey and the sweets that always found their way into my stocking.

MORE CHRISTMASES WENT BY. I started school and our visits to the garden became less frequent.

Still, whenever we could, we'd walk out in the evenings-my mother laughing to herself when I lost my way in what felt like a maze. If ever I strayed too far or pricked my fingers and started to cry, she would run from wherever she was sitting and sweep me into her arms once more, tucking a fresh flower (carefully stripped of its thorns) behind my ear.

At first, I loved the pink petals best. Once the tears had gone as quickly as they'd come, she'd set me down and leave me to play until I was exhausted enough that she had to carry me home, curled over her shoulder and humming into her overcoat.

If the flowers in my hair wilted or died, the tears would come thick and fast again, especially if my father made me take them off before bed. She taught me to press the flowers between two dictionaries that otherwise resided in the attic— books I'd never seen used for anything else.

She taught me many things in the meadow; how to braid my hair and tie my own laces, how to ride a bike without stabilisers and swim in the river that ran through the fields north of the ruins.

As I got older, a map of the abandoned grounds (everything from the river to the ruins themselves) became muscle memory. My mother could sit and read for hours while I ran around and around— pretending to be a faerie queen. The roses became my subject and the meadow my kingdom. As the games I fabricated became ever more complicated, saplings growing near the creek became woodland nymphs running from a River Monster. I ran with them.

One lazy afternoon, lying across her lap, she read me the story of Artemis. For the next few weeks I became her-battling my way through legend with a bow and arrow carved from a curved branch and wool I stole from the sewing kit. The following afternoon, out of breath from running myself ragged and spread eagled in the grass, I asked my mother what it would be like if we owned all of this land... to build a house even bigger and grander than the old manor and have the grounds all to ourselves.

She just smiled, neatening my hair where it was wild and tangled, picking out the pieces of autumn leaves.

"What we do already", she replied simply. 'Swim in the creek, read in the rose garden, hike in the fields'.

She called it the rose garden. The name felt like an imposition more than anything.A proper name did not suit the tumbling weeds and wildflowers.

In later times, while we still went every Christmas, my mother preferred to stay in the warm and I ventured out to the meadow on my own. I grew to love reading in the very same spots she did. The habit of heading to the garden after school to lie on the grass or perch on a tree branch with a good book became my routine The flowers we'd pressed all those years ago, and the ones we'd done days ago if we remembered, became bookmarks nestled in the pages of whatever had taken my fancy that day.

I visited the world in those pages. I went to the deserts of Africa and the rainforests of South America. I soared above the clouds and floated across space. I swam deep in the ocean and fought in mythical battles. I fell in love with a thousand different characters- soared when they soared, cried when they cried- all from a grassy bank and the sprawling mosaic of roses.

My favourite books, the Atlases, brought me all over the world. I adored the glossy photographs and poured over the information about animals and cultures I could hardly imagine with absolute awe.

They were reserved for the adults section in the town library and I only managed to wrangle them away because the librarian would look at me with a toothy smile.

"*You're my favourite customer.*" She would say.

"*And just because I know you would* never *harm a book,*" as she stamped the date in the cover.

I threw myself into the words of traditions all over the world but mythology always remained my favourite. Nothing absorbed me more than when I fought alongside Odysseus and Thesus in the tombs I found, dusty and yellowing in a forgotten corner of the book store. My favourite stories seemed to be the ones everyone else had forgotten.

As a teenager, a strange nostalgia came over me, of being perched on a fallen tree plucking the dried parchment rose from my book in the garden that it came from. I felt as though my life were a novel, written as a story, the number of pages behind me growing.

I felt trapped in a strange limbo, much too old and much too young at the same time. The feeling that I'd been on this earth forever but not seen nearly enough of it; growing pains perhaps.

That summer- the Summer of in-betweens- I met a boy from the village. He went by Edward, or Wick to his friends for some reason I could never coax out of him. He had sandy hair always escaping whichever way his mother gelled it, and wore well ironed shirts and smart leather shoes. He did well in school, came from a nice family, and my mother had always liked him. He often came for dinner- the kind of boy that would talk about cars and politics with my father over the table and classic literature with my mother over dessert.

He's also the kind of boy that kisses my cheek and my forehead before I was ready for him to kiss my lips, the kind of boy that eats lunch with me as often as possible, even if his friends tease him for it. Wick embodied all that was kind and good and handsome.

So when he eventually, *finally* asked me out I said yes with a giddy smile and peck on his cheek.

He knocked on my door at lunchtime, clutching his hands together and making sure to shake hands with my father and bid a polite hello to my mother, even when she excitedly ushered us out the door with wrapped sandwiches and cookies still warm from the oven.

It took us until the end of the road- lined with blossoming apple trees not just yet in season- that we realised neither of us had planned what to do, too caught up in the newness of it all. I slid my hand into his and told him I knew a place. It was the first time I wished we'd named the rose garden, if only so I didn't seem so strange leading him through the fields with no tangible destination in mind.

When we reached the meadow, we sat on the fallen tree I'd favoured for years as a palace to perch and read or finish school work. We ate the sandwiches and the cookies and we drank lemonade he'd managed to swipe from the cellar. I told him about the different colours and types of roses, something I knew from a bored, rainy afternoon where I found one of my Grandma's old botany books and made it my mission to learn all the different species. Though I got the feeling he wasn't really listening, I stopped minding when he leant in, tasting chocolate chips and sugar.

Being so completely enamoured with a person felt strange; like nothing I'd ever experienced before— the newness and excitement of being in love for the first time. We were determined to spend every possible moment together.

Wickalways preferred to be indoors, so rather than spending time at the old ruins we sat, curled up on his sofa together (the nice kind with ornate legs that we could never afford) and read until we fell asleep, or watched cartoons on the old, stuttering television that my mother said would kill our eyes.

I liked the kissing best though. He always gave me a peck on the cheek before he walked me to school. A proper press full on the lips when I did well on an exam or helped him with an essay. Slow, thorough kisses for hours on end when my parents or his were away and we told them we were just planning to study.

Sometimes, when the clouds cleared, the rain stopped and I could convince him, we'd make the long walk to the rose garden carrying water or lemonade, just like that first time, and spend the afternoon tumbling around in the grass where no one would bother us — so caught up in adoration that we probably wouldn't have noticed if someone did.

The year proved to be one of many firsts. That Christmas, the village held a Fayre in the centre. For the first time a tree was towed in from the woods to stand tall and proud in the square.

At the church service the very same evening it'd been decorated, the Vicar handed around little wooden stars and pens, telling the kids to write their very own Christmas wishes and hang them on the tree. Wick and I drew our names into one, and not for the first time I wished that we would never end.

The second summer came, the summer before the rest of our lives. Wick stayed to learn his father's business. A small fortune waited for him and years more of study waited for me — not that I resented him for it. I felt lucky to have a warm house with a white picket fence and a pretty trellis, parents who provided for me and fields and woodland that could keep any kid occupied for years. But I grew up, and my home, while it would always be my home, was beginning to be stifling. I loved Wick but my claustrophobia, as well as the excitement and properly starting my life far outweighed the distractions of young love.

When I asked him to talk, I took him to the one place I knew would give me the courage to finish things. The walk over the hills, through the ruins, and out into the meadow went by easily, but far too quickly. We talked and laughed and held hands just as well as we always did, I pointed out the little dancing birds and wildflowers and he nodded along just as he always did.

For a minute, I doubted myself. I questioned if I could really let him go.

I remembered all those afternoons spent pouring over books on the grass, frantically writing by the last drefs of sunlight to finish essays and applications. I remembered my mother crying when we got the acceptance form, my father's hand on my shoulder and so much pride in his eyes. I remember being a little girl, coming here and playing a character I'd only ever read about in books. Books I wanted to write, characters I'd always wanted to create. I needed to do the right thing.

I knew too many women, my mother included, who had let love get in the way.

I didn't resent them from it, nor did I ever judge them for it. I just thought that it was perhaps the reason my mother gave me books instead of dolls for Christmas. She'd always wanted me to go to university and I'd always wanted to write, so that's what I was going to do.

Perhaps it was her presence in this place, the walks we took together so many times that reassured me. When we reached the roses, we were honest with each other — we never were people to sugar coat things. That beautiful place where I'd known happiness and youth and stress and sorrow would now be the place where I first knew heartbreak.

We talked, we understood, we cried. The tears were good. Tears meant that it was all worth something- and to me, loving him meant feeling like there was more to life than school, chores and the little village I'd hardly ever been away from. It isn't that he wasn't enough, it's that I was too much. I was too much for the neat hedgerows and cobblestoned streets.

Once our tears dried, and our last kisses were shared, he told me he remembered the story about the pressed roses, and the two big dictionaries gathering dust on a shelf in the kitchen. He picked one and asked me to save it.

When I got home that evening, bone tired and emotionally exhausted my mother wrapped me in a hug and helped me press the flower just as we used to- I used it as a bookmark just as always- until the petals fell and turning the pages crumbled the stem- lost, but not quite in the same way Wick was.

He was my first love. But the nature of first is that there is always a second, something has to come after for there to be a before. Firsts are always bittersweet.

FOR THE NEXT FEW DAYS, packing my room felt euphoric and terrifying all at the same time. The village may have been stifling, but it was pretty, my family were there and it was the only home I'd ever known. Women there tended to grow up, get married and stay there for the rest of their lives. University was for the rich —the people that live in the big manor houses beyond the terraced village centre, past the fields and forest that make up their sprawling estates. I worked hard enough, I think, stacking the countless paperbacks I poured over for years in boxes my mother got from the grocers. I deserved my chance.

Money was tight, just as it always had been, but with the scholarship, a job lined up on campus and a little money saved we'd make it. We always did. I told my parents that I'd write to them every week.

Though my mother was terrified of me being so far away, she knew it was all I ever wanted (it was all she'd ever wanted for me too). My father boasted to all his friends at work about his *"smart as hell daughter with a fine as hell scholarship to a prestigious as hell university"*. They were both so proud it didn't matter that it scared us.

The car journey was quiet, and I could see my parents' clasped hands over the gear shift, tightening as we got closer, my shoe tapped in the footwell with excitement and I chose the middle seat in the car so I could see the dorm building as soon as it appeared ahead.

After hours upon hours it did — big and scary and my new home.

Between the three of us my boxes don't take too long to unpack- part of me wanted to find something nestled away in the trunk to bring upstairs, or to realise I've forgotten something vital and to know I'd see them again in a few hours. It was not so much the leaving that scared me, it was the not knowing. After double and triple checking I'd brought up absolutely everything from the car they still had to leave and I still had to move on.

Of course there were tears when I walked away, from both of them, to my surprise. My father has never been one to cry, but he wrapped his arms around me then and told me he was proud, all while my shoulder dampened a little.

I told myself I'd only use a cafe job as a means to pay for

my classes, but I found it worked perfectly for a cushion of cash I'd never had before. Alongside my articles, short stories (freelance work the papers paid for in cash) and the novel that sat unfinished on my nightstand, I had tried to write a Christmas love story. Next, a thrilling mystery then a horror and back to romance again — but my words fell flat on the page. I could never conjure a world like the authors I'd read as a child.

So I never gave up, but I waited. I waitressed for the meantime to pay the bills. Business was better than good, and when the owners moved from the flat above the shop to a terraced house in town, I moved in. It was a small, cosy apartment with peeling wallpaper and a few creaky floorboards but nothing fresh paint and a rug wouldn't fix.

I even managed to make it home for Christmas that year, on the promise to myself that I'd write plenty over the holiday. I was determined to be published one day.

Sometimes, when my deadlines loomed ever closer or the words simply wouldn't come to mind I picked up my favourite notebook— a heavy, blue leather bound paper (a gift from my father) and walked to the rose garden — still so familiar after all these years away. My words flowed far easier there, not to mention inspiration came naturally. I suppose absence really does make the heart grow fonder.

I stayed there, writing the afternoon away until I got too cold or the sun disappeared behind the old manor and I could no longer discern the colours of the roses, nor see the words on my page.

I left with a promise of a visit to the city soon and a far less tearful kiss on the cheek than the first time I'd made the journey. I felt that I was no longer leaving home, just returning to a different one.

A few days after taking down the Christmas tree in the

cafe window and boxing up the lights (as well as practising the new recipes with mince pies and gingerbread no longer an option for the counter) my eyes were pulled from the book I'd been lost in by the silver bell chiming tauntingly above the door.

It was a short enough time after Christmas (the time when the kids go back to school and we lose the business of little boys sneaking in to buy sweets before their mothers notice) and purse strings are too tight to waste on cakes. I was surprised to see a man, around my age with snow in his dark, curly hair and cheeks rosy from the cold take a seat in the window and pull out books from a fraying messenger bag slung on the chair opposite like he planned on staying a while.

"Can I get you anything?" I asked, my voice quiet from being silent so long.

When he looked up at me, wide blue eyes and unruly curls I was suddenly quite glad I'm the only waitress working the quiet Friday.

"What would you recommend?" He asked, looking up with wide green eyes.

"We're short this weekend so I made the apple pie. Not to boast but it's the best thing up there," I grinned.

"Then that please," he smiled.

I set it on one of the little china plates and a vase of drinking water.

"If you need anything at all I'll be behind the counter or in the kitchen." I stammered, smoothing my apron at my waist, tying and retying the knot as he ate.

Perhaps my flushed cheeks and fiddling hands were because he was the only customer in a few hours, or perhaps they're because of those wide eyes and the way he pushes his glasses up every few seconds.

"Haven't seen you around before," he broke the silence with a timid smile.

"Christmas is the busiest time of year- I've been sequestered behind this counter for the past few months."

"Do you teach at the university?" I ask eventually, only feeling a little bad for keeping him from the pile of essays I saw stacked to the side.

"No," he says wistfully. "Maybe one day. For now I teach literature at the Upper school." He never made a move to leave, even if he had somewhere to be, nor did he try to bring the conversation to a close. We chatted away the last hours of my shift — mainly about books, or the pictures. He begged me to read my work when I told him I was a writer (as well as an aspiring novelist) but I brushed him off with a laugh and insisted that we've only just met.

It was nice. I'd forgotten what it was like to talk about things other than school or work. Forgotten what it was like to exchange casual touches and glances across a cafe table. It was the first time in a while I'd felt like I existed outside of my apartment and the notebooks filled with ideas I should be writing about.

That night I did, the character in my story introduced as a tall, intelligent man with beautiful blue eyes and dark curled hair I wanted to run my fingers through.

I nearly rolled my eyes at myself and the cliches I swore off ever writing, but it fit so perfectly with the story and for the first time in months, I went to sleep feeling like I was making progress.

After that day, he came in every Friday evening with the same smile, the same messenger bag and the same pile of essays to mark in the window seat, always asking which of the treats laid out behind the counter I made and ordering one specifically. We would end up talking when I took him his food — flirting in our casual, private way, laughing along with each other until I remembered there are other customers to serve — he got me in trouble more than once and apologised by buying me a cake or tipping a little better than usual.

One quiet Monday night, he hung back while I closed up, helping to wipe down the counter and stack the chairs on the side, a job that was far more enjoyable with his teasing and my laughter. He asked to walk me home and looked confused when I laughed again, going on to explain I only lived upstairs but he's sweet to offer. I made up for it with the suggestion we walk down to the school together the next morning. I was supposed to be running errands, errands that would be far more enjoyable with good company.

The school, which I was seeing up close for the very first time, was a beautiful, stone brick building that reminded me of what the manor back home might have looked like still standing. While I stared incredulously at the high windows and ornate ceilings of his office, I asked why he didn't do his mark ups here. The light was stunning and the chairs looked far more comfortable than the cafe stools.

"I only really come in for the pretty waitress," he looked at me with a crooked grin and just the right amount of bashfulness in his gaze that I could''t quite help surging forward and pressing a kiss to his mouth. He was bright red when I pulled away and mumbled something about me 'getting him fired,' glancing outside his office before carefully pulling the door closed and kissing me again, one hand on my waist, one in my hair.

I thought everyone kissed the same- that it was just a routine thing humans knew how to do automatically. He was so different from anyone else, the way he pulled me closer to him, the way he tasted of coffee instead of sweetness- the scent of nicotine, cologne and something like libraries curled beneath my hands in his shirt.

AFTER A FEW MONTHS I let him read my work, at first only a feature I'd done for the paper, then the publications for bigger magazines in the city until finally he flipped through the first chapters of my book. My heart between his fingers while I looked through his lesson plans.

My favourite nights were the ones when we curled up on the sofa, Tv and dinner forgotten in favor of arguing over the ideas behind the books he chose for his students or he'd hand me my printed pages with pencil marks dancing across the paper — always a little heart drawn at the bottom of his revisions. He marked while I wrote, or read while I baked.

After finally finishing the my meagre pages, he slammed the manuscript on my lap. I looked up with a laugh.

"You have to finish this because I need to know it's going to end because you can't possibly leave me high and dry like this."

I grinned and pulled him down next to me.

He wrapped his arms around me and pulled me against his shoulder, whispering "You're going to finish it, you're going to get it published and it's going to be amazing."

I laughed at him off. Just like that first time we met though, he inspired me to write.

I thought if I ever settled with another man I'd think about Wick more, worried I'd compare them or feel bad for moving on. Either that or I'd feel the other way around and regret the boy I'd loved before. When we talked about our first kisses and first loves and fumbled first times, I realised that I didn't regret anything, but that didn't mean I should hold on to it either.

It was far easier to fall in love with him than I would've thought.

We first told each other a snowy evening with the fire lit. He stumbled from the storage room with the stepladder and bullied it into place to finally set the star atop the Christmas Tree.It was messy, not at all perfect with mismatched plastic baubles he'd had left over from decorating his classroom.

"THIS IS WHY I LOVE YOU," he says as I brought in a batch of gingerbread from the kitchen, eyes widening as soon as the words slipped out.

It was by no means a shining Hollywood moment that you'd see in the movies. It became part of our routine, replacing goodnights, goodbyes and see you laters.

By Christmas, my first draft was finished and I took him home to meet my family. He came from the same kind of money I did and it was comforting to know he'd worked just as hard as I had to be where we were. My parents liked him (which I always knew they would). He kissed my mother's hand, clapped my father on the back and helped them clear up after dinner. Just like that, they were smiling proudly and adoring over his teaching stories.

I couldn't have been happier.

On Christmas Eve, when he told me he was going to bed with a kiss on the cheek and a brush of his hands over my shoulders. I stayed up drinking wine with my mother.

She looked at me softly, rubbing my shoulder and says 'You've done well, making something of your life.You've built something incredible'

I couldn't do anything but smile.

Later, when I climbed the stairs and crawled into bed, he stirred and threw his arm over my waist, smiling sleepily against my side, I thought, yeah I have.

A few days after Christmas, when he asked to see my old childhood haunts, there was only one place I wanted to take him. We packed up a few leftover slices of Christmas cake and walked arm in arm through the fields, pulling each other closer whenever there was a sharp, cold burst of wind.

This time around, the man sitting next to me on the fallen tree, picking at fondant and gazing across the meadow hung onto my every word when I told him the stories of my mother showing me the garden, playin faeries in the grass and coming here for Christmas.

When I told him of the time I fell in the creek and scraped my knee on the shingle he pokes my leg.

"Did it scar?" He asked, to which I pulled the bottom of my dress to reveal the white crescents right under my knee.

When I told him about coming out one afternoon to try and pick a rose of every colour, he looked across the garden with an unreadable expression.

"We'll do that one day," he promised.

He was completely enamored with the place. On his insistence we visited every day afterwards, at least until the time came to go home.

Where that was shifted when we were reading down by the creek on New Years Eve. He propped himself up on his elbows and looked me dead in the eye.

"Will you move in with me?" He asked.

It wasn't even a question to me.

The time came to say goodbye to the cafe and the apartment over it. The apartment that had been my first beautiful experience of independence. My home, for a while at least.

EMILY JONES

The ending to it all was so sad that I had to clutch at his waist to leave after my last shift at the cafe.

I chose to see it as a new beginning. It was sad, but the sight of my boxes in his living room and the desk he'd built for me in the spare bedroom far makes up for it. He was worth all the goodbyes. He might've just been my favourite beginning.

I thought things might change when I moved in. While we do fight over the silly things a little more often, we spent our days the same; reading, writing and talking.

Over the summer holidays he edited my second draft. I'd worried he was working too much.

"You have all those lesson plans to write".He'd brushed me off with a kiss in the cheek — reaching around my waist to steal the manuscript sitting on the counter, claiming that *'editing is what he's best at.'*

Autumn leaves lined the streets and a chill was creeping into the air when I finished my final draft- a love story of epic proportions.

Or at least that's what he called it when he finished it with tears in his eyes on a crisp Sunday morning. He had a friend from University that worked for a very successful publisher. I mailed the typed up manuscript with fair skepticism but the letter that came back had words like 'advance' and 'distribution' and 'print for Christmas' all over it.

He snatched it out of my hands when I finished reading and twirled me around the kitchen grinning like a madman.

He set me down and told me to "Close my eyes and *stay there.*"

A few minutes later, there was something square and velvety being pressed into my hands. My eyes flew open to see a perfect, shining silver ring.

I looked up at him with tears in my eyes.

"I asked your parents permission at Christmas but could never quite work up the courage," he rubbed the back of his neck. "Now just seemed like the perfect time."

I nodded tearfully and wrapped my arms around his neck, clinging onto the ring for dear life.

"Will you marry me?"

"Yes you idiot! Wasn't it obvious?"

WE WERE married six months later in December, back in the flintstone church a street away from home. Confetti and the light from christmas trees shining through village windows paved our way home.

I could see his lip trembling when I walked down the aisle, my father clutching my arm and my mother's wedding dress flowing behind me. What they didn't know was that he'd snuck into my bedroom half an hour ago, kissed my hurriedly and pressed a bouquet of roses he'd picked from the meadow into my arms, darting away before my mother could catch him — superstition and bad luck be damned

The book paid for a honeymoon to Paris, New Year's, no less. Decorations still lined the streets — far more extravagant than anything I'd seen before; lights wrapped around every streetlamp and towering trees adorning every storefront. From my husband's unwavering grin in the car from the docks to the hotel, to the constant clicking of a film camera his mother had gifted us I could tell he was as excited as me.

Even the suite was beautiful, silk sheets of a blue so deep it's nearly black and shining floors, a balcony that looked over cream terraced houses and a market below. I could smell the bread and something like marzipan from the window.

In the evening the noises from revellers and holiday

makers drifted through the glass with the chorus of the city: cars, people and a million souls doing a million different things.

OUR WORDS BECAME part of that chorus. I'd written about the history of Paris and its occupation (which to the people around us- wasn't quite history yet) but none of the newspaper clippings or artwork I'd researched in the library compared to the city alive and thrumming beneath my feet. Instead of words on a page or a picture in a book looked over in dip light, instead of something I'd only ever imagined it is real — tangible before me and mine for the taking. All those places I'd read about from the rose garden — all those stories, all my dreams of publishing, of falling in love, of living my life- they were finally becoming real.

We lay in bed one morning, curled around each other as the sun shone a little brighter off the snow. He turned to me.

"Where do you want home to be when we get back?" He asked, hand drifting across my abdomen.

"Where I come from," I whispered honestly. "Where I love".

He smiled, and I knew where home was.

THROUGH FIRST LOVES to last loves, the garden remained. It seems only fitting that my daughter — dark haired like her father and kind like her grandma (clever as her mother, my sanity be damned) dances through the very same meadow four years later. Skin snow white against the snow and the roses red as holly berries. The new ribbons she'd found under the tree on Christmas Eve trailing behind her, the baubles in her hair jingling with every step.

She whips her head around at every ring — determined it's Santa flying overhead — leaving my husband to tousle her ponytail, setting them jingling all over again. When the sky starts to darken and we all start to feel the cold, he swoops her over his shoulder and wraps his spare arm around me.

The tree in the square of the village lights just as we're approaching- the timer setting off with a ding that wakes my sleeping girl with a start.

"Honey-" I whisper, handing her a cardboard star I've been keeping in my pocket. "Make a wish."

She huddles over her star as she writes, my husband's arms wrapping around me from behind when she waddles up to the tree and hangs it from the highest branch she can.

"Go ahead," I whisper to them, lingering a little longer.

I bring a rose from my pocket, holly berry red against the pine and nestle it in the branches. There's no need to read the star. We have all the time in the world to provide her with everything she could ever want. The next morning, she'll fly into the bedroom at 6:30 sharp, burrowing between us to escape the crispness of the air. Shouting 'Mummy, Mummy, Mummy Santa's been.' Later, we'll eat roast chicken and potatoes. I never could get quite as good as my mother's. I'll unwrap a fresh leatherbound notebook from my husband and kiss him when no one's watching. I'll watch firelight dance across his face in such a way that makes him look younger, but look beautifully forward to growing older, here in the village where the wild roses grow.

DAYS GONE BY

R.A. GERRITSE

PAST JOY

*D*ebrah stood by the window and looked at the dark clouds that painted this already melancholy holiday in a dreadful gradient of gray. She rubbed her aching hands, absently turning the dented and worn golden ring on her wrinkled finger and shivered. Despite the cozy warmth inside the house, she could feel the chill outside by just looking at the tragically depressing scene—December twenty-third, and still not a flake of snow in sight.

Nothing but mud, bare trees, and dreadfulness, she thought, stretching — carefully turning her sore neck to relieve her tense muscles.

"Better get to work, old woman. That tree won't decorate itself," she chided herself with a smile, and turned to slowly make her way to the kitchen. "But first, some nourishment and holiday cheer. Cannot decorate a tree without cheer, now can we, Mr. Sandals?"

The fat black cat looked up but briefly, then laid his head back down on the mantle of the fireplace with a lazy meow—

sticking out his hind paws with the characteristic white lines that got him his name, basking in the warmth of the flames. Debrah couldn't help laughing.

"No, no, please do take it easy, I insist. Let me take care of everything."

A little under ten minutes later, she sat in her favorite leather reading chair in front of the large tree in the living room with a steaming cup of cocoa and marshmallows in hand, gathering courage. As she gave the distribution of the glittering strings of twinkle lights in the otherwise still bare tree a final inspection, she breathed in the smell of pine, mixed with the scent of her cocoa, and let it warm her. As much as it took out of her, Debrah never dreaded the task before her—on the contrary. This yearly ritual had grown to be one of her favorite holiday traditions. Still, as the years accumulated, and with it, the memories, even this most wonderful of activities started to take an increasingly heavy toll on her emotions.

"The price of past joy," Debrah sighed. With the lights aligned as perfectly as they would ever be and all out of excuses, she put down her mug on the side table, right next to the box of tissues and her weathered copy of Dickens' *A Christmas Carol*.

She slowly bent, taking the first old candy-striped hat box full of ornaments, pulling it onto her lap and lifting the lid. Gently she reached into the tangle of crumpled white wrapping inside, took out the first of her treasured ornaments, and carefully unwrapped it—her eyes already moist before the paper touched the floor, as the memories the little item held flooded in.

ECHOES OF SUMMER

DEBRAH SAT at the lakeshore grumbling as she threw another pebble onto the water. It bounced but twice, then sank— such an excellent metaphor for her summer holiday. She looked across the water in disgust to her annual prison, situated on the other bank.

I loathe this place, she thought. The rustic Banks family lakehouse could not be further from civilization. After over a decade of vivid memories of spending her summers here, she knew every single square inch of the surrounding woods and mountain trails by heart. They held no more mysteries to her, but nor could they offer her any more adventures.

She turned nineteen this year and dreamed much bigger dreams than the naive kid she used to be — a dreamer who still saw wonder in everything and loved wasting a summer in a place even the sun had trouble penetrating.

"I wonder when I misplaced those pink glasses," she whispered, immediately feeling a pang of guilt at her dissatisfied train of thought.

Caprecia Lake and the surrounding woods held a type of beauty and serenity that couldn't be found anywhere else. But did they have to spend *every* summer here? Maybe things would have been different if she had any brothers or sisters, but as an only child, and a young adult at that, it was hard to hear the birdsong over the sound of the world calling to come and play.

"Is it too much to ask for a seaside holiday, or at the very least, a place with other people?" She blew the hair out of her face and sighed deeply. Overhead a flock of birds soared towards the distant horizon, filling her with a wistful longing.

"I don't know. Are you certain you've looked for any here?" A calm male voice spoke behind Debrah. 'Startled to find out that she was not alone and suddenly afraid, she spun on her heels, lost her balance, and with a yelp, tipped backward into the lake. "Ooooh... I'm so sorry about that — I didn't mean to frighten you!" the stranger exclaimed, hurrying over to help her out of the water.

Looking up at her rescuer as he towered over her with an outstretched hand, she felt her fright inexplicably evaporate. Standing at least a solid 6"2, probably around her age, with dark curly hair and unsuccessfully trying to hide an embarrassed but wide grin, he radiated a sincere friendliness — which struck Debrah as odd.

Keep it together, Deb, she thought as she took his hand and got to her feet. *Stop eyeballing the friendly heartthrob giant that just caused you to soak your clothes.* But it was hard to stop looking.

"Where the hell did you come from," she said, a little too hostile, and winced at the unintended ferocity in her words. "And how long have you been spying on me?" she added, a little more insecure.

At that, the stranger stepped back and held up his hands in a comforting gesture, his cheeks flushed. "Spying? Uhm. I wasn't... This situation *so* did not play out as I intended," he said. "I'm sorry. My stupid sense of humor will one day be the death of me. Let's start over, shall we? My name is Josh. My parents and I are camping just about a mile..." He stared in eastern direction. "That way. I just happened upon this lake while checking out the neighborhood and heard you talking to yourself. I just wanted to say hi."

Debrah stared at him and shivered through her soaking wet clothes. "Well, eh. Hi, I guess. I'd love to say nice to meet you, but it wouldn't be the full truth right now. I must look like a drowned kitten."

"I truly am sorry," Josh said. "At least it wasn't seawater..."

Debrah gave him a death stare. "Not funny."

"I know, sorry. I'm worse when I get nervous." He rubbed his forehead as if trying to find the right words to diffuse the situation he caused, and it looked adorable.

"You apologize a lot, don't you?"

"I do. At least, I do if I'm in the wrong."

"It's fine," Debrah said. "You're forgiven. I am known to be clumsy." Distracted, she wrapped her arms around herself in a futile attempt to get warmer.

"You must be freezing. Hold on." He unbuttoned and took off his tweed shirt, revealing a suspiciously tight-fitting white t-shirt underneath, accentuating his uncomfortably masculine body. Debrah felt herself turn red, but luckily, Josh did not seem to notice. "Here. Put this on. Are you camping around here as well?"

"T-thank you," Debrah stuttered, unsure if the cold, or the absurdity of the whole situation caused it. "And no. I am not camping. We have a house here." She pointed to the other end of the lake.

"Would you mind if I walked you home? I feel it's the least I can do."

She looked at him and considered, but only for a moment. Something about this boy made him more likable than a stranger in the woods had any right to be — a sincere kindness in those brown eyes that dismantled all her defenses. *I hope I am not going to regret this.*

"Sure," she said. "It would indeed be the least you could do. Bonus points for the shirt, though. Thanks." She gave him an insecure smile and felt her cheeks burn. "You can call me Deb. Debrah. My friends call me Deb."

"Wonderful to meet you, Deb. Now, let's get you warm and dry, shall we? Lead the way."

DEBRAH STILL REMEMBERED everything about that summer, now almost fifty-five years ago — annotated and in full color. She could still picture her father's distrusting look as Josh brought her home, and how quickly Josh had won him over by simply being... Well, Josh. She fondly remembered the following days in which she got to know him better, as her mother invited Josh and his parents over for dinner and drinks. She'd never forget the blossoming friendship, the warmth, and the laughter of that summer, nor the eventual passion it birthed. *A bittersweet reflection,* she thought, wiping her eyes, for it was also the last summer she and her mother got to spend with her Dad. Cancer unexpectedly claimed him later that year.

"I'm glad you got to meet him, Dad. And that you liked him." Debrah smiled through her tears, as she held the seashell Josh had gifted her that September. He'd told her that it symbolized the marvels hidden in plain sight, the wonder in the mundane, and the miracle of imagination.

"Keep it to your ears, and you can hear the echoes of Summer," he'd said. "You don't need to be at the ocean to hear it, Deb. Just like I only need to think of you to see your smile and feel it warm my heart."

She got up and placed the shell in the tree and smiled. "One ornament up, a few boxes to go. I fear I might be turning too emotional with my old age to be doing this alone, Mr. Sandals. What do you think?"

The cat sat under the tree, mesmerized by the lights.

"You're right. Better get a move on." She walked back to

her chair, breathed deep, and took the next wrapped ornament from the box.

SHADES OF PINE

THE WINDS HAD TURNED, and with it came a chill that pierced both walls and hearts. A shadow had fallen over the Banks family as Debrah and her mother mourned. The death of her father felt surreal. Her last memory of him, in his Sunday suit, laying in that pine casket, still haunted her. Meanwhile, the house felt too quiet in his absence, as if it waited silently for his return. The transience of life, like the cruelty of winter that year, struck mercilessly.

Debrah sat in the living room, staring at a chemistry book, but her thoughts drifted. From the corner of her eye, she watched her Mom, sitting in her reading chair, absently staring out the window.

Ever since her father passed, Debrah buried herself in her studies and spent as much time as she could with Josh, whenever her classes allowed — anything to distract from the helplessness she felt. Still, she worried over her mother, who now had no one left but Debrah.

Her father's sickbed had been a short and traumatic one, and it had left them with little time for goodbyes. *Could there ever be such a thing as enough time?* she wondered.

With that thought came unexpected clarity. *No. There would never have been such a thing as enough time. And I'm wasting the time I have left with Mom, too.*

Debrah closed her book, grabbed a notebook and pen, and started writing. She saw her mother struggling and felt her happy childhood slipping. As a writer, she knew where that road led — she could not watch that happen. Not this close to the holidays. Somehow she knew that if they allowed this darkness to pull them under it would damage them beyond repair, and so she wrote. When she finished, she walked over to the piano, opened the lid, and sat down, placing her hands on the keys.

For a moment, she just sat, eyes closed, contemplating in silence. It had been a long time since she'd played, but somehow the melody she sought to express her words wove itself together in her thoughts. Before she opened her eyes, her fingers had already started moving as if by their own volition. It startled her mother out of her silent reverie — she turned her full attention to Debrah, nodding to the melody, and gave a sad smile as Debrah started singing.

> *"Each holiday, this feeling comes again.*
> *Every gathering, each celebration,*
> *My thoughts just drift away.*
> *However great things are,*
> *They're not the same*
> *As in most cherished memories,*
> *Spent with those not here today.*
> *Seeking a smile*
> *In days gone by*
> *It dawns that*
> *There are others by my side.*
> *Everyone has stories,*
> *No one is spared in life.*
> *Tell me about your lost ones,*
> *And I'll tell you about those who left my path.*
>
> *Let's sing a song for the fallen ones*
> *For the loved ones that we've lost,*

For the lost ones, never found again.
For lovers left behind and absent friends.
Let's raise our glass to the missing ones,
And make a toast to all the those people,
Who got us here, but can no longer see
Who we are,
How our lives turned out to be."

At those last words, Debrah hit a false note, and her voice faltered, as tears welled up in her.

"Oh, honey. That was beautiful," Mom said. "Did you...just write that?" She had a hand on her heart, and tears fell from her eyes.

"Y-yeah. I did. There's more to it," she stammered, trying to suppress her flailing emotions. "If you give me a minute, I can probably..." Before Debrah could finish that sentence, her mother had gotten up from her chair and wrapped her in a firm but silent embrace. At that, Debrah's floodgates opened, and she released all her pent up pain, anger, and frustration in a river of tears.

After what seemed an eternity, long after the tears ran dry, her mother let her go and looked at Debrah with so much love and pride, it made her choke up all over again. "You seem in some serious need of cocoa. I must say, I believe that I can use a cup as well. Marshmallows?"

Debrah smiled. "Wonderful idea, mom. Yes, please."

She was still drying her eyes when the doorbell rang.

"Can you get that, honey?" she heard her mother calling.

"Sure, mom," she said, and hurried to answer. To her surprise, it was Josh — completely unplanned and unexpected, and for a moment, she could only stare at him.

He must have noticed, for he grinned and spread his arms.

"Surprise!" he said. "I felt like you could use some quality time with me, and cleared my week for y…"

Debrah smothered him in an embrace, and started crying all over again.

"Well, seems like I was right," Josh whispered, and kissed her neck, then tightened his arms around her.

"Josh?" her mother's surprised voice sounded, seemingly far in the distance. "Guess we're going to need a third cup."

Roughly an hour later, Debrah and Josh walked arm in arm through Crawford Forest, the little patch of green a minute walk from the house, and talked about everything. About her feelings, her worries, her song.

He's such a good listener, she thought as she looked at him and for the first time fully realized how much she loved him.

"I'm glad I came", Josh said. "You can use some happy thoughts and pleasant distraction."

"You don't know half how welcome that distraction is", Debrah said, and stopped to pick up a pinecone. She held it up and gestured with it at the trees, most of them bare. "It at times feels like my whole world is dying, Josh. And that's so hard to cope with. Dead trees, rotting leaves…"

Josh took the pinecone from her hand and turned it around., inspecting it. "I think you're looking at that a bit more bleakly than is warranted," he said, and nodded to the trees. "Yes, life is ever changing, but what you see is not death. It's merely the start of a new cycle. And yes, some things change to never return to what they were…" He handed her back the pinecone and wrapped her hands around it. "But we get to hold on to the memories."

❄

"It's your story, tell it proud. Sing it loud, sing it every-where — to anyone who wants to hear," Debrah sang softly, as she placed the pinecone in the tree, and grabbed another tissue. "I'm going to need a bigger box of those next year," she laughed through her tears.

But mostly, these are tears of joy.

MEMORIES ON STRINGS

"Josh had an idea," Debrah exclaimed. "And it's a great one!" Smiling, she took Josh's hands and squeezed them. It felt good to smile again, and mean it.

I love you, I love you, I love you, she thought. *And one of these days I'll probably tell you, too.*

"Well, spill it," her mother said. "You got me all curious and have my undivided attention. Don't stop there!"

"Right. Sorry, I got distracted."

"I can tell," her mother teased. "Maybe I'd better ask Josh directly, hmm?"

It felt great to spend Christmas together with the two of them. Debrah felt blessed that Josh's parents decided to go on a winter vacation in Europe by themselves this year, leaving Josh free to spend the holidays with her and her mother.

"Well, Josh?" Her mother said. "Maybe I need to go check on the roast, so you two can first find your words, eh?" She laughed. It felt good to see her laugh.

"Oh, sorry, Mrs. Banks," he said. "But it's your own fault, you know, for raising such a wonderful daughter."

"For the last time, young man, it's Joanna. None of that 'Mrs. Banks' nonsense, please."

R.A. GERRITSE

"Well, alright, Joanna. I was telling Debrah about a tradition we have in my family and she seemed to like it."

"Like? Adore!" Debrah said.

"It must be quite something, given her reaction," Mom said.

"It's a simple thing, really," Josh said, his cheeks flushing as he rubbed the back of his neck as if in search of words. "Whenever big events happen in our lives, or memorable things happen, or milestones are achieved, we always try to capture these memories, by choosing something — a little keepsake, a trinket, to remember the moment. Like... the tassel from my graduation cap. Or a lock of hair from my childhood dog. We use those to decorate our tree at Christmas."

"It's like memories on strings, Mom!" Debrah said. "And I love that! Can we start doing that too?"

"Memories on strings eh," Mom said. "I like that. We have plenty of those memories."

At that the room fell quiet for a few seconds. Debrah was the first to speak. "Yeah. Yeah we do. Pretty darned good ones too."

Her mother smiled again. "Let's do it. We can use a few new traditions."

And so they did. They spent the day gathering keepsakes from around the house, telling Josh about the memories they held, and putting them on strings. One of Dad's old baseball cards, symbolizing his endless love for the sport, and how much it used to annoy the women in his life. A fountain pen Mom had used to write her very first novel. Debrah's first toy harmonica, that sparked her love for music.

But Debrah and Josh also shared several items that were new to Mom, like the seashell, and the pinecone. They recounted their memories while Mother listened, and smiled, and smiled, and smiled.

When they ran out of stories and ideas for things to put in the tree, they sat by the hearth, each with a steaming cup of tea, and admired their work.

"That is indeed a wonderful tree," Mom said. "And a beautiful new tradition. But I've been thinking as well."

Both Debrah and Josh looked at her. "What's that, Mom?" Debrah said. "You sound serious."

"Nah," Mom said. "Nothing serious. I just want to make certain you're up for it. I wouldn't want to spoil such a perfect day." She put down her cup, and took Debrah's hands. "Do you remember the song you wrote a while back, and partly sang for me, the day of Josh's surprise visit?"

"Of course I do, Mom."

"What would you say we'd make that another new tradition. To sing that. For the ones not here."

Debrah smiled. Not a sad smile, this time either, but one that filled her with warmth and love. "I think that would be wonderful."

SOFTLY SINGING, Debrah unwrapped one ornament after another, smiling and crying with every memory — and before she knew it, the first box sat empty. "Two more to go, Mr. Sandals. Time for a refill." She picked up her mug, and the now empty box of tissues. "On both of these, I guess."

OF SNOW AND WARMTH

THE NEXT CHRISTMAS felt even happier for Debrah — it had been quite the year. As she and Josh drove from their home, a hundred-and-fifty-five miles upstate to spend Christmas day with Debrah's mother, she almost bounced in anticipation of the new memories she got to share with her Mom on the tree. She felt slightly guilty for once again stealing Josh from his family for the holidays, but after his parents had told her for the seventh time that it was okay as long as they got them for new years, she felt that weight drop off her shoulders.

"Aren't you the cheerful one today," Josh said as he turned down the music.

"Ain't I always?" she grinned at him. "That's why you love me, right?"

"That, and so much more, babe. Ooh, I love this song!" He turned the radio back up and started to sing along loudly with "Last Christmas."

Your voice will never be one of your strong points, I fear, Debrah thought, but couldn't help loving him for his musical enthusiasm, and joined in.

When they arrived at the house, Debrah's eyes lit up at the sight, for it had been decorated in thousands of little lights for the first time since she'd been a little girl. "How did she manage this by herself?" she whispered.

"Who said she did it by herself," Josh said and gave her a sly grin. "Remember I had to work late a few nights last week?"

She hit him, playfully. "You didn't! You drove all the way up here to do this? Why?"

"To make this the most perfect Christmas yet," he said, and kissed her. "He placed a loving hand on her belly. "We have some great news for 'grandma' after all.

"Is it possible to love you more?" She sighed, as she placed her hands over his.

That Christmas was filled with love and stories, with tears and smiles, and of course, many new memories to decorate the tree. Two joined golden rings, to symbolize Josh and Debrah's marriage that summer. A silver key to symbolize Mother's upcoming move to the lake house. Although there would be no more Christmases in the house in which Debrah grew up, she did not mind much, for she had a new home to build. Her mother's happiness mattered most, and if she were honest, having her mother over an hour's drive closer, felt good too.

"I saved the best for last," her mother said, just before Debrah wanted to drop their big news.

She swallowed it down and gave Josh a quick meaningful glance. "What's that, Mom?"

"I'm so thankful for the joy you two found together, and by extension, the happiness you bestowed on me. You have no idea how much these last two Christmases have meant to me."

"I think I do, Mom," Debrah said and sat next to her. "This means the world to us too."

"You two brought light and warmth back where there was none, and pulled me from my darkest times. John was the love of my life. Losing him, I thought, that's it for me. There goes my smile."

"Oh, Mom…" was all Debrah could say.

"But I was wrong. You two showed me that. So thank you." She pulled a little box from behind the couch, and handed it to Debrah. "This memory isn't just mine. It's ours. And as you were the catalyst, I'd like for you to do me the honor of first placing it in the tree."

With trembling fingers, Debrah unwrapped the box and took out a little snow globe which held a miniature of her childhood home — complete with Christmas decorations."

"There's a switch on the back," Mom said, and turned it on. The house lights illuminated, and the snow started to twirl inside the glass sphere. "May we have many more of these happy nights together, wherever we might meet."

"It's perfect, Mom," Debrah said, and walked to place it in the tree. "But you are wrong, though."

Her mother gave her a puzzled look. "You don't like it?"

"Oh, I love it. But it's not the best, nor the last." With that, she took a little envelope from her purse, and handed it to her mother, who took it while trembling, biting her lower lip, and looking at her with glassy eyes. Debrah smiled and nodded her on to open it.

Two sets of blue baby socks lay nestled inside.

DEBRAH HUNG the tiny socks in the tree and wondered where the years had gone.

Hard to believe that my boys ever fit into those. Her men, she should say, but in her heart of hearts, they'd always be her little boys. *They sure as heck acted like kids most of the time*, she thought to herself, and grinned.

As she pulled the next ornament from the box and recognized its shape, she shivered. "I'd better sit down for this one..."

LAST WISH

THEY STRUGGLED through the last Christmas Debrah got to spend with her mother. She remembered how she'd once wondered if one could ever have enough time to say goodbye

— her mother's last months became an endless goodbye. In the spring of that year, the doctors gave Joanna the diagnosis that tainted her last days. Although she never stopped fighting her disease, once the treatments failed to work, they faced an imminent truth: they needed to say goodbye.

In the following months, Debrah spent every spare moment at the lake house. She saw her mother deteriorate and suffer more with every passing day. It drove Debrah to try and make every single moment of every day the best it could possibly be. The stress of putting so much weight on everything did not help — it made things even less bearable. She knew that, and yet... what else could she do?

As they gathered around the tree that year to exchange their memories, it felt forced to Debrah. She felt the unsuppressable urge to keep her smile on for Mom. She felt the irrational need to make this loaded holiday a perfect future memory.

"Sit down, sweetheart. Please stop tiring yourself out," Mom said, for the dozenth time that night. "We're all fine. We've got our drinks, there are snacks on the table, please take it easy. You are stressing me out."

With a guilty smile, Debrah took a seat next to Josh, who gave Jonah a bottle. "I know," she said. "Sorry." She glanced over to the box, where Jake still lay sleeping ever so peacefully.

At that her mother grimaced. "She learned that from you, you know? That habit of endless apologies," she said, then broke into a coughing fit, waving off Debrah to stay seated. "I'm fine."

Debrah knew her mother tended to be stubborn. *At least I know where I got it from,* she thought wistfully. She found it so hard not to smother her Mother with well-meant care.

"So, what did you bring for the tree this year?" Mom said

when she'd finally gathered herself again. "I bet it's got something to do with those two little angels of mine again?"

"You're right about that, Mom," Josh said, and nodded to a little box on the table. "Can you get that for her, honey?" he asked Debrah. "I've kind of got my hands full at the moment."

As Mom unpacked the little box and smiled at the two pacifiers inside, she broke into another cough.

How I hate to see you like this, Mom, Debrah thought. *I hate to see you suffer.* It felt like the universe decided to play a cruel joke on them, after the way it took her father from them. *At least he didn't suffer long. I'd almost have wished the same for you.* She pushed down the immediate wave of guilt following the thought, for she knew it not to be true. Each moment with Mom felt like a gift. Tears welled up, and she made a lame excuse about having to check on something for dinner, hurrying from the room.

She snuck out to cry several times that weekend. She knew she'd need several times more. Deep down she felt both Josh and her mother probably knew as well.

When Debrah made it back to the living room, Josh held Jake, feeding him his bottle, and her mother had Jonah on her lap.

"Are you okay, Mom?" she asked.

"Wonderful," her mother said. "I'm surrounded by the ones I love most on this Earth," and gave her a happy smile, as she held her grandson. "Which brings me to my contribution to the tree. Could you get it, sweetheart? It's on my desk."

When Debrah returned with the small, but heavy, pinstriped box, her mother told her to open it. Inside she found a beautifully carved wooden heart, wearing a holly crown, and she almost melted.

"That," her mother said, "which will probably be the last memory I get to contribute to our tradition, is to remind you of the love we share. Don't ever let that light inside you fade, sweetheart. Keep those memories alive in your heart, and don't forget to let them out for air once a year to share them with your loved ones — your wonderful husband, and those two darling angels of yours, by the tree. That way, you will never lose us, me and your father. Whatever darkness life may bring."

THERE WOULD NOT BE a Christmas celebration the next year, Debrah recalled, as she hung the wooden heart in the tree, with a pang of guilt and regret.

"It's not that I did not want to honor your last wish, Mom. But losing the both of you in the span of a few years time... It took its toll. I just... couldn't."

'Meow?'

When she turned, Mr. Sandals sat on her chair, looking at her expectantly. "You're right. Life does go on, and we have our obligations to our family and loved ones. Like providing a happy home environment for our children. And, I guess, feeding our gluttonous cat."

Mr. Sandals gave a content purr, jumped off the chair and preceded her to the kitchen. She followed, shaking her head and rubbing her temples in relief — she'd once more made it through the worst.

GUARDIAN ANGELS

"AND THIS," Debrah said, choking down a rush of memories, "was your Grandmother's pen. She wrote her first book with it!" She held it up and slowly spun it in the light of the almost filled-up Christmas tree, so her two mezmerized toddlers could see it from all sides.

"Pretty!" Jonah said for the hundredth time that night, as Jake clapped his hands and grinned.

"You find everything pretty, don't you?" She smiled at her boys, then turned to hang the pen in the tree. As she did she looked over all the ornaments — she'd missed them. Or, their memories, actually. Even though she hadn't seen the decorations for almost two years, she still remembered each of them by heart. "I think we should be just about done," she said as she picked up the box, intending to move it back to the attic. The weight of it surprised her.

Didn't I already unwrap all the ornaments? Debrah thought, wondering if she could have overlooked something. When she stuck her hand into the crumpled wads of wrapping paper and started to feel around, she noticed the box contained a false bottom. Her heart skipped a beat as she moved it aside and pulled out a large, heavy package from under it — wrapped in dark blue paper with golden stars, with a card tied to a red bow on top, in her mother's handwriting. *What on Earth...*

"Oooh, pretty, mama!" Jonah exclaimed again, but Debrah barely heard it. She untied the card with trembling fingers and started to read.

I couldn't resist sharing one more memory with you all, even if I will not be there in person to do so. I promised you that me and Dad will always be there for you, but a thought away. My last gift to you, something I had custom made,

symbolizes just that. We're proud of you, sweetheart, and
wish you all the happiness in the world. Make it a good life.
— *Mom & Dad.*

Tears poured down Debrah's face as she held the carved wooden tree topper depicting two guardian angels in a loving embrace, looking down, when Josh returned from the store.

"Mommy sad," Jake told him.

"Oh no, honey," Debrah said, and leaned over to kiss both her sons. "These are tears of joy." She then stood and handed Josh the tree topper, and the card. "I miss her so," she whispered as she watched him read, and tear up.

"That woman…" Josh said, and looked at his wife with nothing but love. "It's no wonder you turned out so wonderful, having been raised by such a loving Mom. I miss her too. Shall I put it on the tree?"

Debrah nodded. "Please."

When the topper was in place, they sat down on the floor with the twins to marvel at the beauty of the tree and the loving memories it held. For the longest time their perfect little family sat there in loving embrace, under the watchful eyes of Debrah's parents, eternalized as their very own guardian angels.

HERE AND NOW

DEBRAH GENTLY PLACED the tree topper on the table. She'd need to wait for help to put it on the tree — it'd been quite a few years since she last trusted herself on a ladder. Next to it stood the last, and largest box of ornaments, yet to be

331

unwrapped — all the ones that she, Josh, and the boys made in the years after her mother's final gift.

Her thoughts played through the many happy moments she knew the items in the box symbolized, and she smiled warmly. "I've had a blessed life so far. Yes, I have," she whispered.

Behind her, she heard Mr. Sandals meowing loudly, and she turned to see what all the noise was about. "What is it, silly cat, are it the birds again?" He sat by the window looking outside and she hurried over.

Josh's van had turned up the driveway. "They're here!" she said joyfully, and scratched the cat under his neck. "And so early! Thank you for alerting me."

When Debrah opened the door, her family already started exiting the van — she felt a wave of joy, even though she already knew they could all make it that year. She took another tissue from her pocket to stop the flow of happy tears.

"Back, safe and sound. Did you miss me?" Josh said, as he walked over and kissed her. "I hope you did not use *all* the tissues again this year, or I might need to make a quick store run," he teased.

"Oh stop it, you goof." She slapped his shoulder with a grin. "Now, where are my sons, grandkids, and other in-laws? Grandma needs some hugs!" She looked at each of them — Jonah and Merith with their two daughters Lizz and Maggie, Jake and his husband Ben, and spread her arms as wide as her smile.

"WE DID WELL, DIDN'T WE," Josh whispered to Debrah, as they sat together under a blanket by the fire, listening to their family sing their traditional song by the piano.

Debrah looked at him, and brushed her hand through his still handsome head of silver hair, and kissed his lips. "That we did, my love, that we did," then placed her head on his shoulder, as they softly sang along.

Each holiday, this feeling comes again.
Every gathering, each celebration,
My thoughts just drift away.
However great things are,
They're not the same
As in most cherished memories,
Spent with those not here today.
Seeking a smile
In days gone by
It dawns that
There are others by my side.
Everyone has stories,
No one is spared in life.
Tell me about your lost ones,
And I'll tell you about those who left my path.

Let's sing a song for the fallen ones
For the loved ones that we've lost,
For the lost ones, never found again.
For lovers left behind and absent friends.
Let's raise our glass to the missing ones,
And make a toast to all those people,
Who got us here, but can no longer see
Who we are,
How our lives turned out to be.

It's your story, tell it proud.
Sing it loud, sing it everywhere,

To everyone that wants to hear.
Open the vault that is your heart,
And let out the ones that live in there
In memories the world may not forget.

Every trip to a place I've been before,
There are those who travel with me,
And those I bring along.
As we ride familiar tracks well known to me,
At each landmark I recall
All the things we've seen.
I will tell with a smile
About days gone by,
To those that came along
The loved ones by my side.
Together we share stories
As we share this life.
These memories are precious,
Way too beautiful to lock inside.

So sing your song for the fallen ones
For those lost along the way.
For the ones that have moved on or went
*   away.*
For all the ones we wished they could have
*   stayed.*
Let's raise our glass to the absent ones.
They will never be forgotten.
Let us drink and share their stories when
*   we can,*
With our family and friends for whom we care.

ABOUT THE AUTHORS

Seamus King has been fighting dragons and foul knights in his dreams and imagination since before he can remember. He grew up on Tolkein, Alexander, and Cooper, and will always be grateful for them opening doors to faraway places in his mind. Historical, Epic, Low, and Medieval Fantasy will always be his first loves, with Urban Fantasy and Horror close behind. He attended Middle Georgia College, Fordham University, and the University of Georgia, and now lives in the beautiful Smoky Mountains of Tennessee while working as an editor for Better Words and Jazz House. In his spare time, he enjoys hitting people in the head with sticks.

Mileva Anastasiadou is a neurologist, from Athens, Greece. A Pushcart, Best of the Net and Best Small Fictions nominated writer, her work can be found in many journals, such as Litro, Jellyfish Review, Maudlin House, Moon Park Review, Okay Donkey, Bending Genres, Open Pen and others.

Perla Nasser is an old, lonely, misunderstood soul trapped in the body of a 21-year old who is trying to put feelings into words, and loves embodying memories and thoughts into fictional characters. She is half-Syrian and half-Lithuanian medical student living in Romania, with a burning love for writing sci-fi, and creating fantasy worlds where she knows that she would rather be. She is eternally grateful for everything she has in this life, but always seeking for more.

H.R.Schwartz is a stay at home mom to a beautiful little girl. She can often be found riding her bicycle towing a trailer, filled with her daughter and a large stuffed bear, behind her. She loves action packed fantasy stories that are intertwined with some elements of romance. She has been previously published in a Zimbell House Anthology and is in the process of writing a full-length novel.

Katie Kent is a writer of both fiction and non-fiction and lives in Oxfordshire in the UK with her wife, cat and dog. Her fiction has been published in *Youth Imagination*, *101 Fiction* and *Flash Fiction Magazine* and is forthcoming in *Flash: The International Short-Short Story Magazine*, *Small Loves (Hybrid Ink)*, *Smoking Pen Press'* time travel anthology and *This is Not a Punk Rock Anthology, It's a New Wave Anthology (Bone & Ink Press)*.

CJ Mattison stumbled into Dallas in search of love, great sushi, and access to big box stores. Having found all three, he now inhabits the city with his wife Cee and their sweet black-and-tan hound, Saber-girl. Retired from the reckless adventure of engineering, he now designs and builds contemporary fiction, space fantasy, gothic horror, cozy mysteries, and even a little romance, while working on his MFA. CJ has self-published three novels and has placed several shorts stories in various genres.

Breanna Bright has a Master's degree in English Professional Writing and has published a plethora of works since 2009, including the stories "Those We Meet In Between," "A Girl Who Forgot Her Name," "The Storyteller," and "For Cornelius."

Sadie May has a Masters degree in Learning and Instructional Design and hopes to one day earn a PhD in Postcolonial literature. She has two cats named Honey and Beam. She enjoys reading anthologies, memoirs, and mysteries. She was a writer for Spine Magazine and now she writes whatever she feels like for herself.

Alexandra Rose was born in Wisconsin during a hospital-shaking thunderstorm in 1980. She studied literature and creative writing at Lakeland University after serving 10 years in the Air Force where she daydreamed of fantasy worlds and would lay the groundwork for all the stories that would follow. She is now a fantasy author, living with a witch-friendly black cat and howling winds in Northern Michigan.

LT Ward writes mostly speculative fiction shorts and novels while spending her days raising her children and satisfying her never-ending thirst for knowledge through reading, meeting people, and first-hand life experiences. She writes for various age groups and has several published short stories in the literary fiction, historical fiction, and speculative fiction genres. She currently volunteers with WriteHive, an online writers' conference.

Tiffany Putenis holds a Masters degree in English and Creative Writing from Southern New Hampshire University. Her love for the written word started at an early age. She works as a Senior Editor and handles Acquisitions for Jazz House Publications in addition to writing her own works of fiction. Tiffany lives in the American Northeast with her husband, three kids, and 2 cats. She finds solace in hiking through the beautiful forests that surround her home. You can find Tiffany on Twitter (@PutenisWrites) and Instagram (@TPutenisWrites).

Emily Jones is a student from a small town in East Anglia who has loved reading and writing her whole life. This story is inspired by Ickworth Park but far from autobiographical- she grew up nearby and it's always inspired her. At the moment, she writes as a way to make a little money and de-stress from sixth form life. Christmas has always meant so much to her- as a family that is quite spread around the country it's the perfect time to come together- this story is a combination of some of the most beautiful inspirations in her life.

R.A. Gerritse. As an author, host of the Twitter poetry prompt tag #vsspoem, and as lyricist for four different bands (Dissector, The Lust, GOOT, Loudborn), poetry is part of Randy Gerritse's every day—it even found its way into his novels. The social platform, in a way, has become the drafting pad for his poetic thoughts, where he is ever self-editing. He self-published a large bundle of his micro poetry, forged into a single, two-act epic poem called "The Rhythm of Life," while he is seeking representation for his debut Sci Fi-thriller novel "Clear Sight," and works on its sequel.